THE BIBLICAL KIERKEGAARD

COLLEGIUM

CHRISTI REGIS

FROM THE COLLECTION OF

GEORGE SCHNER, S.J.
1946 - 2000

THE BIBLICAL KIERKEGAARD

READING BY THE RULE OF FAITH

Timothy Houston Polk

MERCER UNIVERSITY PRESS

MACON, GEORGIA

—1997—

0.86554.539.1
Timothy Polk
The Biblical Kierkegaard
Reading by the Rule of Faith

Mercer University Press
Macon, Georgia 31210
© 1997

∞The paper used in this publication meets the minimum requirements of the American National Standard for Information Sciences—Permanence of Paper for Printed Library Materials, ANSI Z39.48-1984.

Cover design: *Burt & Burt Studios*
Set in TimesNewRoman/ColonnaMT
Printed in the United States of America

Library of Congress Cataloging-in-Publication Data
(applied for and available)

Table of Contents

PREFACE

The service began with our pastor reading the second chapter of Acts in its entirety. The chapter recounts how the pouring out of the Holy Spirit on the disciples led to their proclaiming the gospel in tongues that all the pilgrims to Jerusalem clearly understood, including Medes and Elamites who had been long extinct even then. One might well wonder who among the living in the pews would notice this presence of the dead in the story, much less take it seriously. Or would the text be to us an alien tongue, unintelligible even in English?

The Jews were celebrating Pentecost as the giving of the Law, or Torah, we were told, of which the present vehicle is the scripture, itself called Torah, so close is the connection between the vehicle and its freight. Christians, of course, celebrate Pentecost as the birth of the church through the gift of the Spirit, whose vehicle (essential, but not sole) is, again, scripture. Reading that scripture in our liturgy (originally a Greek word for "public works") is supposedly one of our identifying marks and (not exactly *self*-) constituting acts. In the reading we invite the Spirit of the One whose story scripture tells to re–animate us as his Body—to be our Lord, even.

So many facets of this mystery are disconcerting, besides the claim on our obedience. Not least is the fact that the words of dead people are, we say, a Living Word. But then we have so many ways of trying to make scripture a dead letter. One way is by ossifying it into the proverbial "tablets of stone." That is, we forget scripture's character as a historical witness and absolutize it into an idol. Even now some elements of the church would enshrine Paul's anti–Judaizing polemic, which underlies his "written code/new covenant" contrast (2 Cor 3), and turn it into a warrant for anti–Semitism. We thereby become unwitting perpetrators of the very legalism—indeed, arrogant bigotry—that Paul was attacking. We shrink from the burden of discernment that the gospel itself lays upon us as the good news of a living Lord/Word, whose sovereign summons calls us beyond the cultural prejudices and limited horizons of the biblical writers themselves, privileged prophetic and apostolic witnesses though they be. Scripture's authority does not simply extend—and must not naively be extended—to all the historically conditioned customs, values, and habits of mind of its writers.

Another way to kill scripture is to abandon it *because* the writers are dead, *because* we can see their prejudices, or *because* their witness is disconcerting. Sometimes the abandonment is accompanied by the illusion that a biblical text, or even an isolated metaphor, can be flatly equated with an out–of–favor ideology, and that substitutes can be found immune to corruption. Sometimes the abandonment is accompanied by the gnostic notion that Jesus is less significant as a person than as a disembodied idea, or that precisely as an embodied and gendered person he cannot represent us all, or that he cannot—in the telling of his story—be contemporaneous with us all. Sometimes the abandonment is accompanied by the modernist assumption that the words of the "historical Jesus" must carry more authority than those fictively imputed to him by the early church, or that Jesus' ethical teachings can and should be abstracted from the redeemer cult that his followers are said to have manufactured around his death. Sometimes the abandonment is just the witless expression of another modern bias, illustrated by the baccalaureate speaker who sought to commend "authentic life" to the graduates of the liberal-arts college where I teach, by contrasting authenticity with "tradition" *per se*.

This book celebrates "the Tradition" by celebrating the way one of its contributors, another dead witness, read scripture 150 years ago. Part of the power of the dead man's witness is the way he defies the "conservative" and "liberal" labels by which those Spirit–deadening misreadings I describe above are typically characterized. I have persuaded myself that by championing Soren Kierkegaard I can help us avoid those misreadings (and their labels) today.

But celebrations can get tedious, or outright delusional, particularly when they dress in academic expertise and follow the old formula: identify a crisis, name the enemies, and prescribe the proper correctives. I am reminded that there is yet another way of driving the Spirit out of scripture: namely, by waxing professional and talking it to death. Ecclesiastes refers to the the vanity of making books as "a striving after wind."

Back in the church pew, the question was whether anyone has the patience to listen to all of Acts 2. I have to admit, it's a suspicious question. And obviously, my suspicion is the projection of my own inattentiveness, for look what I've been dreaming in the meantime! The fact is—and I should have learned this in the fourteen years that they have been cradling my family and me—this is a congregation full of rapt, discerning listeners, and just as defiant of the conventional labels as my champion. They excel at hospitality, not least toward "the Tradition," gladly entertaining the presence of the dead, who knows how many "angels unawares." For what I talk, they do: daily receive all things as gifts, proving what the pastor, now well into his sermon, just said, that the Spirit blows where it wills, that we cannot domesticate it, that it is not within our power—particularly mine, thank God—either to kill it or vivify it. Rather, it vivifies us.

"Watch out!" he says. "Your soul could catch fire at any moment, even now, even here in church! I would hate to see nice, respectable people like us, with mortgages to pay, run out of here as if they were drunk."[1] No he wouldn't. And they really might.

To Olivet Congregational Church I dedicate this book.

Pentecost, 1996

---

[1] My pastor was quoting William H. Willimon, Pulpit Resources, 24 (1996): 31.

Acknowledgements

Over the fourteen years that this book has been in the writing, I have accumulated more debts of gratitude than I can count. Certainly, Hamline University has been uncommonly generous, not just in awarding me numerous Hanna Summer Research Grants, but also in allowing a biblical-studies person to wander a bit out of his field and regularly teach a Kierkegaard seminar. I am no less grateful to the students who were so ambitious as to take that seminar and whose responses to it have been so enriching for me. Without the grants, the seminar, or the students, the book simply would not have been possible.

Likewise, I want to thank the MAHADH Foundation for supporting the two sabbaticals that it took to complete the project. The first sabbatical was spent at the Institute for Cultural and Ecumenical Studies in Collegeville, Minnesota, where I received wonderful help and support from my fellow residents and from the Director, Patrick Henry. I was able to spend part of the second sabbatical in St. Andrews, Scotland, where I was fortunate enough to sit in on the Kierkegaard seminar of Professor Daphne Hampson.

I am grateful to Harper and Row Publishers for permission to use a revised version of a previously published essay for chapter 4, and to the many friends and colleagues who have read and critiqued drafts of various chapters: Dale Ahlquist, Lee Barrett, Richard Bell, Alexandra Brown, Bill Cahoy, Marc Cox, Garvin Davenport, Josh Doane, David Gouwens, Abrahim Khan, Roger Larson, Bob Robinson, Gerry Sheppard, Karyn Sproles, Terence Tilley, and Margaret Wurtele. Especially crucial was the insightful and rigorous editorial work done by Patricia Dean. Needless to say, what errors remain in the book are fully attributable to my own oversight or obstinacy.

Finally, I remain ever more in the debt of love to my wife, Lucy, and our children, Ben, Sam, and Martha, all of whose exceptional good humor helped bear the burden of Kierkegaard longer than the normal limits of sanity would seem to allow.

Abbreviations

The following abbreviations for Kierkegaard's works will be used after the initial citation in each chapter.

AUC   *Attack Upon Christendom*, Walter Lowrie, trans. Boston: Beacon Press, 1956 (originally, Princeton: Princeton University Press, 1944).

CUP   *Concluding Unscientific Postscript*, David F. Swenson, trans.; trans. completed, intro. and notes by Walter Lowrie. Princeton: Princeton University Press, 1941

ED   *Edifying Discourses: A Selection*, Paul L. Holmer, ed. New York: Harper & Row, 1958. This edition is used in chapter 4, in conjunction with the *Eighteen Upbuilding Discourses* (below). For chapter 5, again in conjunction with *EUD*, the following edition is used: *Edifying Discourses*, 4 vols., David and Lillian Swenson, trans. Minneapolis: Augsburg, 1944.

EUD   *Eighteen Upbuilding Discourses*, Howard and Edna Hong, trans. and eds. Princeton: Princeton University Press, 1990.

FSE   *For Self-Examination and Judge for Yourselves!*, Walter Lowrie, trans. Princeton: Princeton University Press, 1941.

FT   *Fear and Trembling and Repetition*, Howard and Edna Hong, trans. and eds. Princeton: Princeton University Press, 1983.

JP *Journals and Papers*, 7 vols., Howard V. Hong and Edna H. Hong, trans. and eds. Bloomington: Indiana University Press, 1967-78.

OAR *On Authority and Revelation: The Book on Adler, or, a Cycle of Ethico-Religious Essays*, Walter Lowrie, trans. Princeton: Princeton University, 1955.

PC *Practice in Christianity*, Howard V. Hong and Edna H. Hong, trans. and eds. Princeton: Princeton University Press, 1991.

PF *Philosophical Fragments*, Edna and Howard Hong, trans. and eds. Princeton: Princeton University Press, 1985.

PV *The Point of View for My Work as an Author: A Report to History*, Walter Lowrie, trans. (New York: Harper & Brothers, 1962.

SUD *The Sickness Unto Death*, Howard V. and Edna H. Hong, eds. and trans. Princeton: Princeton University Press, 1980.

WL *Works of Love: Some Christian Reflections in the Form of Discourses*, Howard Hong and Edna Hong, trans.; R. Gregor Smith, preface. New York: Harper & Row, 1962.

INTRODUCTION:

INFLUENCES AND TRAJECTORIES

Over forty years ago, New Testament scholar Paul Minear remarked on the academic neglect of a powerful biblical dimension in the work of Søren Kierkegaard, predicting that future generations would reckon Kierkegaard more as a biblical exegete than as either a poet-philosopher or theologian.[1] Whenever Kierkegaard's light has fallen upon a subject, the resulting illumination has always been more than academic. If Christian faith and theology are grounded in scripture, as the church has always insisted, then recovering Kierkegaard's grasp of scripture would seem an urgent task indeed. But only recently has the neglect Minear spoke of begun to be remedied and his prediction fulfilled.

L. Joseph Rosas's *Scripture in the Thought of Søren Kierkegaard* (Broadman& Holman, 1994) is the first work in English to provide a systematic overview of the subject. Much of that work this study presupposes: the biographical background, the philosophical and theological context, and the change in Kierkegaard's employment of the Bible from his philosophical works to his "second literature."[2] But I want to ask a different set of questions from those that occupy Rosas, in order to venture a constructive hermeneutic proposal.

What I propose is that Kierkegaard's integration of individual subjectivity with political consciousness, devotional passion with blistering culture critique, illustrates a discerning and principled way of reading the Bible that merits the attention of the Christian church.

---

[1]Paul S. Minear and Paul S. Morimoto, *Kierkegaard and the Bible: An Index* (Princeton: Princeton Theological Seminary, 1953), 8.

[2]I would also refer the reader to Rosas's exhaustive bibliography. The bibliography for the present study will list only works cited.

Kierkegaard's way of reading I want to identify, first, with the ancient church's Rule of faith, formulated in terms of love, and second, with a deft sensitivity to the canonical shape of the literature. I would commend his vision of scripture as an aptly Christian alternative to those scripture-killing styles of misreading that I spoke of in the Preface, what technically would be called the hermeneutics of either suspicion or naïveté. By articulating the proposal through a set of close readings of selected Kierkegaard and biblical texts, I hope to bring a degree of clarity to the current debates over biblical interpretation, in particular, to the debate over the theological interpretation of the Bible as "scripture."

I. An Intersection of Disciplines:
Narrative Theology and Canon

Since I harbor more than descriptive intentions, it might be well for me to identify my more tendentious biases at the outset and situate them in the context of the relevant disciplines. For starters, one reason for the neglect of Kierkegaard as exegete, of which Minear spoke, may be the way a century of technical specialization has combined with a positivist model of history to open a breach between the disciplines of biblical studies and theology, diminishing both. With respect to Kierkegaard studies, the effect on theology has been to slight the biblical-exegetical writings that constitute Kierkegaard's "second literature" (the Edifying Discourses and Christian Reflections), despite their occupying what Kierkegaard expressly regarded as the strategic center of his authorship.[3] Perhaps theologians have felt a closer kinship with philosophers than with biblical scholars, amid all the latter's esoteric apparati. In any event, they have heavily favored the overtly philosophical and pseudonymous works, which Kierkegaard saw as being propaedeutic to the non-pseudonymous, biblically oriented writings.[4]

I want to redress the imbalance by concentrating on the second literature. Part One of this book will focus on the 1847 *Works of Love* as the epitome of Kierkegaard's biblical hermeneutic. Part Two will explore key elements of subjectivity correlative with love in two of

---

[3]Kierkegaard, *The Point of View for My Work as an Author: A Report to History and Related Writings*, Walter Lowrie, trans. newly edited with a preface by Benjamin Nelson (New York: Harper & Row, 1962), 18f.

[4]Paul L. Holmer, "Introduction," *Edifying Discourses: A Selection* (New York: Harper & Row, 1958), vii-xix.

the 1843 *Edifying Discourses*, "Every Good and Perfect Gift Is from Above" (James 1:17) and "The Lord Gave, the Lord Took Away; Blessed Be the Name of the Lord" (Job 1:20-21).

Positively, from the theological side, this book leans heavily on the work done in the last two decades under the rubric of narrative theology, particularly that wing of the movement associated with Hans Frei and George Lindbeck. They and their colleagues and students have done much to redirect the attention of theologians to matters of scripture, not by just arguing for practical exegesis as constitutive of the theological task, but by actually practicing it. Several of my central emphases reflect the influence of this group of scholars.[5] First, I share their anti-foundationalist stance in epistemology, and I shall refer to their works frequently for supporting argumentation on that issue.[6] Second, I embrace their

---

[5]The works most prominent in my study include, first, those of the movement's standard bearers, Hans Frei, *The Eclipse of Biblical Narrative* (New Haven: Yale University Press, 1974), and George Lindbeck, *The Nature of Doctrine: Religion and Doctrine in a Postliberal Age* (PPhiladelphia: Westminster Press, 1984). Scarcely less important are: David Ford and Daniel Hardy, *Praising God and Knowing God* (PPhiladelphia: Westminster, 1985); David Gouwens, *Kierkegaard's Dialectic of the Imagination* (New York: Peter Lang, 1989); Garrett Green, *Imagining God: Theology and the Religious Imagination* (San Francisco: Harper, 1989); works of Stanley Hauerwas and David Kelsey discussed below; and Charles Wood, *The Formation of Christian Understanding: An Essay in Theological Hermeneutics* (Philadelphia: Westminster, 1981).

Undefinable by party affiliations, nevertheless deeply influential for many of the scholars above as for me, is Paul L. Holmer. Seminal for this study was his brief introduction to *Edifying Discourses: A Selection* (see above). Also important is his later set of essays, *The Grammar of Faith* (San Francisco: Harper & Row, 1978).

[6]Not noted in subsequent chapters but especially compelling in their articulation of the anti-foundationalist case in theology and ethics are William Placher, *Unapologetic Theology: A Christian Voice in a Pluralistic Conversation* (Louisville: Westminster/John Knox Press, 1989); Jeffrey Stout, *Ethics After Babel: The Languages of Morals and Their Discontents* (Boston: Beacon Press, 1988); and Ronald F. Thiemann, *Revelation and Theology: The Gospel as Narrated Promise* (Notre Dame: University of Notre Dame Press, 1985).

It perhaps bears stressing that, in our context, the term "anti-foundationalism" refers very specifically to the rejection of the Enlightenment and "modern" epistemological project of trying to establish objective and personally neutral bases for one's claims to knowledge. Hence, my reference to an "anti-foundationalist stance in epistemology" is deliberate and technical. It does not imply a rejection of foundations per se, only an acknowledgement that one's foundations are as much a part of the web of personal convictions and commitments as the superstructure of ideas and values built upon them. That is to say, as I shall have frequent occasion to reiterate throughout this study, they have something of the character of faith. For the narrative theologians, Christian foundations are given and held narratively.

interest in performative language, an aspect of the speech-act theory coming from the later Wittgenstein via Austin and Searle. These two emphases are closely related projects that characterize the Frei-Lindbeck form of narrative theology as pronouncedly "postmodern." Because I find Kierkegaard anticipating both projects, I refer to Kierkegaard's exegetical work, however anachronistically, as postmodern, too. His is a speech-act hermeneutic that grounds itself non-foundationally in the canon. A third prominent idea stemming from this school, that of an "imaginative construal" of scripture, I shall introduce in some detail shortly.

As for the discipline of biblical studies: as a member of the guild, it is predictable that I would be hyper-conscious of its foibles and feuds. The idea of the canon represents one of the feuds, the neglect of Kierkegaard (and of much pre-critical exegesis) one of the foibles. The two are related. Kierkegaard's practice of a style of exegesis that takes the interpretive role of canon seriously is one of the reasons for the neglect. I should explain.

The discipline of biblical studies developed for the better part of two centuries under the paradigm of historical-critical objectivity—a paradigm that Kierkegaard attacked. Many of the historicist principles supporting that paradigm remain prevalent in the field, e.g., the "foundationalist" assumption that social-scientific knowledge is either the same as or requisite for religious understanding. The discipline was therefore not well positioned to regard Kierkegaard's rejection of that assumption and his countervailing emphasis on subjectivity as much more than an idiosyncratic pietism. Scholarly interpretive proposals, like older systems of orthodoxy, have typically aimed at establishing the proper methodological procedures, the sure theoretical bases, or the authentic levels of tradition that will insure valid biblical interpretation. Kierkegaard believed there could be no such impersonal guarantees, not if we intend to understand the Bible as "scripture." No objective grounding is firm enough to prevent ingeniously self-interested readers—i.e., each and every one of us— from making malevolent use and self-deceptive sense of scripture. Moreover, an elaborate scholarly apparatus or a "doctrinalized" text, by appearing to secure validity, can aid in the readers' self-deception, tempting us to forfeit precisely the qualities within ourselves that validity requires. When it comes to scripture, valid reading requires a passionate interestedness, a risk of faith in the face of uncertainty, a resolute love of God and neighbor, a posture of gratitude toward the past and hope for the future, and a relentless self-scrutiny, which are what Kierkegaard means by "subjectivity."

It is precisely this subjectivity that the concept "canon," properly understood, embraces. Kierkegaard's own use of scripture illustrates this canon-contextual subjectivity; in the process he helps clarify what the category "scripture" implies. The major purpose of this study is to chart that use and the significance it may hold as a paradigm of reading for the interpretive communities for which the Bible functions as canonical literature.

Properly understanding the concept "canon" is no easy task. I shall be using the term in the manner of Brevard Childs, the leading exponent of one of two rival forms of "canon criticism" in biblical studies.[7] The concept is complex enough in either form, but Childs's presentation of it is especially subtle. Add to that the polemical edge of Childs's critical blade, and it becomes understandable why his view of canon has not always had a fair hearing. The common mistake is to think that a canon-contextual approach[8] is utterly antithetical to historical-critical methods, that it works on a purely synchronic plane excluding considerations of the diachronic dimension of the text's production and reception, and that it dogmatically aims at a univocal meaning.[9]

---

[7] The most significant of Childs's works for purposes of this essay are his *Introduction to the Old Testament as Scripture* (Philadelphia: Fortress Press, 1979) and *The New Testament as Canon: An Introduction* (Philadelphia: Fortress, 1984). Many of the narrative theologians listed above have taken note of Childs's work. The one who has addressed the issue of canon most directly is Charles Wood in *The Formation of Christian Understanding*.

Interestingly, Childs is no longer content to use the term "canon criticism," largely because the rival approach employs the rubric in a way parallel to the historical-critical methods (e.g., source-, form-, tradition-, and redaction-criticism) from which Childs wishes to distinguish his effort. The leading voice for the rival school is James A. Sanders; see his *Torah and Canon* (Philadelphia: Fortress Press, 1972) and *Canon and Community* (Philadelphia: Fortress, 1984).

In sharp contrast to Childs, Sanders tends to dismiss the theological significance of the final shape of scripture, preferring to locate the normativity of "canon" in a pre-biblical hermeneutic process, which he identifies in religious terms as a monotheizing impulse. Childs, on the other hand, wants to insist that the final shape of the literature effected a shift in how the material was seen to function and established a new context for theological reflection. For a fuller statement on these differing approaches, see Gerald T. Sheppard, "Canonical Criticism," *Harper Bible Dictionary* (San Francisco: Harper, 1992), I, 861-66.

[8] The term is that of Gerald T. Sheppard (n. 7, above), a leader among the second generation of Childs's students.

[9] Perhaps the most influential misreading of Childs has been that of James Barr, *Holy Scripture: Canon, Authority, Criticism* (Oxford: Oxford University Press, 1983). Unfortunately, one of the scholars Barr's misreading has influenced is Rowan Williams, whose fine work in "The Literal Sense of Scripture" (*Modern Theology*, 7

It takes more than flat denial to overcome such a caricature. What is needed is repeated practical illustration, which is one of the reasons for the close readings prominent in each chapter of this study. While the more abstract and technical argumentation will occur in footnotes, I want to say something here by way of orientation to the concept.

For present purposes, what needs to be stressed about the idea of canon is that it implies both a literary and a social context for making religious sense of scripture. Literarily, canon privileges the final form of the biblical text over against the earlier forms that discrete sources and units of tradition may have had, without denying the heuristic significance of those earlier sources and units.[10] It thus encourages reading intratextually, interpreting one passage in light of others, under the assumption that scripture can function as a complex whole. Conversely, it discourages atomistic readings that presume a unit can only be understood in terms of its original historical context and that the parts of scripture, more or less randomly arranged, have at best an accidental relation to each other.

Socially, canon is the application of the principle that there can be no understanding of a text apart from the socially informed commitments and purposes that determine its uses. A text's meaning by this view is not simply an objective property of the print on the

---

[1991]) is marred by a tendenz reflective of Barr's slant on Childs, as in the phrase " a new totalitarianism of canonical context, understood without reference to history" (124). To understand canonical context without reference to history is not the way Childs understands it.

In a note to the phrase above (124, n. 14), Williams quotes Barr to the effect that "canons do not give us hermeneutic guidance" (Barr, 67). If the statement is taken to mean that the canonical shape of the biblical text does not give such determinative guidance as to preclude different, even conflicting readings, and thus to direct all readers to one and the same interpretation of any given passage, then, despite being too broadly formulated, it is at least tolerably accurate. If, however, it means that the canon provides no guidance whatsoever in identifying the semantic range of a text (in which any number of significant differences in sense-making may nevertheless occur) while ruling certain construals as out of the ballpark, then it is badly mistaken.

[10]As Childs and Sheppard have been at pains to point out, the source-, form-, tradition-, and redactional-analyses that seek to identify and describe the earlier stages of the biblical material's development can be of immense importance in helping to clarify the canonical shape and—if you will—intention of the text. I would add that, simply in terms of the pragmatics of reading, the experience of analyzing the text diachronically and thereby becoming informed of the history of its composition and reception cannot help but inform one's sense of the whole and one's perception of the dynamics at work within it.

page, much less an intention in the head of an author, but an intersubjective phenomenon involving readers in its production. In the case of canon, this implies reading the Bible in light of the religious commitments and purposes of the historically specific communities that originally shaped it and have since received it in its final form as a normative, if complex, witness to their faith and practice. Explicating the Bible in its canonical context (and explicating Kierkegaard's explication of the Bible in its canonical context) is therefore a kind of reader-response criticism. If my explication has a confessional ring to it, that is because it entails looking at the Bible from the perspective of the interpretive community known as the church, to which I belong, and as a text that speaks of and to Christian tenets and values, which I hold.

II. The Fish Connection

I have used the term "interpretive community" twice already. It comes from Stanley Fish's *Is There a Text in this Class? The Authority of Interpretive Communities*.[11] Now well-worn by a generation of scholars trained in post-structuralist theory and reader-response criticism, Fish's book remains vitally influential for my study at a number of points. First, in Fish, we find an anti-foundationalist stance and a sophisticated employment of speech-act theory, both rigorously argued and lucidly illustrated with practical exegesis.[12] Next, and corresponding with these concerns, is Fish's belief in the Wittgensteinian maxim that meaning is in use.[13] I hope to show how

---

[11]Stanley Fish, *Is There a Text in This Class? The Authority of Interpretive Communities* (Cambridge, Mass.: Harvard University Press, 1980). Except for discursive notes, page references will be given in the body of the text.

[12]See especially Fish's chapter, "How To Do Things with Austin and Searle: Speech-Act Theory and Literary Criticism," 197-245.

[13]It is only a short step to this principle from Fish's explicit contention that the meaning of an utterance is in what it does (25-32, 88). He takes that step when he proposes an alternative view of language to the cognitive-propositionalist view: "The alternative view would be one in which the purposes and needs of human communication inform language and are constituent of its structure" (106); so also when he comments on the difference between "literary" and "nonliterary" speech: the distinction "is not between illocutionary acts and some other kind but between illocutionary acts put to differing uses" (222, my italics); and finally when he explicates the literal sense of various utterances according to those human purposes and needs, i.e., uses (on "literal sense," see below, n. 14). Interestingly, Fish makes explicit reference to Wittgenstein in regard to the latter's concept of language games,

Kierkegaard's work demonstrates the same belief. Third, Fish offers a discussion of "literal sense" that complements a similar interest among narrative theologians and that strongly colors my own way of talking about the canon.[14] Some of the methodological argumentation over the "literal sense" will be conducted in footnotes; the main discussion will come in the body of chapter two. Fourth, to return to Fish's title, I embrace his idea that specific communities of readership generate and inherit distinctive readerly conventions, competences, and expectations, which in turn generate family resemblances among the interpretations the members make of scripture and which determine, among other things, what counts as a literal sense. For my purposes, "interpretive communities" means "church," defined either in the broadest, catholic terms, or in the narrower terms of denominations, local congregations, and cells within congregations.

What actually triggered the thesis of this book, however, uniting the other four themes, was a brief reference Fish makes to the Rule of faith. He makes the reference while arguing that the sense we make of texts is a function of the interpretive strategies we use, which is also to say that our interpretive strategies determine the nature and substance of the texts we read. In short, different strategies produce different texts, even of the "same" piece of writing (168f.). On the other hand, the same strategy can produce the same text, even from ostensibly disparate writings, like those that make up the Bible.

Augustine urges just such a strategy, for example, in *On Christian Doctrine* where he delivers the "rule of faith" which

---

by which Fish critiques the foundationalist remnants in the speech-act theory of John Searles (241). On meaning as use, see below, pp. 57 n. 9, and 132 n. 37.

[14] See especially Fish's chapter, "Normal Circumstances, Literal Language, Direct Speech Acts, the Ordinary, the Everyday, the Obvious, What Goes without Saying, and Other Special Cases," 268-92, as well as a key remark on p. 333f. The concept "literal sense" is one of the great cruxes in both literary and theological hermeneutics. In addition to Fish's discussion, the following have been most helpful for me: Owen Barfield, "The Meaning of the Word 'Literal,'" in *Metaphor and Symbol, Proceedings of the Twelfth Symposium of the Colston Research Society*, L. C. Knights and Basil Cottle, eds. (London: Butterworths, 1960), 48-63; Brevard S. Childs, "The Sensus Literalis of Scripture: An Ancient and Modern Problem," in *Beitrage zur alttestamentlichen Theologie, Festschrift fur Walther Zimmerli zum 70. Geburtstag*, Herbert Donner et al., eds. (Göttingen: Vandenhoeck & Ruprecht, 1977), 80-93; Gerald T. Sheppard, "Between Reformation and Modern Commentary: The Perception of the Scope of Biblical Books," *A Commentary on Galatians by William Perkins*, Gerald T. Sheppard, ed. (New York: The Pilgrim Press, 1989), xlviii-lxxvii; Rowan Williams, "The Literal Sense of Scripture" (see above, n. 9).

is of course a rule of interpretation. It is dazzlingly simple: everything in the Scriptures, and indeed in the world when it is properly read, points to (bears the meaning of) God's love for us and our answering responsibility to love our fellow creatures for His sake. (170)

The crucial thing to observe here is the formulation of the Rule of faith in terms of love. In every chapter I shall be paraphrasing Fish's version of Augustine's "dazzlingly simple" formula. At the very least, I hope to show that the readings Kierkegaard produces by following it are far from simplistic. Rather, they are challenging and true, true because they generate faithful vision.[15]

Further along in his book Fish returns to Augustine to comment on a contemporary sports phenomenon. He describes the case of a professional baseball player who, after a conversion experience, had come to "*literally* see everything as a function of his religious existence," including the home runs he was suddenly hitting. The point Fish wants to make is that what one *sees* is dependent upon one's verbal and mental categories. In the case of the born-again slugger, his verbal and mental categories made it natural for him to perceive the hand of God in everyday occurrences, whereas the categories of the exasperated reporter covering the hitter's streak yielded a different perception—"'mere athletic competition.'" "What is perceived to be 'in the text' [or 'in the world'] is a *function* of interpretive activities," Fish asserts (273). It is the same principle articulated by Augustine's Rule:

The eye that was in bondage to the phenomenal world (had as its constitutive principle the autonomy of that world) has been cleansed and purged and is now capable of seeing what is really there, what is obvious, what anyone who has the eyes can see: "to the healthy and pure internal eye He is everywhere." He is everywhere not as the result of an interpretive act self-consciously performed on data otherwise available, but as the

---

[15]I should point out that Kierkegaard's reliance on the Rule of faith is implicit. To my knowledge, the closest he comes to explicitly citing it is in the 1843 Edifying Discourse, "Every Good and Perfect Gift Is from Above," when he speaks of "worthily interpret[ing] the apostolic word to the honor of God." (See chapter 4 below.) For more on this only implicit reliance, see below, chapter 2, n. 41.

result of an interpretive act performed at so deep a level that it
is indistinguishable from consciousness itself.[16]

For all practical purposes, my study of Kierkegaard began with
the thin Augustinian connection Fish draws between the Rule of faith
qua love and a capacity for seeing. What is at stake is how to
"literally see" the Bible as scripture, with Kierkegaard in his preferred
role as "midwife" to this rebirth of vision.[17] Let me try to thicken
Fish's connection now, by situating it within the narrative-theology
movement mentioned earlier.

III. Vision and Construals

At about the same time that Paul Minear was urging the study of
Kierkegaard's biblical exegesis, the novelist-philosopher Iris Murdoch
was urging a shift of governing metaphor in ethics from *krisis* (choice,
decision) to "vision." Important as decision-making may be for an
analysis of the ethical, such an analyis can only understand life as
episodic, a collection of discrete moments. Insofar as our lives exhibit
patterns of behavior and thus have an element of continuity, ethical
analysis needs to attend to the formation of character, which includes
the formation of the imagination and the role it plays in how we
construe the world.[18]

Murdoch's call found a responsive hearing in Stanley Hauerwas.
Beginning with his *Vision and Virtue* (Fides, 1974; Notre Dame,
1981), Hauerwas has been applying Murdoch's proposal to a
specifically Christian ethic informed by the aesthetic categories of
vision, imagination, and story. Murdoch's re-conception of the moral
life as "a way of seeing the world" through selfless nonviolent love is
projected by Hauerwas into the Christian task of learning faithfully

---

[16]Fish, 271f., quoting Augustine's *City of God*.

[17]The metaphor of the midwife pertains to the strategy of "indirect
communication" that underlies all of Kierkegaard's writings (even when he thought
he was being "direct"). It is an integral aspect of the aesthetic and imaginative
dimension of his discourse, by which he hoped to induce his readers to find the
"truth for themselves," knowing that religious truth could not be directly
transmitted from one person to another. Chapters 1 and 3 below attend to
Kierkegaard's interest in biblical parables and the parabolic quality of his own
writing, parable being the genre of indirect communication par excellence.

[18]Murdoch, *The Sovereignty of Good* (New York: Schocken, 1970). See further,
below, n. 28.

"to attend to reality under the mode of the divine."[19] Because
Hauerwas believes that faith's perspective on reality finds its
paradigm in scripture, he argues for the primacy of scripture in
shaping Christian life. By his account, the Bible's narrative structure
and metaphorical language prove indispensable both for articulating
the Christian vision and for capacitating Christians to live out the
vision. This point about the primacy of scripture will be explored in
chapter 1.

Hauerwas's linkage of vision with scripture was a decisive move.
While securing the role of imagination in ethics, it affirmed the
authority of scripture and gave ethics the responsibility to be
exegetical. Where exegesis appears, however, hermeneutics cannot be
far behind, waiting to raise the questions that Hauerwas skirts. For
example, given that the Bible may generate vision in its readers, what
vision *of the Bible* is most apt for enabling it to work as Hauerwas
suggests? How are readers to "see" the Bible in order best to see the
world and themselves in its light? Historical-criticism has been posing
versions of this question for two hundred years,[20] but in terms of our
ocular metaphor its force was perhaps best captured by David Kelsey
in his study of the diverse ways modern theologians have used
scripture to authorize theological proposals.[21]

By Kelsey's analysis, the diverse *uses* of scripture evince
different *concepts* of scripture (14, 103), and these concepts in turn
are rooted in different "imaginative construals" (161) that
theologians make of the Bible as a whole. The Bible may be imagined,
for example, and frequently has been, in principally didactic terms as
an inspired set of inerrant doctrines (21f.), or as "a lexicon
containing a system of quasi-technical terms" (28). It can also be
construed narratively as a story of the "acts of God in history" (33),

---

[19]See the chapter, "The Significance of Vision: Toward an Aesthetic Ethic," 36,
46.

[20]For example, historical research has prompted scholars to ask not only which of
the notably diverse biblical stories is the biblical story (e.g., Matthew's, Mark's,
Luke's, John's, Paul's), but also at which level of the material's development one
locates its authority: oral, pre-redactional, canonical. Of course, for any answer to the
latter question there are infinitely finer discriminations still to be negotiated, all of
which may further problematize the already difficult determination regarding the
relation between the two Testaments, while leaving untouched yet another kind of
question raised by research. Why, among the variety of biblical literary genres (song,
proverb, prophecy, letter and law), should story be privileged? Proponents of
narrative theology have not always adequately addressed these questions.

[21]Kelsey, *The Uses of Scripture in Recent Theology* (Philadelphia: Fortress
Press, 1975). Page references will be given in the body of the text.

or as rendering an identity description of an agent who intends and enacts his own identity (39-47). Again, it may be viewed mythico-symbolically as a set of images expressive of religious experience, whether conceived as cosmic processes of creation and recreation (61), as individual release from existential alienation (68), or as a coming to authentic self-understanding (74). The possibilities are limited only by the imagination as it encounters the shifting historical situations of human communities.

It is clear that the accent in "imaginative construal" is on "imaginative" and that there is a bias toward the visual. Kelsey will refer to such construals as "syn*optic*...metaphorical judgments" (107, 159, 163) that "yield something like a 'gestalt'" (206). Even his technical term for the most rationalized stage of the imaging process, "*discrimen*" (160ff.), recalls a rootage in visual perception.

The root differences among construals are both deep and primal. "Logically irreducible," Kelsey says of the construals' diversity (102).[22] And because each construal grows out of "the concrete particularities of the common life of the community" of which the theologian is a product (193; cf. 170, 200), the construal is always "logically prior" to any particular textual exegesis the theologian might perform (166, 199).[23] The point is clear: vision is not only a

---

[22]The "irreducible diversity" of construals surely relates to the fact that they are irreducibly imaginative, but by no means does either fact (their diversity or their imaginativeness) imply to Kelsey that they are merely fanciful projections immune to rational critique and reformulation. Rather, construals are accountable to the common life of the church and the bi-polar structure of tradition (170-75). Moreover, scripture itself places constraints on the imagination in the sense that, if the theologian expects his theological proposals to be persuasive, he must be prepared to articulate the determinate patterns of textual features that constitute the construal in the first place. (In this case, one might ask, isn't the construal's accountability to scripture just a more specific instance of its accountability to the church?) The construals remain, however, "free and creative," Kelsey insists.

To my knowledge, the best discussion of the place of the imagination in theology is that of Garrett Green's *Imagining God.* (See above, n. 5.) Especially helpful is his distinction between: 1) our use of the word "imagination" to speak of flights of fancy unnormed by the rules of specific kinds of discourse, and 2) our use of it for speaking of highly rational activities. Such rational activities, or ruled kinds of discourse, would include theology and quantum mechanics, among others.

[23]It should be emphasized that the form of exegesis under discussion here is *theological* exegesis, which Kelsey will not allow to be simply conflated with historical exegesis (198-201). But the matter is complex. The theologian's imaginative construal, Kelsey maintains, will not affect how she goes about the historical task. Yet her historical findings may well influence the construal. However, the construal does become "decisive" as soon as one begins to specify

product of reading, as Hauerwas reminds us, but its prerequisite and (slippery) foundation as well, conditioning even the literal sense of the text being read, as Fish observed.

Here let me restate my thesis in question form. Might Kierkegaard's "vision of love" constitute a construal prior even to the logically prior construals Kelsey speaks of, one that might then be capable of ruling those other construals so that, despite their irreducible diversity, they retain a family resemblance as Christian? In other words, shouldn't Christian love, as Kierkegaard understands and practices it, govern the Christian use of scripture? Or to put it in terms familiar to a wider cultural debate, can Kierkegaard's construal by love help Christians read the Bible as canonical scripture even in a milieu that has discovered systemic prejudice and vice deep within the fabric of the writings themselves? In each case, this would be to speak of love in its role as *regula fidei*, the Rule of faith definitive of Christian sense and community. The primary case for this conception of love-*qua*-Rule will be made in chapter 2.

---

how the historical and theological tasks are related—if one judges them to be related—because that judgment itself trades on one's construal. The judgment trades on the construal, according to Kelsey, because at the bottom of one's construal of the Bible qua "scripture" (i.e., sacred writings authoritative for the faith and practice of the church) is a notion of how God is present to the church in its use of scripture. And that is clearly a theological, not a historical, judgment.

While I agree with the basic thrust of Kelsey's analysis, I would question his belief that the imaginative construal does not influence the way historical exegesis is executed. The results of what Kelsey calls "exegesis 2," in which the aim is to determine what a biblical text "meant" for its writers/redactors and original audience, would seem especially open to a theological contamination-by-construal. Since the task would typically entail assessing how the writers and their early readers understood how God was present to them through their tradition and writings (including the text before them/us)—an assessment for which the primary evidence is usually that same biblical text, among other sources, including other biblical texts, which were already functioning as religious texts—, would not one's own sense of who God is and how God is present now influence one's ability to "seriously imagine" (172) the who and how then?

In other words, I would ask, doesn't one's present imaginative construal incline one to "see" one's historical evidence one way rather than another, to recognize some textual features and overlook others, to foreground some and suppress some, to construe their inter-relationship one way rather than another? However self-conscious and critical one may become with respect to one's own theological imagination, it remains one's own, both capacitating and limiting one's (historical-critical) reading of theological literature. I would think the deconstructionist principle holds here: the fact that reading a text in its *differance* depends on reading it in its familiarity means that some of the difference will be deferred.

The logical source for a discussion of love-*qua*-Rule within the Kierkegaardian corpus is *Works of Love*. Designed to show the "sociality" of faith,[24] this set of discourses comprises Kierkegaard's "Christian ethics." *Works of Love* also provides one of the most sustained threads of biblical exposition in the Kierkegaardian corpus.[25] That exposition everywhere shows the imaginative colors of its foundational vision. Evidence of the positive relation Kierkegaard sees among scripture, the imagination, and vision is abundant, as in this comment on the Bible's imaginative language:

> Under many metaphors and with many concepts Holy Scriptures seek in various ways to give our earthly existence festivity and dignity, to win air and vision through the relationship to the eternal. And certainly...a need is felt for the enlivening vision of a great expectation.[26]

Accordingly, it is more than a verbal tic when, in a passage on the radically metaphorical character of biblical language, Kierkegaard begins a paraphrase of Luke's Parable of the Great Banquet with, "*Imagine* a man who gave a banquet feast"[27] As we shall see in chapter 2, such appeals to his reader's imagination are deliberate and systematic.

The favorable attitude toward "vision" and the imagination should go a long way toward dispelling the popular misconception of Kierkegaard's ethics as mere "decisionism." David Gouwens has addressed this misconception head-on by emphasizing Kierkegaard's appreciation for the way the imagination informs the ethical person's *disposition*.[28] I shall have occasion in every chapter to comment on

---

[24]Kierkegaard intended *Works of Love* as an answer to the charge of privatistic individualism that was leveled even then against his account of faith (see the "Introduction" to *WL* by Howard and Edna Hong, 17-18, citing a passage from the Journals). The persistence of the charge indicates a continuing failure to comprehend the plan of the Kierkegaardian corpus and its dialectical, polemical character.

[25]The only clear rival would be *Practice in Christianity*, Howard V. Hong and Edna H. Hong, trans. and eds. (Princeton: Princeton University Press, 1991).

[26]*WL*, 231f.

[27]*WL*, 90 (my emphasis). See also his discussion of "the secret of transferred language," on 199f. For further evidence on vision, which is a major *leitmotif* in *WL*, see 23, 32f., 79f., 85, 87, 95-97, 107, 153-64, 216f., 227, and 350f.

[28]Gouwens, *Kierkegaard's Dialectic of the Imagination* (New York: Peter Lang, 1989). See especially the following statement:

> Contrary to popular portrayals of Kierkegaard's thought, to be ethical is not only "making choices" as if—to use Iris Murdoch's phrase—the self were

this formative dimension of the imagination, especially in relation to the reading of scripture.

However, *Works of Love* is not without condemnations of the "poetic." The "poetic" is a category equivalent to that of the "aesthetic," which Kierkegaard closely associates with the imagination. His suspicion of the aesthetic play of the imagination in religious discourse (including his own) is shared by Brevard Childs. This in turn proves a bit inconvenient for my effort to have Kierkegaard illustrate Childs's canon-contextual approach to exegesis.[29] For the present, I can only say by way of defense that Kierkegaard is working through a complex dialectic here. I want to defer discussion of this dialectic, and whether the scandal of "aestheticism" in his own work—and in our reading—can be resolved, for the concluding chapter.

IV. Annotated Table of Contents

Given the maze of themes and issues just laid out, it may be useful to provide a more sequential, chapter-by-chapter preview of the book. Chapter 1, "A Kierkegaardian *Sola Scriptura*," contrasts two rival construals of the Bible, "classic" and "scripture," using Frank Kermode's *The Genesis of Secrecy* to illustrate the first, *Works of Love* to illustrate the second. The chapter concludes with a summary account of Kierkegaard's notion of Christian love. The biblical texts under discussion in chapter 1 include the Parable of the Sower in Mark 4, the Parable of the Good Samaritan in Luke 10:27-34, and the parabolic snippet in Luke 6:44 about the tree that produces good fruit.

Chapter 2, "Imagining Scripture," takes an extended passage from the Discourse "Love Hides the Multiplicity of Sin" in Part Two of *Works of Love* to illustrate in some detail the relevance of the Rule

---

merely an "agent, thin as a needle," who "appears in the quick flash of the choosing will" [Murdoch, *The Sovereignty of Good*, 53]. Kierkegaard's picture of the ethical self is much richer, concerned with the ethical person's continuity through time in developing long-term dispositions. In the ethical sphere, not only the will but the imagination is raised to a constant factor in one's life. The ethical person not only does ethical deeds, but with originality envisions a way of life and acts upon it responsibly. The ethical person does not simply "image" at particular times, but is dispositionally imaginative. (208; cf. 253.)

[29]See Childs's *The New Testament as Canon*, Excursus III, "The Canonical Approach and the 'New Yale Theology,'" 541-46.

of faith to Kierkegaard's exegetical practice. Here is where the Rule is explicitly characterized as a form of "imaginative construal." I chart its historic development within ancient Israel and the early church to explicate its peculiar, characteristically hermeneutic, circularity.

Chapter 3, "Hiding Sin: Kierkegaard's Hermeneutic Scandal," further investigates the Discourse introduced in chapter 2, but now with respect to the moral and exegetical offense it seems calculated to give to contemporary readers, especially those sensitive to feminist concerns. The chapter takes two seemingly unrelated tacks to bring the offense into focus. First, it develops a comparison between Kierkegaard's Discourse and Nathaniel Hawthorne's short story, "Young Goodman Brown," stressing the parabolic nature of the two pieces. Second, it relates Kierkegaard's rhetorical strategy to the current scholarly debate over the audience and address of the Epistle of 1 Peter, the biblical text on which the Discourse is based. Audience and address are typical focal points of canon-contextual criticism.

As indicated earlier, these first three chapters constitute Part One, "Hermeneutic *Works of Love.*" Part Two, "Elements of Subjectivity," investigates the hermeneutic significance of a set of love-related affections and their antitheses. Chapter 4, "'Heart Enough to be Confident': Doubt, Receptivity, and the Epistle of James," features the dispositions of gratitude and defiance, double-mindedness and purity of heart, besides the dispositions named in the title. The canonical issues of apostolic authorship and intratextual referentiality figure prominently in this discussion.

Chapter 5, "The Praise of Job: Edifying Discourse Against Theodicy," inspects a paradoxical interdependence of blessing and cursing, praise and complaint. Kierkegaard's doxological way of reading the Book of Job is contrasted with several current sociological and metaphysical readings that take Job as the *locus classicus* of biblical theodicy. Besides the 1843 Edifying Discourse on Job, the chapter also makes use of *Fear and Trembling* and *Repetition* from that same year.

The final chapter, a postscript on "the canonical imagination," will return to the topic of aesthetics and the imagination, drawing together the relevant threads from the previous five chapters so as to sort through the problematic nature of the intrusion of aesthetics into religious belief and discourse.

V. Close Reading

Finally, by way of prefatory warning, I should say something about the book's internal dynamic: its oscillation between meta-discourse and micro-analysis, broad argument and close reading, where the point is never quite fixed, always multiplying, and forever recurring. It is partly a matter of finding a methodology appropriate to Kierkegaard's own pre-systematic style. Specifically, in *Works of Love* and the *Edifying Discourses* Kierkegaard does not so much talk *about* the Bible as kaleidoscopically *use* it. Certainly, correlations can be made between the practice and the relatively few programmatic remarks elsewhere. Chapter 2, for example, will explore an absolutely crucial correlation between the practically oriented *Works of Love* and the programmatic "Mirror of the Word" in *For Self-Examination*. Nevertheless, insofar as *praxis* does not just vary from theory but often outstrips it, it will be the actual practice that receives the major scrutiny.

No better demonstration of praxis outstripping theory exists than that offered by Kierkegaard's pseudonymous works, in particular, Johannes Climacus's *Philosophical Fragments* and *Concluding Unscientific Postscript*, where much of the "theory" is to be found. Climacus's notorious reduction of the significance of the historical material in the Gospels to the simple claim that at such and such a time and place one Jesus of Nazareth lived and died—and his implicit trivialization thereby of the four-fold character of the canonical story—belies the emphasis Kierkegaard places on the imitation of Christ when he writes under his own name in the religious discourses. To assess the relevance of Kierkegaard's theory for his actual hermeneutics, one cannot ignore the rhetoric of pseudonymity and the dialectical structure that shapes Climacus's polemic against speculative idealism. The style is of the essence.

In any case, given Kierkegaard's belief that scripture exists for religious use, not for disinterested discussion, it is his use we want to examine. This means that the hermeneutic at work has largely to be induced. Add to that the peculiar knot of concerns we want to address, and we risk perpetrating the very hyper-abstraction Kierkegaard devoted his life to combatting.

The danger can only be averted by close and continual attention to his actual practice as it unfolds in specific texts. Progress along this route will be slow. Attending to the practice, giving space to the textual details, allowing time for their subject matter to develop, patiently teasing out the intratextual logic—in sum, disciplining oneself by the *explication de texte*: this process must maintain its privileges vis-a-vis quick "results." For the approach to be inductive, it must be doggedly exegetical.

Last but not least: a practical consideration. This "canonical hermeneutics of the Rule of faith," as I would term Kierkegaard's approach to scripture, is not a simplistic enterprise. "Getting it," I've become convinced by my own experience, requires seeing the ideas developed repeatedly in varying texts and contexts. For fellow slow learners, I trust the repetitions will be helpful. For "quick studies" among my readers, any forbearance will be deemed a work of love. For both, it might help to know that Kierkegaard regarded repetition not as a mental crutch, but as an existential necessity.[30]

---

[30]See below, chapters 5 and 6.

CHAPTER 1

A KIERKEGAARDIAN
SOLA SCRIPTURA

The primary task set for us by the Introduction is how to see the Bible as scripture, or to put the question in Kelsey's language, under what imaginative construal should the Bible be viewed in order for it to be scripture? Before proceeding to that task, however, it might pay us to pursue the prior question of whether and why we would want to see the Bible as scripture in the first place. After all, "scripture" is a construal in itself, implying that the Bible has authoritative, canonical status for the religious communities that receive it as such. The phrase in the chapter title, "sola scriptura," was coined by the Protestant Reformers for underscoring just those implications. The slogan asserted the singularity and indispensability of the Bible as a norm for Christian faith and practice and served the Reformers as a critical principle for purging a tradition of what they believed to be distorting accretions.

The point is that not everyone committed to Christianity today remains content with those implications. For many contemporary theologians, Protestant and Catholic alike, "sola scriptura" belongs to a rhetoric of conservative opposition wielded against their struggle to reform the tradition anew. For the new reformers, "authority" has become equated with the opponents' perceived authoritarianism, and to speak of "scripture" is to view the Bible as the opponents do, i.e., as a source of doctrine, a deposit of right teachings, "an archetype binding and confining Christians to patterns of thought and behavior laid down once and for all in the past."[1] Accordingly, many liberals feel they must abandon the traditional language to search for more suitable conceptualities. Elizabeth Schüssler Fiorenza, for instance, describes the Bible, rather than as a source and archetype, as a "resource" and "prototype," meaning "a first attempt, from which one may learn both positively and negatively, and which may and probably should be surpassed."[2]

An attractive alternative to Schüssler Fiorenza's model of the Bible-as-resource, accommodating a wider range of attitudes toward the Bible's religious value, has been to construe the Bible as a "classic." In the work of David Tracy, one of the two principal formulators of this conception, the term "classic" is not meant to negate the Bible's role as scripture, only to redefine its role in terms of a broader cultural phenomenon so as to enhance its public intelligibility. For Sallie McFague, on the other hand, the term accomplishes what "prototype" does for Schüssler Fiorenza: it negates the status of scripture and the oppressive authority accompanying that status. Positively, for McFague, "classic" draws attention to the Bible's extraordinary literary value and cultural impact and encourages the sort of literary approach to the text that McFague endorses, an approach more sensitive to the play of metaphor intrinsic to first-order religious discourse than the more traditional, dogmatic approaches typically are. Citing the other principal formulator of the concept, the literary critic Frank Kermode, McFague wants to emphasize a non-imperial view of the classic as "open, relative, pluralistic in interpretation" in contrast to the privilege, rigid fixity, and closure connoted by "canonical scripture."[3] The category "classic," conceived in this way, grants a certain autonomy and critical authority to individual experience over against an absolutist tradition. The fact that Kermode himself writes on the Bible illuminatingly from a secular standpoint, and with an intertextual hermeneutic of suspicion that relativizes the biblical text, must confirm for McFague the suitability of the category to the contemporary pluralistic situation, since ecu-

---

[1]Charles M. Wood, "Hermeneutics and the Authority of Scripture," in *Scriptural Authority and Narrative Interpretation*, Garrett Green, ed. (Philadelphia: Fortress, 1987), 12f.

[2]Wood, 7, citing Schüssler Fiorenza's *Bread Not Stone: The Challenge of Feminist Biblical Interpretation* (Boston: Beacon, 1984), 61, *et passim*.

[3]Sallie McFague, *Metaphorical Theology: Models of God in Religious Language* (Philadelphia: Fortress, 1982), 60f.

menical conversation in a "nonbelieving time" is one of her major concerns.[4]

Kierkegaard's situation was different, of course, since in mid-nineteenth-century "Christendom" nonbelief was still disguising itself as belief, at least as far as Kierkegaard was concerned. "Sola scriptura" would have been one of the basic tenets of faith the nominal confession and practical nonobservance of which he would have satirized by juxtaposing with the concept's radical implications. His point would have been to provoke either a deliberate recommitment or an honest rejection by his professedly Christian audience.

Or so one would think. Indeed, the abundance of entries in the *Journals and Papers* on the topic of scripture's authority, not to mention the strident reminders in the *Attack Upon Christendom* about "the Christianity of the New Testament" and "the requirements" of "God's Word," attests as high an estimate of the singularity and indispensability of scripture as one would expect of Luther himself.[5] Nevertheless, Kierkegaard rarely, if ever, actually uses the phrase "sola scriptura." His avoidance suggests he was aware that it had ossified into just another piece of doctrinal orthodoxy, which he was as eager to combat as he was the Bible's cultured despising or mindless neglect. He avoided the phrase, I suspect, precisely because the kind of authority that orthodoxy asserted was alien to the way he saw scripture really working—in the tensiveness of its language and the de-

---

[4]McFague, ix-x.

[5]Howard and Edna Hong, trans and ed, *Søren Kierkegaard's Journals and Papers*, 7 vols. (Bloomington: Indiana University Press, 1967-78). E.g., I, 73, no. 182; III, 265-304, nos. 2854-2921. In the vol. III entries, it is primarily the satire on the way Christians seek to evade the claim of scripture upon them that attests Kierkegaard's high estimate of scripture's authority. Typical is the following, under the heading "God's Word":

This word of God, very simply, contains God's will for us and his commands—and this we evade in such a way that we pretend as if everything were in order. We have God's word, we are a Christian nation, and so on—and the only things which occupy us are the artistic, the scientific-scholarly...While the pastors dispute about who can write most beautifully, while journals and periodicals with deep seriousness criticize the artistic aspects of the language, the construction, etc., we completely forget that we are to act according to this, that God has not really given his word as material for a literary exercise to see who is able to present it most elegantly. This is so completely forgotten that to say it in earnest would be regarded as ridiculous.

The remarks in the *Attack Upon Christendom* (Howard and Edna Hong, trans. and eds. [Boston: Beacon Press, 1956; originally, Princeton: Princeton University Press, 1944]) go to the same effect. See, for example, "A Eulogy Upon the Human Race, Or, A Proof that the New Testament Is No Longer Truth," 105f.

mands it makes upon the imaginations of its readers. I hope to show in this and following chapters that Kierkegaard's actual use of scripture manifests a far more nuanced and sophisticated sense of its authority than the view presupposed either by the pillars of orthodoxy in his time or by proponents of the Bible-as-classic in ours.

For the present it might be helpful to examine the construal of the Bible-as-classic more closely. If Kierkegaard were available to comment, I have little doubt he would regard the "classic" construal as a category mistake analogous to his own age's confusion of the concept "genius" with that of "apostle."[6] Whether "classic" is meant to replace the category "scripture" *à la* McFague or only reposition it *à la* Tracy, it misses the point and obscures the issue: namely, that in and through the Bible, with the marks of historical contingency all about it, the Word of God again breaks in upon human experience to awaken, challenge, transform, and shape the reader in its own unique, cruciform image.[7] For Kierkegaard, the Bible's aesthetic quality and cultural impact are only relative goods (and potential distractions). What is decisive about it as scripture is that it is a unique occasion for contemporaneity with Christ, which itself is a unique revelatory event—moreover, a unique learning event. Through scripture one learns—not doctrines—but to speak, feel, think, see, and imagine Christianly. Through scripture, one learns the grammar of Christian faith.

The Kierkegaardian critique of the Bible-as-classic construal resembles what we heard Hauerwas say of scripture in the Introduction, i.e., that it is a paradigm for faith's perspective on reality. It also anticipates an important contemporary theological critique. This critique observes that the "classic" construal trades upon an "experiential-expressivist" model of religious language and literature. By this model, the Bible is thought to give expression to a prelinguistic, universal human experience of the divine, an experience which finds analogous expressions in other historical media and in

---

[6]See *On Authority and Revelation: The Book on Adler, or, a Cycle of Ethico-Religious Essays*, Walter Lowrie, trans. (Princeton: Princeton University, 1955). See also the useful commentary on both the work as a whole and the "genius"/"apostle" distinction in L. Joseph Rosas, *Scripture in the Thought of Søren Kierkegaard* (Nashville: Broadman & Holman, 1994), 46-52.

[7]McFague's paired reference to "an incarnational christology or a canonical Scripture" (x), both of which she rejects, makes an association that accurately describes Kierkegaard's position. Indeed, so close is the association one could switch the adjectives and describe his position as a "canonical christology and an incarnational Scripture."

other cultures. The critique challenges this notion of pre-linguistic universal experience, however, to propose that language, embedded in specific forms of life, shapes human experience in culturally specific ways, and does not merely reflect it.[8] Experience, then, cannot function as it does in the "classic" construal, as a pristine criterion for judging the adequacy of particular linguistic expressions (e.g., the Bible). Rather, the expressions are what make any given experience available. Human communities come into existence as certain expressions attain the status of large-scale "imaginative paradigms,"[9] and learning to "see" the world through such a paradigm generates experience distinctive of a particular community.

It is important to notice what is and is not being said here. To use the phrase *sola scriptura* approvingly from the cultural-linguistic perspective is in no way to deny the role of metaphor and the imagination in religious language and experience. In fact, it is to insist on the unsubstitutability of the metaphors that go together to constitute the Bible as the Christian imaginative paradigm, and, as a consequence, it is to expect a difference in the experience produced by that paradigm from the experiences produced by other religious paradigms. Neither is it to succumb to a fideism that renders questions of scripture's truthfulness moot and choices among rival imaginative paradigms as purely arbitrary and subjective. Rather, it is to say that such questions and choices entail extraordinarily complex verification procedures, which: (1) do not admit of simplistic fact/fiction, reason/faith dichotomies or allow recourse to a supposedly neutral epistemological

---

[8]As applied to the study of religion, this critique is perhaps most closely associated with George Lindbeck, who develops it as part of what he calls a "cultural-linguistic" model of religion drawn from the work of such figures as Ludwig Wittgenstein in philosophy, Clifford Geertz in anthropology, T. S. Kuhn in the philosophy of science, and Karl Barth and Hans Frei in theology. See Lindbeck's *The Nature of Doctrine: Religion and Theology in a Postliberal Age* (Philadelphia: Westminster, 1984). Garrett Green has sharpened the critique with specific reference to Tracy and McFague's construal of the Bible as a classic. See his *Imagining God: Theology and the Religious Imagination* (San Francisco: Harper, 1989), 119-23, 127-34.

[9]The term "imaginative paradigm" is Garrett Green's and is at the heart of his thesis in *Imagining God* (n. 8, above). He applies the term to the Bible as a way of describing its normative status as canonical scripture. The term highlights the fact that in canonical perspective, "the various parts of the Bible are grasped in a single gestalt," the unity of which "is not a uniformity but a wholeness, that is, a holistic pattern" (116). The authority of this imaginative paradigm is exercised as it renders God—via the "image of God" (83-104)—to the reader/hearer's imagination. Or as Green puts it, "Scripture, rightly employed, enables its hearers to imagine God" (119).

language or stance, and (2) entail a holistic logic characteristic of the paradigm shifts we see in the natural and social sciences.[10] Finally, *sola scriptura* is not meant to immunize scripture from criticism, whether historical or ethical. The problems associated, for instance, with the patriarchalism manifest in both the content of scripture and the way it has been marshalled by the tradition are intensified, not obscured, by this emphasis on the uniqueness of scripture. It is precisely such problems that necessitate our exploration of the Rule of faith as a prior construal governing how we are to see the Bible as scripture.

Of course, it is also such problems that make the Bible-as-classic construal an attractive alternative to "scripture." So far the discussion of this construal has been theoretical. To test the actual difference it can make when the Bible is read as a classic, shorne of the authority denoted by "scripture," we need to look at a practical application that might exemplify the approach. One of the strongest examples is provided by one of the formulators, Frank Kermode, in his widely read and influential *The Genesis of Secrecy*.[11] Following a probe of this book, a classic in its own right, we shall turn to Kierkegaard's *WL* to inspect the contrast Kierkegaard provides to Kermode's reading. The final portion of the chapter will be given to elaborating the notion of love that underlies the contrast.

I. The Bible as Classic: A Contemporary Effort, or, Reading Beyond the Pale: What's Missing?

Like all Kermode's forays into biblical literature, *The Genesis of Secrecy* is brilliant. Kermode is sensitive, sympathetic, and profoundly humane throughout—enough so that the presumptive critic might well feel a certain embarrassment at tilting with giants. In this case, the embarrassment is exacerbated by Kermode's anticipating exactly how someone like me would go about the tilting.[12] Nevertheless,

---

[10]For amplifications of this argument, see Lindbeck, 130-34, and Green, 134-45. See also Green's "'The Bible As...': Fictional Narrative and Scriptural Truth," in his collection of essays, *Scriptural Authority and Narrative Interpretation* (Philadelphia: Fortress, 1987), 79-96.

[11]Frank Kermode, *The Genesis of Secrecy: On the Interpretation of Narrative* (Cambridge, MA: Harvard University Press, 1979). Page numbers will be cited parenthetically in the text.

[12]My critique shares certain of the lines laid out in an article by Joel Marcus, "Mark 4:10-12 and Marcan Epistemology," *Journal of Biblical Literature*, 103

Genesis provides a kind of parable of blindness, a story of how hermeneutical construals structure our seeing and, in this case especially, our unseeing.

Kermode says his book is about interpretation, and he claims, rightly, that interpretation is typically institutional: it occurs in institutional settings with the institutions claiming privileged access to their canonical texts and a special understanding among their members. Thereby lines get drawn between insiders and outsiders. With respect to the church and its canon, Kermode takes a deliberate stand as an outsider; the book is dedicated "To those outside." And here is how institutional interpretation works, he says: "Outsiders see but do not perceive. Insiders read and perceive, but always in a different sense" (144).

That is exactly what I am going to say. The key text is the Gospel of Mark, which Kermode wants to interpret "in a wholly secular way," i.e., as an outsider (15). Well and good, but for "insiders," I shall argue, Mark makes not just different sense, but a different *kind* of sense from that which Kermode expects, a kind of sense that his wholly secular way takes him out of position to perceive.

Mark's fourth chapter is the linchpin of Kermode's argument. Not coincidentally, Mark 4 is a chapter about perception, about hearing and understanding God's Word. The chapter begins with the parable of the sower. The perception language has been highlighted:

> Again he began to teach beside the sea. And a very large crowd gathered about him, so that he got into a boat and sat in it on the sea; and the whole crowd was beside the sea on the land. 2) And he taught them many things in parables, and in his teaching he said to them: 3) **Listen!** A sower went out to sow. 4) And as he sowed, some seed fell along the path, and the birds came and devoured it. 5) Other seed fell on rocky ground, where it had not much soil, and immediately it sprang up, since it had no depth of soil; 6) and when the sun rose it was scorched, and since it had no root it withered away. 7) Other seed fell among thorns and the thorns grew up and choked it, and it yielded no grain. 8) And other seeds fell into

---

(1984): 557-574. No doubt Kermode would find my similarities with Marcus rather telling. They would be seen as "lines" of defense, sociologically grounded in our role as "interpreters de metier" (*Genesis*, 45), and psychologically wired by our anxiety to recuperate the institutional privileges Kermode has exposed. (On my differences from Marcus, see below, n. 14.)

good soil and brought forth grain, growing up and increasing and yielding thirtyfold and sixtyfold and a hundredfold." 9) And he said, "**He who has ears to hear, let him hear.**" 10) And when he was alone, those who were about him with the twelve asked him concerning the parables. 11) And he said to them, "To you has been given the secret of the kingdom of God, but for those outside everything is in parables; 12) **so that they may indeed see but not perceive, and may indeed hear but not understand**; lest they should turn again, and be forgiven." 13) And he said to them, "Do you not understand this parable? How then will you understand all the parables? 14) The sower sows the word..." (RSV)

Kermode's interpretation focuses on Jesus' scandalous account of his parabolic pedagogy: "I teach in parables so outsiders won't understand, repent, and be forgiven." In this formula of exclusion Kermode hears not the voice of Jesus necessarily, much less that of God, but the voice of the early church, as a redaction critic might—and as we might (even if "we" happen to be believers who also hear it as the voice of the "Christ, the Son of God" [Mark 1:1]).

To put it more sharply, Kermode hears the formula as the self-legitimating effort of an ecclesiastical institution jealous to guard the gates of understanding against intrusion by impious, unwanted outsiders. Interpretation, Knowledge, Salvation—all of that has become a privilege of the institutional elect, a "spiritual" secret reserved for a "spiritual" elite, "insider information" *par excellence*. But a word of caution: Kermode treats the "secret" in Mark's Gospel as if it were a matter of information.

Kermode goes on to say that Mark's Gospel, like his own book, is about interpretation in general, or rather about the *un*interpretability of texts, the obscurity of all narrative. The "parables are about *everybody's* incapacity to penetrate their sense" (27, my emphasis), and what the Gospel reveals, if anything, is the predilection of religious institutions for mystification in the service of exclusion.

Admittedly, Kermode's account is compelling. It makes sense both of much empirical history and the welter of conflicting interpretations that always confront us. And Kermode surely has a right to pursue his interest in a secular reading of the Bible. More, it is important for the church that he do so, since in the judgments passed on scripture by the world, in the person of such an astute observer as Kermode, the church may be called to hear God's judgment upon itself.[13] I want to ask, however, what falls out of sight when he pursues that interest?

There is a short answer. What falls out are the text's imperatives.[14] Kermode makes no mention of the fact that Jesus both begins and concludes the parable with the command to "listen"/"hear" (vv. 3, 9). He fails to mention that Jesus twice employs the idiom "Whoever has ears to hear" (vv. 9 and 23)—a phrase suggesting that proper hearing takes a certain willingness, a readiness, a disposition to hear. Our interpreter seems undisposed to hear that phrase. In a secular world, obedience grates.

What's in an imperative, we ask? The very character of the gospel narratives as religious literature, for one thing. For it is precisely at the imperatives that the Gospels break out of the strict confines of story form to address readers directly and make ultimate claims on their lives. Or better, it is the imperatives that extend the narrative's boundaries to include the readers in a story of everyone's ultimate destiny.[15]

---

[13]This point is made with special cogency by Rowan D. Williams, "Postmodern Theology and the Judgment of the World," in *Postmodern Theology: Christian Faith in a Pluralist World*, Frederic B. Burnham, ed. (San Francisco: Harper, 1989), 92-112.

[14]My difference from Marcus ("Marcan Epistemology") is precisely the emphasis I place on the text's imperatives. Marcus argues that this softens the picture of divinely appointed limitations on human perception (only those whom God gives ears to hear can hear, 562), a theme basic to the apocalyptic scenario that informs Mark's epistemology and which, after all, is the crux of the problem posed by Jesus' statement in v. 12. However, I would insist on the tension, irreconcilable as it is, between the two themes of divine determination and the human responsibility implicit in the imperatives. This same tension is maintained throughout the biblical literature: pentateuchal (the hardening of Pharaoh's heart), sapiential (Prov 16:9), apocalyptic (Dan 11:32-36 and Rev 20:12-15), and prophetic, including the Isaiah text (6:9-10) that Mark has Jesus quote here. The point of Mark's depiction is clear: it is to show that Jesus in his teachings, actions, and death is fulfilling the Isaianic vision of the divine word which sovereignly effects first hardening and then opening, utter judgment followed by unimaginable salvation, all the while demanding human response. Kierkegaard, too, sees that paradoxical tension as one not to be dissolved.

[15]That Mark intends Jesus' words to address the reading audience as well as the hearers within the narrative proper is indicated at two points in particular. First is the superscription in 1:1 that places the readers on the same ostensibly inside track as the disciples with respect to "the secret of the kingdom" (4:11): the secret is "Jesus Messiah, the Son of God." The proclamation of the gospel thus pertains to both the explicit and the implied audiences. Second is Jesus' comment-with-imperative at the end of the apocalyptic discourse of Mark 13: "And what I say to you I say to all, Watch!"

Naturally, one can always avoid inclusion by disregarding the imperatives, but that would be to disregard significant features in Mark's design: such as the fact that the proclamation of the gospel begins with Jesus' imperatives, "Repent and believe" (1:15); and that the first word to the disciples is the command "Follow me" (twice: 1:17, 2:14); and that right before our parable Jesus has said, "Whoever does the will of God is my family" (3:35). These summons to obedience are the literary-contextual preconditions for reading Mark's fourth chapter. But they are outside Kermode's interest, certainly his outsider's purview.

Kermode also omits the Marcan Jesus' own interpretation of the parable. Verses 14-20 say that the parable is about hearing and heeding the "word." "Seed," "secret," and "word" are all rough (if shifting) equivalents, and according to Jesus the word wants to work, to be "fruitful." But in order for the word/seed to "bear fruit," which it can in miraculous abundance, Jesus says, one must "accept" it. "But those that were sown upon the good soil are the ones who hear the word and accept it and bear fruit, thirtyfold and sixtyfold and a hundredfold" (v. 20). Obviously, the resolve to remain "outside" is a decision not to "accept."[16]

What continually confounds readers in Mark's Gospel, "insiders" and "outsiders" alike, is that the secret/word is Jesus himself,[17] not "information," not a cognitive proposition with a meaning that can be stated (like a doctrine), but a life to be lived, receptively.[18] What Mark represents is not hopeless obscurity but the conviction that ob-

---

[16]The decision either to accept or not to accept is, by definition, an exercise of human freedom. Kierkegaard would insist on the paradox that it remains such even when those who choose to accept acknowledge their power of acceptance as a gift of God (cf. n. 14, above). My concern in these pages is not to untangle the freedom/necessity conundrum; much less is it to condemn Kermode for his choices. It is only to observe the consequences of his choices in how he reads, or, more specifically, in what he perceives or doesn't perceive in what he reads.

[17]The point is widely shared in Marcan scholarship. See Luke T. Johnson, *The Writings of the New Testament: An Interpretation* (Philadelphia: Fortress Press, 1986), 162, 168; Donald H. Juel, *Mark*, Augsburg Commentary on the New Testament (Minneapolis: Augsburg, 1990), 29f., 120, and 206f.; and Jack Dean Kingsbury, *Jesus Christ in Matthew, Mark, and Luke*, Proclamation Commentaries (Philadelphia: Fortress Press, 1981), 32-35.

[18]This phrase has a double reference. Jesus lived his own life receptively, i.e., as a gift from God. And believers are invited to receive Jesus' life as their own and to live it in his manner, receptively. On receptivity as a dimension of love and the Rule of faith, see chapter 4.

scurity comes from wanting one's salvation in the form of a bloodless gnosis. But Jesus insists on the bloody way: "Follow me!"

Indeed, under closer inspection the Gospel of Mark is not about interpretation-in-general. To read it as if it were looks like a way of dodging what in fact it is talking about. What it is talking about is a very *particular* problem of understanding, which resides not in texts per se, but in people, like the disciples.[19]

The disciples in Mark are the paradigmatic insiders, those entrusted with "the secret of the kingdom of God" (4:11), the ones to whom Jesus "privately explains everything" (4:34). Nevertheless, they persistently misunderstand him.[20] In effect, the insiders prove themselves simultaneously to be outsiders by misreading the Word even during his ministry. For instance, in 7:18 Mark subtly amplifies Jesus' question from 4:13 ("Do you not understand this parable?") with the word "also" so as to associate the disciples, not just with the general crowd (7:14), but with the Pharisees whose hostile question (7:5) prompted the parable. "Then do you also fail to understand?" Jesus asks, incredulously. The association of the disciples' misunderstanding with that of Jesus' opponents is reinforced by 6:52 and 8:17-21 when Mark attributes to the disciples the same hardheartedness by which he had characterized the lethal hostility of the Pharisees and the Herodians in their early resolve to "destroy" Jesus (3:5f.).[21]

Moreover, like that of Jesus' hardened enemies, the disciples' misunderstanding proves to be motivated. Their confusion is not simply imposed upon them by the ambiguities of language itself, though language itself—cut off from the relevant forms of life—has ambigu-

---

[19]As we shall see below (n. 31), this distinction in where one locates the "problem," in text or people, is one which divides Kierkegaard and the later Wittgenstein from many postmodern critics and theorists whom they otherwise anticipate.

[20]The disciples' misunderstanding of Jesus is thematic in Mark (e.g., 4:13, 41; 5:31; 6:51f.; 7:18; 8:16-21, etc.), as all the commentators observe, e.g., Juel, 72, 74, 76-78, 233; Paul J. Achtemeier, *Mark*, Proclamation Commentaries (Philadelphia: Fortress Press, 1975), 93; R. C. Tannehill, "The Disciples in Mark: The Function of a Narrative Role," *Journal of Religion* 57 (1977): 386-405.

[21]It is worth noting that the heart-hardening motif belongs to the immediate context of the Isaiah passage quoted in 4:12 and is readily invoked by that quotation. The allusion to Isa 6:9f. is especially clear in Mk 8:17, when Jesus asks the disciples directly, "Do you still not perceive or understand? Are your hearts hardened? Do you have eyes, and fail to see? Do you have ears and fail to hear?" Further, the latter passage reinforces the association of the disciples' hard-hearted misunderstanding with that of Jesus' lethal enemies by referring to the Pharisees and Herodians in an emphatic warning three verses earlier: "Watch out—beware of the yeast of the Pharisees and the yeast of the Herodians" (8:15).

ity aplenty. Rather, it is driven by fear. Roughly seventy percent of the instances of the word-family "fear"/"afraid" in Mark's Gospel apply to the disciples' response to Jesus.[22] The first instance is noteworthy in that it comes at the end of our chapter thematizing perception, acceptance, and (mis)understanding. After Jesus stills the storm at sea, he asks the disciples two questions, connecting their fear with faithlessness: "'Why are you afraid? Have you no faith?'" (4:40) The narrator then reiterates the connection: "And they were overcome with enormous fear, and said to one another, 'Who then is this...?'" (4:41). Both the fright and the bafflement are focused on the person of Jesus.

Still more significantly, three instances occur in the context of the three passion predictions that structure the central part of the Gospel (chaps. 8-10), in which Jesus makes his way to Jerusalem and execution. Thus, the fear motif gets linked with the theme of death. Specifically, right after each prediction by Jesus of his death, the disciples evince a misunderstanding of the teacher, compelling him to instruct them further in the meaning of true discipleship. True discipleship means sacrificial service (9:35, 10:43), drinking the cup of suffering that Jesus drinks (10:39), and taking up one's cross to follow Jesus (8:34). In an atmosphere thick with personal foreboding, the disciples experience terror that renders them foolish (9:6), uncomprehending (9:32), and perplexed (10:24, 32). In short, the disciples are scared to death of dying, which is where Jesus' imperative to follow will lead them.

Not incidentally, Mark brackets this central section of the Gospel with two stories about the healing of blind men (8:22-26 and 10:46-52). Bracketing is a typically Marcan device by which the author provides parabolic commentary on the bracketed material.[23] In this instance he is commenting ironically on the disciples' blindness, i.e., their slowness in coming to understand and faithfully accept their master. Afraid to accept the Word precisely because of where it/he will lead, they deceive themselves into thinking they do not understand it/him. Their misreading is an act of self-deception. They blind themselves.

I would not want to push too far the analogy between the disciples' "misreading" and Kermode's. Suffice it to say that a universal-

---

[22]*Phobés/phóbos*: 4:41; 5:15, 33; 6:50; 9:32; 10:32; 11:18; 16:8. Also, *deilós* ("timid") is used of the disciples' response to Jesus in 4:40, and *tarásso* ("be troubled") accompanies *phobés* ("be afraid") in 6:50.

[23]Johnson, 151.

izing move to the secular rubric "classic" has not guaranteed greater precision in the analysis of the biblical text. In this case, in fact, where the interest was in reading the text for what it shows us about reading any text (i.e., for interpretation-in-general), Mark's particular point about the singularity of the person of Christ and about the human condition revealed by that singular person is lost. On the other hand, we might note, by attending to Mark's particularity as scripture one finds oneself positioned for a rigorously critical self-scrutiny. After all, the effect of Mark's depiction of the disciples, precisely in their paradigmatic status, is to subvert the very insider/outsider hierarchy that Kermode thought himself to be discovering, and to do so from within the stance of faith.

Kermode's exegesis of the parable of the Good Samaritan in Luke's Gospel (Lk 10:25-37) confirms the pattern of his blindness. Without pursuing in detail his otherwise exquisite analysis, I can only mention the characteristic omission. He observes that the parable ends, open-endedly of course, in a question: "Who proved neighbor to the man who fell among thieves?" (24). In fact, it does not. If we are going to accept Jesus' application as the parable's endpoint, the parable "ends" in the imperative: "Go and do likewise!" The parable still ends open-endedly, for the task of understanding remains with the hearer.[24] The understanding will be given, and get enacted, in the doing. That is where love comes in. "Go and love that way!" is the imperative force of the gospel. By assimilating the Bible to the general category, "classic," so as to talk about narrativity in general, Kermode misses that peculiar force and its distinctive content.

II. Judgment Judged and the Grammar of Love

Surely if anyone saw the imperatives in scripture, it was Søren Kierkegaard. Kierkegaard lived in a milieu of nationalistic Lutheran orthodoxy that had sloganeered the doctrine of "justification by faith" into a device not just for avoiding the idolatrous meritoriousness of works, but for avoiding works per se—that is, sloganeered it into a device for divorcing faith from practice, the practice being in-

---

[24]By polemicizing against Kermode's version of hermeneutic openness, I am by no means promoting a model of scripture as "a closed book whose meaning is exhausted by the standard theological lexicon," as Mark Wallace neatly puts it ("Theology Without Revelation?" *Theology Today*, 45 [1988], 212). When interpretation is tied to the whole of life, as the canonical literature would have it, then it is more open-ended than ever.

creasingly one of making capital.[25] Living in that milieu, Kierkegaard made it his task to rub the face of all Denmark in the imperatives of the gospel.

Congruent with his insistence that Thought was not Being, nor Hegelianism Christianity, Kierkegaard knew that interpretation was not just a mental process. As he saw it, all of scripture had a shingle hanging out saying, "Follow Me!" Or as he says in chiding the poet's (or literary critic's) tendency to aestheticize[26] scripture, "Ah, but with invisible letters behind every word in Holy Scriptures a disturbing notice confronts him—for there it reads: go and do likewise."[27] And he knew that the "likewise" meant loving the neighbor. By Kierkegaard's reading, it is the life of love that interprets the text.

This is curious. It implies that only by the activity of following can those "invisible letters" be read. "Walking with God," with Love's very self, Kierkegaard says, "constrains us to see in a new way" (*WL* 87)—i.e., so that we see the imperatives. But if we are walking with God, we are already following the imperatives that say to walk that way. More than curious, where and how this circle of seeing-walking/walking-seeing all begins is a great mystery.

Theologians have been wise to circularity for a long time. Those of the early church made it the substance of the ancient Rule of faith, which is basically a normative definition. Defining what Christian scripture is, the Rule prescribes how to read it as such. Essentially, the

---

[25]For a detailed analysis of Kierkegaard's relation to the social, political, and economic currents of mid-nineteenth-century Danish culture, see Bruce H. Kirmmse, *Kierkegaard in Golden Age Denmark* (Bloomington: Indiana University Press, 1990). For a bitingly ironic statement by Kierkegaard himself illustrative of my point, see the following from *For Self-Examination and Judge for Yourselves!*, Walter Lowrie, trans. (Princeton: Princeton University Press, 1941), 41:

There is always with us a worldliness which would have the name of being Christian, but would have it at a price as cheap as possible. This worldliness became observant of Luther. It listened, and it took the precaution to listen a second time for fear it might have heard amiss, and thereupon it said, "Capital! That suits us exactly. Luther says, 'It is faith alone that matters'; the fact that his life expresses works he does not himself say, and now he is dead, so that this is no longer an actuality. Let us take then his word, his doctrine—and we are liberated from all works. Long live Luther!

[26]Kierkegaard's sense of the term is: to adopt a speculative, hypothetical approach to something (in this case a text); to render the text an object of purely disinterested consideration in that the possibilities it represents are not taken on as tasks to be actualized in one's concrete existence.

[27]*WL: Some Christian Reflections in the Form of Discourses*, Howard and Edna Hong, trans. and ed. (New York: Harper & Row Publishers, 1962), 62. Hereafter pages will be cited parenthetically in the text.

Rule legislates that scripture, read rightly ("rightly" for the Christian), everywhere speaks the love of God, and that it is only by God's love that one can thus rightly read it. There is the circle. That this love is not our own creation, however, means that it can come only as a gift, to be received in faith, even as we choose it.[28] There the circle mysteriously opens to the transcendent grace of God.

In the next chapter I shall develop more fully the Rule's odd logic and Kierkegaard's reliance on it. Suffice it to say here that Kierkegaard's *Works of Love* is a comprehensive exercise in the Rule of faith. Appropriately enough, the book begins by stating love's dependency on faith. Let me try to chart the argument and begin to delineate the grammar of love as Kierkegaard presents it. Three points of emphasis will be: (1) the fact that love has implications extending beyond private relations and into the public sphere, (2) the idea of love as a skill, and (3) our difficulty in identifying it. In the course of the discussion we shall come across a second parable of blindness and self-deception.

A biblical passage heads *WL*'s first chapter. It is a saying from Luke's Sermon on the Plain: "the tree is recognizable by its fruits" (Luke 6:44). Kierkegaard will develop the text dialectically, as evident from the chapter's title, "Love's *Hiddenness* and its Recognizability" (my emphasis). Why is love hidden? Because God is its source: a hidden source, undetected by the casual observer, nondemonstrable apart from the faith that confesses God. And because God is hidden, love has a hiddenness, too; it is eminently susceptible to different interpretations. What the believer calls love in her neighbor, the skeptic will doubt, the cynic will call sentimentality, and the neurologist will read as a printout of diverse electro-chemical blips, none of which decodes as anything like "love." Kierkegaard's point is that love must be believed in to be seen. It requires faith.

Faith is clearly a risky business, and Kierkegaard makes much of the way we worry over the possibility of being mistaken. On that same first page, he introduces the idea of being deceived, of self-deception in the matter of love. But he adds an interesting spin. We are accustomed to being suspicious, he says; we are wary of falling for love, surrounded as we are by so many glib love hucksters. But which would be worse, he asks—to be fooled by believing that there is love in your neighbor, hidden with God, or to be deceived by a "superficial shrewdness" that, in a resolve not to be taken for a fool, refuses to

---

[28]See nn. 14 and 16 above, on this paradox of freedom and necessity.

believe in love? He answers unequivocally: "To cheat oneself out of love is the most terrible deception" (23).

Kierkegaard would have us notice the dynamics of the deception, how it comes out of a comparative-competitive posture vis-à-vis the neighbor. He refers to the self-deceiver's "superficial shrewdness" as a "flattering conceit" indicative of a desire for superiority—as if one's integrity were established not just by avoiding looking foolish to others, but by keeping the upper hand over them. What Kierkegaard will show in the rest of the book is how demonic such a posture becomes when a whole culture adopts it. Self-deception can turn ideological. Skepticism toward love, like its cousin, sentimentalism, can get harnessed to political, economic, and social programs of self-aggrandizement. For Kierkegaard, part of what is at risk in the issue of faith and whether one believes in love or not, is the health of the human community.

So love has its source in God and requires faith. That is its hiddenness—or "inwardness," as Kierkegaard liked to say. The other side of the coin is its recognizability, or outwardness. Though having a hidden and inward source, love will OUT. Like most emotions, love is not a strictly internal thing. It is a behavior; it has behavioral manifestations and reasonably determinate targets. It is part of the logic of love to express itself, to act toward its targets. Nor are the actions a by-product separable from the thing itself; they are part of the love, which is incomplete without them. The actions are the lov*ing*. Love works; hence the book's title.

Now if love entails action, it is a practice. Rather, it *is* praxis, for there is no loving-in-theory. And love has practice*s*, which can *be* practiced. This means that love is not just a feeling state or a mood, which may come and go uncontrollably at the caprice of glands and external circumstances. Neither is it simply an attitude, a private state of mind. Rather it is a skill, learned and practiced in social contexts, not least that of reading.

The point about praxis is crucial to our thesis in this chapter about the singularity and indispensability of scripture for the church. Kierkegaard will develop it emphatically. Further along in *WL* he insists that love "is sheer action":

It is not that secret, private, mysterious feeling behind the lattice of the inexplicable, which the poet wants to lure to the window, not a soul-mood which fondly knows no laws and hearkens only to singing—it is pure action and its every deed is holy, for it is the fulfilling of the law....Love in [Christ] was pure action. There was no moment, not a single one in his life, when love in him was merely the inactivity of feeling, which hunts for words while it lets time slip by, or a mood, which is self-satisfying, dwelling on itself with no task to perform—no, his love was pure action. (106)

And in a passage that will be the centerpiece of our next chapter, he describes love as an artful skill entailing—through practice—the education of one's tastes, the enhancement of one's powers of observation and attentiveness, the development of creativity and one's ability to discern novel possibilities (271f). For Christians, scripture is the paradigmatic occasion for getting the practice.

The significance of the category "skill" for religious life and sense-making has been highlighted by George Lindbeck.[29] Stanley Hauerwas develops the idea in a way especially relevant for our purposes when he describes truthfulness and rationality as two particular skills that Christians learn from the gospel in order to combat self-deception.[30] Mark's deconstruction of the insider/outsider dichotomy, which we observed earlier in this chapter, illustrates how his narrative might inaugurate a process of critical self-scrutiny for the believing reader. Here we might observe that truthfulness and rationality are love-related skills, or aspects of love, insofar as they belong to the self-scrutinizing practices known as confession and repentance, practices generated by learning to see the world and oneself under the sign of God's forgiving love, i.e., in light of Mark's narrative, the gospel story of Christ and the cross. The bite of that story is that the love it depicts also entails a judgment on human sin, which our impulse to autonomy and self-righteousness impels us to deny. We would rather listen to other, less offensive stories, or blunt the Bible's edge by assimilating it to other stories.

An unhappy consequence of the denial and assimilation is that, given the notion of love as a skill, if the love is not exercised, it will atrophy. What then, Kierkegaard (and Hauerwas) would have us ponder, if a whole culture should forget that love, like peace and justice, is a skill to be developed, not just an accident of nature, history, and temperament? What if the church should forget that reading scripture

---

[29]*The Nature of Doctrine*; see in particular chapter 6, section IV, "Intelligibility as Skill," 128-34.

[30]Stanley Hauerwas, *Truthfulness and Tragedy: Further Investigations into Christian Ethics*, with Richard Bondi and David B. Burrell (Notre Dame: University of Notre Dame Press, 1977), 79-98, and *Against the Nations: War and Survival in a Liberal Society* (Minneapolis: Winston Press, 1985), 6-9.

in love is an art to be practiced, and that without intentional practice the scriptures cease to be scripture—and the church ceases to be church?

In any event, Kierkegaard insists that love manifests itself in works, and, if so, then in principle it is recognizable, like the tree known by its fruit. But—here we see the dialectician—if love's works are recognizable in principle, in practice they are still eminently susceptible to misunderstanding. It is as with texts. Just as there is no one way to read and no one meaning to make but rather senses shift with shifting contexts, so there is no one way of construing an action. *For there is no one expression or no one deed which guarantees that love is present in it* (*WL*, 30). What might be love in the charitable deed of one person might be self-love in that same deed done by another—in which case the deed is not charitable, nor quite the same.

As Kierkegaard will say later in *WL*, "God and Christianity have no infallible signs" (146). Coupled with the remarks about indirect communication elsewhere in the authorship, such statements articulate a hermeneutic principle for Kierkegaard anticipating the notion of linguistic indeterminacy characteristic of contemporary poststructuralism. What distinguishes him from most deconstructionists, however, is what distinguishes Mark the evangelist from Kermode in the latter's emphasis on the uninterpretability of narrative per se. Like Mark and *contra* Kermode, Kierkegaard locates the responsibility for making sense in people, not in language itself.[31] Thus, with respect to the difficulty of interpreting love, Kierkegaard says, "It depends on how the deed is done" (30).

So the hiddenness of love has returned. The intention, the attitude, the inwardness—while not a sufficient criterion of love—is a necessary criterion. What conclusion are we to draw regarding Jesus' statement about the tree? Jesus says the tree is recognizable by its fruit. We just can't tell for sure what the fruit is. Love is known by its works; but given the hiddenness of the intention, how can we tell if someone's works are loving or not? And why the emphasis on recognizability?

Kierkegaard seems to have turned Jesus' meaning obscure before our very eyes. What was plain a moment ago now darkens. Jesus' words are a mini-parable, and to crack it Kierkegaard works intra-

---

[31]Accordingly, there is a clearer connection between Kierkegaard and the later Wittgenstein, whose emphasis on language games and forms of life he directly influenced, than between SK and most post-structuralist/deconstructionist theorists.

textually, citing a parable from the Old Testament (2 Sam 12:1-7).[32] Kierkegaard reminds us how the prophet Nathan tried to bring King David to a recognition of his royal crime in killing Uriah and taking Bathsheba. Nathan tells the story of the rich man who takes a poor man's only possession, a lamb, which was like an only child to him. It used to sleep in his bosom and drink from his cup. David turns livid with indignation at the rich man's lack of compassion and pronounces royal judgment, at which point Nathan's discourse turns direct: King David, "you are the man!"

"The tree is recognizable by its fruit," says Jesus. "We are the tree!" says Kierkegaard. Our position is not outside the parable, but inside it if we are to read the text religiously. Our task is not to "interpret" the fruit, but to produce it. And to get the point, we have to hear the text as addressed to us:

> The holy words of our text are not spoken to encourage us to get busy judging one another; they are rather spoken *warningly* to the individual, to you my reader, and to me, to encourage each one of us not to let his love become unfruitful but to work so that it is capable of being recognized by its fruits, whether these are recognized by others or not. (31; my emphasis.)

Read lovingly, Jesus' point is to get us busy with actual loving, not to provide a criterion for judging others, or even for recognizing love's fruits. The saying works exhortatively to motivate loving, not propositionally, to assert some objective norm that leaves us untouched while we apply it to someone else. As soon as judging becomes our interest—as it typically does, being one of our pet devices for justifying ourselves *vis-à-vis* others—we lose the sense of the text and the love that it calls for, condemning ourselves to unlovingness in the process. We thereby effect a self-judgment, claims Kierkegaard.

"Judge not that ye be not judged." In chapter six Luke places that famous maxim in the same context with "By your fruits...." Kierkegaard in turn strings the notion of reciprocal judgment, which Luke links with the "By your fruits" saying, like a red thread through-

---

[32]While each chapter of this book will illustrate Kierkegaard's "intratextual" practice, chapter 2 will develop more systematically its significance for his canonical hermeneutics and the Rule of faith. See especially pp. 82-84.

out the length of *WL*.[33] In the linkage we catch the sense. Our situation with respect to the Bible is like David's with respect to Nathan's parable. David hears the parable as an occasion[34] to exercise the royal prerogative to judge his subjects, and in so doing manifests his blindness to the fact that he himself is subject to God. By self-interestedly and unlovingly reading the text Nathan puts before him, which here means reading as if the parable were not about him but someone else, David misreads it, and inadvertently judges himself.

Who then is to judge? Kierkegaard would insist that it can only be Love who judges, since "like is known [recognized] only by like" (33; cf. 183-84), and in concluding the chapter he states that human love is recognizable to God who is Love. But love can also become recognizable to faithful humans, to the extent that they become loving like God (cf. 74). Does this mean that, having become God-like, we are permitted to judge one another after all?

Kierkegaard provides a check on false self-divinization. If we are loving like God, we will not be exercising our heightened powers of recognition against our neighbors (and to our advantage), but in their favor, so as to love forth the love we see in them, building up ("edifying" in its original sense) the love in them and building them up ("edifying" them) with love (206).[35] This is behavior singularly atypical of human beings—so atypical we have to be told to do it.

---

[33]Lk 6:36. Kierkegaard cites the text explicitly on 220 at the culmination of a discussion parallelling that of his first chapter on the task of believing in love and the danger of self-deception in refusing to believe. For Kierkegaard, passing judgment and self-deception are deeply wedded habits. Similarly, the theme of judgment often occurs in connection with a comparative, book-keeping, quantitative approach to love grounded in rebellion against God; see in particular the discussion of comparison on172-84, which culminates in the affirmation that "God is judge" (183). For the judgment theme elsewhere in *WL*, see 113-18, 127, 230, and 272-73.

Finally, the Conclusion of *WL* presents an especially intense admonition against judgment, relating God's role as judge with the principle of "like-for-like," just as in the beginning chapter. Here Kierkegaard cites yet a third saying from the same Lucan pericope: "Why do you see the speck in your brother's eye, but do not notice the log that is in your own eye?" (6:41). The log is the self-blinding impulse to judge others, Kierkegaard comments, by which impulse we get what we give: judgment.

[34]On scripture as an "occasion" that one may take for either love or hate, sin or salvation, see 276-77 where Kierkegaard cites Paul on the Law (Torah), Rom 7:8. The concept of scripture as occasion is one of Kierkegaard's many hedges against the form of misplaced objectivity that today goes by the name of fundamentalism.

[35]On "edification" as a principle in Kierkegaard's hermeneutic, see below, chapter 2, part III, 4, c. On Kierkegaard's employment of the term's original sense, see chapter 2, n. 74.

Hence the repetition of the biblical imperative. Kierkegaard treats that imperative directly in the second and longest chapter of *WL*, titled, "You shall love your neighbor as yourself" (the Royal Law). At this point, however, rather than follow him into his second chapter with further close reading, it might better serve our purposes to take a more synthetic and systematic view of what *WL* says about neighbor-love.

III. Transcendence Means Difference

Kierkegaard's concept of neighbor-love may be summarized as follows:[36] it is transcendent; it is inclusive, nonpreferential and noncomparative; it is transformative, edifying, and creative; it is sacrificial; and it is different, so different as to be offensive.

1. *Transcendent.* How different can Christian love be? So different, Kierkegaard argues, that it will look for all the world like hate (114), and so different that it has to be commanded: "You shall love!" Yet how can love be commanded? There is a first offense. The command—and its implicit claim on our obedience—is an offense to human autonomy, a heteronomous assault on our moral freedom.[37] Nothing makes plainer the outrageousness of the biblical notion of love than this imperative. And it makes an imperious claim, implying that love itself is imperative, essential, even ultimate.

Who would be in a position to make such a claim about what is ultimate? Only God, and of course it is God who issues the command (if scripture is read as scripture, i.e., as Word of God). That the command to love comes from God is another mark of this love's difference. As Kierkegaard says—three times in one paragraph—no human heart would invent such a command, or such a love (40-41; cf. 117-18). Nor, we might add, would the heart know such love apart from the witness of scripture.

---

[36]Apart from the orientation to the scriptural imperative, my explication of love owes much to that of Sylvia I. Walsh, "Forming the Heart: The Role of Love in Kierkegaard's Thought," in *The Grammar of the Heart: Thinking with Kierkegaard and Wittgenstein*, Richard H. Bell, ed. (San Francisco: Harper & Row, Publishers, 1988), 234-56.

[37]Kierkegaard would agree: the command would be heteronomous if God were not Love and the "law" were not proper to authentic selfhood. But alienated ears hear Love's voice as alien, Kierkegaard would observe, and what seems to us the "natural" urge to autonomy is but the (barely) disguised form of a rebellious desire to be God ourselves.

That is what is meant by saying that Christian love is transcendent. We are not its author. Rather, Love authors us, authoring and originating the love in us. Here Kierkegaard points us in the direction of a genuinely biblical, and nonadjudicatory, concept of biblical authority. Scripture is authoritative primarily as it works performatively to author the life of love in its readers—not primarily in its use as a static resource for constructing doctrine and drawing lines of distinction between insiders and outsiders, much less as a bludgeon for coercing opponents.[38] So, the witness of scripture being "original" (originative) in this strong sense (42-44), love does not originate with us; it confronts us from beyond. When left to our own devices, it is not something we do naturally. Hence love is given to us as a duty, undergoing thereby what Kierkegaard calls "the transformation of the eternal" (41, 47-57). Transcendence makes a transforming, qualitative difference.

Further, the Royal Law has it that we are first to love God above all, which is another way of expressing love's transcendence and ultimacy, and then the neighbor as the self. It is as if we cannot love the neighbor rightly without loving God first, that is to say, without loving Love—who after all "first loved us" and then told us to "go and do likewise" (70, 74). That is why Christian love has constant reference to God.[39] God is the crucial factor in every true love relation-

---

[38]For a contemporary critical effort to explain the term "authority" in terms of an "authoring" power, see Delwin Brown, "Struggle till Daybreak: On the Nature of Authority in Theology," *Journal of Religion* 65 (1985): 15-32.

Admittedly, a non-adjudicatory concept of authority does not easily meet our practical administrative and disciplinary needs. But could it be that love intends the transformation of our notions of what constitutes both "administration" and "discipline"?

David Kelsey has shown that in actual practice Christians use the concept "biblical authority" in at least two broad senses (within each of which a plethora of finer distinctions can be made). In the sense I call "primary," scripture is authoritative as it shapes a person's life. In a secondary sense, it functions authoritatively "for theology" as theologians appeal to scripture in performing their task of critiquing and reforming the church's life and speech. (*The Uses of Scripture in Recent Theology*, 135, 139-55.) As I read it, tensions will exist between the two senses of authority to the degree that theological criticism passes over into personal judgment. Indeed, unless there is a difference between "criticism" and "judgment" in the first place, which is not at all self-evident, such tensions could become quite unbearable. (See further, chapter 2.)

[39]On this important point, see further, *WL*, 143, 158-59. The final stroke against all sentimental "coddling" talk of love, Kierkegaard says in the Conclusion, is that "Christianity...makes your every relationship to other human beings into a God-relationship" (345). That we are so typically unaware that we are making "constant

ship, the mediator of love, a kind of "third-party," says Kierkegaard. Every true love relationship is really a triangle: the lover, Love, and the neighbor (280; cf. 118).

Kierkegaard knows this will compound our sense of outrage.[40] Should we not love people for their own sake? To love them for God's sake would seem to violate both their integrity and ours.

2. *Nonpreferential, Noncomparative, Inclusive.* The fact is, Kierkegaard argues, loving others for their own sake is a fiction (253). As if they had a sake apart from God! In reality it is a nefarious self-love.[41] For if God is not the middle term in the love relationship, then *preference* is (65-70). The real rival to Christian love is, not eros, but preferential love, love based on the tastes, desires and demands of the self. If God is not the source of the imperative, then it seems we issue our own and become a law unto ourselves, impelled by our preferences.

Such is how it usually is in the forms of love commonly celebrated in the world, erotic love and friendship. Preference is their principal dynamic. The "beloved" and the "friend" appeal to us on the basis of our preferences, our likes. We select them. And of course that means we exclude others. Preference is exclusive.

Kierkegaard is utterly relentless in showing how the dynamics of preference penetrate every dimension of "Christendom," that *nomos* in which Christianity has been put to ideological (i.e., preferential) service in the interests of capital and the nation-state. Preference pervades class structure, top to bottom; it permeates economic, political, and religious institutions, not to mention the media; it informs both the social forces of reaction and those of (apparent) change; and

---

reference to God" in our "every relationship" is somewhat unsettling, to say the least.

[40]See Walsh, 236, where she paraphrases Kierkegaard to this effect: Is it not especially in love relationships that we say, three's a crowd?

[41]The form of self-love under discussion here is to be distinguished from what Kierkegaard calls a *"proper* self-love" (35, my emphasis). The latter he defines, playfully, as the sort of love with which you love yourself when you love your neighbor as yourself (39). Basically, he means self-respect: i.e., the healthy self-regard and independence that "has the law of its existence in the relationship of love itself to the eternal" (53) and therefore has the strength not to mistake love's task of seeking the neighbor's genuine good with complying with their every whim (36). In other words, the proper self-love that belongs to neighbor-love must be sharply distinguished from masochism.

it structures the so-called private relations of erotic love and friend-ship.[42]

The preference operative in all these areas really is self-love. To the extent that we deal with others on the basis of preference, the others are not genuinely other (37-38). They are either another me, a projection of myself which I love in my egotism, or they do not exist for me humanly. Maybe I call them the enemy and demonize them with hatred.

On its way to robbing others of their selfhood, preference makes invidious distinctions. It is obsessed with marking distinctions between people, seizing upon the distinctions between me and you, us and them—in order to make a self-serving discrimination. On the other hand, the likenesses we find in certain others become marks of dis-tinction that unite us only in order that we may form with them a new united "selfish self" against others who lack such "distinctions" (68).

But how can we dispense with distinctions? Are not the distinc-tions what make the other 'other'? Yes, indeed, unless I seize upon one or another distinction only promptly to eliminate it by using it as the basis for an identification of you with me, loving only that in you which feeds my image of myself. Again your otherness disappears, as it also disappears if I seize upon your marks of distinction as a pretext to remove both you and your distinctions from my regard because they do not suit my preferences.

But Kierkegaard sees neighbor-love as genuinely other-wise. When you love your neighbor as yourself, you love the other, not as the other-I, but as the other-you (69), a person whose integrity is given by and owed to God, a someone not at the I's disposal, thus nei-ther self-possessed nor prepossessing. Hence, your neighbor's other-ness, distinctiveness, remains intact.

---

[42]See 60-65, 81-96, 118-29, 292-305. For Kierkegaard, modern culture is one of thoroughgoing materialism, and he sees a direct relation between materialism and self-love. When one ceases to refer one's love in faith to the invisible God, one finds substitutes among what is visible, beginning with the self (or a deluded notion of the self as independent of God). Thus, preferences generate comparisons ("This is better, more effective, more valuable than that"), by which in turn a calculating, quan-titative orientation is insinuated into all one's relationships. The fact that material-ism goes hand-in-hand with abstraction—and individualism with the evisceration of the individual—was of course one of the ironies Kierkegaard relished, and lamented. For more on this topic, see John W. Elrod, *Kierkegaard and Christendom* (Princeton: Princeton University Press, 1981); and Merold Westphal, *Kierke-gaard's Critique of Reason and Society* (Macon, GA: Mercer University Press, 1987).

So, as it turns out, it is because love has been made a duty commanded by God that we can respect another's integrity, loving the person concretely. And it is only as we love the other for God's sake, and not on the basis of our likes, that love can be radically inclusive. God's command purges the preferentiality and selfishness out of love, demanding that we love without distinction everyone in his or her concrete distinctiveness—or as Kierkegaard says, "loving everyone in particular and no one in partiality" (78). This is also the basis of authentic human equality, which for Kierkegaard adheres not in abstract natural rights, but in the historical particularity of God's having loved all indiscriminately. "Every individual has equal kinship to God in Christ," and everyone is equally addressed by this command, "You shall love the neighbor" (80, 122). So everyone is the neighbor, even the enemy.

3. *Transformative, Creative, Edifying.* This imperative works a nifty transformation, by a Word transforming the enemy into the neighbor. One would think that among Christians it would wreak quiet but inexorable havoc with the idea of the nation-state. Kierkegaard suggests as much.[43] What, after all, is the nation-state but a structure of institutional coercion whose purpose is to enforce the preferences, called the "interests," of some "clique" organized on the basis of one or more distinctions—ethnic, racial, religious, geographic, etc.— against other cliques (92-95)? And what other coercive institutional arrangements might be loved into oblivion were each to love the neighbor as the self? Not that it is optional for Christians to love so. For there stands the eternal imperative: "You shall love!"

When one loves as commanded, transformations are wrought— and not just forensically, by redefining people's status (from enemy to neighbor) and thus merely altering how you regard the neighbor

---

[43]The dialectic Kierkegaard plays between leaving worldly distinctions and their supporting structures in place and relativizing them into insignificance through neighbor-love is extremely subtle (see especially 80-90, 136-46). It may be too subtle to be fully coherent. The danger of directly attacking the distinctions is that broad socio-political action tends to de-personalize human beings and eviscerate individuality, reducing personhood to abstraction. At the same time, such activism can hardly fail to succumb to materialism (e.g., 302). Elsewhere Kierkegaard's term for this complex process is "demoralization" (*Concluding Unscientific Postscript*, David F. Swenson, trans.; tr. completed, intro. and notes by Walter Lowrie [Princeton: Princeton University Press, 1941], 120, 129, 135, 179). But the fact is that, when one makes love one's aim, a new world comes into view, and Kierkegaard explicitly credits Christianity with certain material changes in this world, such as the end of serfdom (80). Further on this inconsistency, see Walsh, 238-39, 249.

(now no longer as enemy); but even materially, by winning a change
in how the neighbor regards himself, thus changing the neighbor in
fact (277, 286).[44] Once you start loving forth the love in him, who is
to say what new creation might not emerge? After all, a Transcendent
Power is at work here, a Sovereign Love, whose Word calls worlds
into being and makes all things new.

Transformative love is therefore edifying, constructive, creative.
Kierkegaard calls it revolutionary and says it is the only thing that
truly is (248). Our reluctance to see it so may be because we tend to
measure our efforts at it by the tangible results and by comparisons,
inappropriate standards for the realm of the Spirit. Much less should
we expect the results to conform to our preferences and preconceptions, for then we would be adopting the same self-deceptive criteria
of effectiveness as govern the nation-state game. And our love would
suffer deformation—into coercion.[45]

Now, neighbor love is transformative not just in the relationship
with the enemy but also in the erotic relationship with the beloved
and in the relationship with the friend. Certainly, one does not stop
loving them because of having preferred them. They too become the
neighbor under the force of the command. And what an extravagant
claim that is! Imagine, learning to love one's spouse both bodily and
unselfishly,[46] the beloved whom one no doubt selected out of preferentiality but who now stands before one to be loved as neighbor, to be
loved after all the distinctions that attracted one's attention in the
first place may have passed away, to be loved after the passion of
preference has cooled, been deflected, or suffered redirection—still to
be loved! There would be a miraculous transformation, and a task for
a lifetime (73-74; cf. 140-45, 168).

4. *Sacrificial.* And obviously, as in all these cases, the miracle
would have to apply to the self as well. For love works its tranforma-

---

[44]Of course, even in the first case the change is not merely forensic, since a change
in how you regard the neighbor is a real change in you.

[45]For Kierkegaard, because neighbor-love is self-sacrificial, and because "Christ
is the pattern" (267-68, cf. 233), it must be non-coercive. See 121-22, 206, 308-13,
322-25.

[46]There is no necessary contradiction here. To think there is, Kierkegaard says, is
"a misunderstanding, an extravagance of spirituality." Kierkegaard proves a keen
interpreter of Paul when he points out that the conflict posed by Christianity is not
between spirit and body but between spirit and *flesh*, since "body" stands for material, sensuous reality, created good by God, while "flesh" means sensuality, a spirit
of selfishness, rebellion. The opposition, therefore, is between two forms of spirit,
two ways of valuing the world. (*WL*, 65.)

tions in both directions, inwardly and outwardly.[47] "Love forms the heart," Kierkegaard says (29), which is to say, it creates a new heart, an unselfish, sacrificial heart. Neighbor-love turns out to be sacrificial love, inevitably, and what gets sacrificed must be the self—namely its preferences, prejudices, its every impulse of acquisitiveness and self-aggrandizement.[48] All are eligible for offering up on the altar of love (123; cf. 132-34).

Again, how different a self this would be: loving without thought of reward, sacrificing without expecting to win the neighbor's admiration or approval—much less the world's—loving even without expecting the love to be reciprocated (cf. 133). For one's love is not dependent on the neighbor, on who he is or what she does; it depends on God. Again, sacrificial love is radically noncomparative; it cannot be measured by any standard other than God (cf. Matt 5:48; *WL* 247), and so makes no reference to how well or badly other people are doing at their task of loving.

If reciprocation is not the aim, and the goal is not to win the neighbor for oneself, what *is* the goal, what *is* the aim? According to Kierkegaard, it is to help the neighbor to love—to help her love God above all and then her neighbor as herself (113, 118, 124). For this is the neighbor's greatest good, as it is one's own. Love seeks the good, for it "seeks not its own" (247-60). Thus love works justice, and here Kierkegaard helps us rework that concept back toward its biblical sense (248-51). For, in the biblical sense, love and justice are not opposed but correlative.

Moreover, as a function of love, justice is not blind. Our concern throughout this book is with vision. Indeed, the sacrificial love which creatively forms the heart will also give the heart eyes to see the neighbor's need. For neither is it a merely procedural notion of justice but a substantive one that scripture presents and that love works.[49]

---

[47]Kierkegaard's term "reduplication" pertains to this phenomenon. See *WL* 150, 261-62; also Walsh, 246-47.

[48]As we shall see in chapter three, feminist criticism often faults Christian love for its emphasis on self-sacrifice. For the many women who, for historical reasons, suffer an under-developed sense of self, the ideal of self-sacrifice seems only to exacerbate their dilemma. But for Kierkegaard, this under-developed self is acknowledged as no less false a self than the masculine, overdeveloped false self, and is just as necessary—and painful—to surrender. For an excellent treatment of this issue, see William Cahoy, "One Species or Two? Kierkegaard's Anthropology and the Feminist Critique of the Concept of Sin," *Modern Theology*, 11 (1995): 429-54.

[49]On this distinction, see Robert Bellah, et al., *Habits of the Heart: Individualism and Community in American Life* (Berkeley: University of California Press, 1985), 26, 29.

True justice is seeing by love the needs of the neighbor and lovingly striving to satisfy them. So sacrificial love will give one vision and make one just. Of course, only as we do it for the neighbor, "even the least of these," will justice be formed in us.

Utopianism is always the charge against this vision of sacrificial love, when the weight of the imperative has grown too burdensome and its sacrifices too dear. Kierkegaard is only too glad to remind us of the grace by which God forgives failures.[50] First, however, he would have us consider the sort of "realism" that often makes the charge and bristles at the command. "Variously concocted tough slime," he calls it, "prepared by the help of habit, prudence, conformity [comparison], experience, custom, and usage," out of which never comes "the miracle," i.e., "the possibility of the good!" (235). Disregarding the eternal in a tragic self-deception, such "muddied realism" (180) has no edification, no hope. For Kierkegaard, it is not real. When it comes to what is real, there is another, truer story to be told. Only in the context of that story's honest realism can true grace be heard.

The story has it that the life of sacrificial love was lived out to its end and offered, sacrificially, on behalf of all. With the Evangelist Mark, Kierkegaard reminds us that the love of which we speak is not an abstract ideal, not a what but a who, with a name and a story that now incorporates its believers (106, 247). Likewise, with Paul, Kierkegaard insists, "Love/Christ is the fulfilment of the Law," available to all for appropriation by faith (106-08). However impossible the love command seems, the Christian's reality is that the command has been accomplished by Christ and its love eternally promised to us. However heavily its burden weighs upon us, the transcendent fact is that Christ's life of love has been pledged to be fully ours at the last.

The story of Christ speaks of one more transformation—that of the imperative itself. What we first heard as a command has become a pledge and promise, historically enacted, eternally grounded, eschatologically secured, given on the highest authority: "You shall love"—*ágapēseis*, future declarative (55, 73; cf. 183). Kierkegaard has made a subtle and yet enormously important observation, and what an enormous difference it makes: now, because of Christ, Christians read an imperative also as a promise; law has become Gospel in

---

[50]See the comments on love's "mildness" in *WL*, 111f., 348, and 353. For a clear explanation of his strategy of restraint in speaking of grace, see his essay, "What Do I Want," in the *Attack Upon Christendom*, 37-40. In a nutshell, grace cannot be heard as "grace" if one does not hear the command of the Christian ideal.

one and the same sentence, not in abrogation but in fulfilment. Therefore, the Christian life of love, always presently striving, should also be one of hope and futurity, hope in the promise of the Gospel. How both edifying and unnerving that what one reads should turn on *how* one reads and lives it.

To conclude as polemically as I began, we see that it is not just how one reads that matters, but *what* one reads as well. Just as Kermode's hermeneutic will not serve as a Christian hermeneutic, so it is not just any story that speaks the love Kierkegaard describes. Not just any and all literature will do, nor just any narrative. Much less is narrativity per se adequate for so uniquely conceiving faith and hope and justice and weaving them together with the transcendent grace that intends of humans a new creation. Christ is too heterogeneous, the love of God too different. For getting in on that difference, Christians need scripture. Kierkegaard permits no substitutes.

CHAPTER 2

KIERKEGAARD AND THE RULE OF FAITH: IMAGINING SCRIPTURE

With its initial survey of Kierkegaard's conception of Christian love, chapter 1 gave us a taste of Kierkegaard's way of working with scripture in *Works of Love* and a sense of what is at stake in the Rule of faith: namely, a capacity to see what scripture seems plainly to say—plainly to practiced believers. In this chapter we shall explore in fuller detail the logic of the Rule and Kierkegaard's application of it. The metaphor of vision will remain in the foreground as a reminder of the thesis that the Rule is a primal *imaginative* construal of scripture.

For the approach to remain inductive and exegetical, we shall need a Kierkegaard text to serve as a hermeneutic candidate, a kind of paradigm to bring a complex configuration of issues into focus. Introducing this focus text and justifying my analogical use of it will occupy parts I and II of this chapter. In part III, I return to the Rule to survey its historical development and to locate its intersections with Kierkegaard's practice, as the latter is illustrated by the hermeneutic candidate, our focus text.

I. A Hermeneutic Candidate:
"The Art of Interpretation in the Service of Love"

The focus text comes in the middle of Part Two of *WL*. In Part One Kierkegaard worked through the biblical imperative to love one's neighbor as oneself; in Part Two he develops love's attributes as found mainly in Paul's paean to love in 1 Corinthians 13. Our text is an exception; Kierkegaard interrupts his Pauline sequence of chapters ("Love Believes All Things," "...Hopes All Things," "...Seeks Not Its Own," "...Abides") to insert a Petrine episode: "Love Hides the Multiplicity of Sins" (1 Pet 4:8). Explicating that interruption and the scriptural thinking behind it must wait until the following chapter. Our concern here is with the combination of key terms—*"imagination,"* *"interpretation,"* and *"love"*—that commends the passage as a prime entry point for discussing Kierkegaard's use of the Rule of faith. It is a classic piece of hermeneutic reflection. I quote the paragraph in full. Particular points for exposition appear in bold type. (The bold-type quotations that follow throughout the rest of this chapter all come from this passage and will be cited without further attribution.)

It is always the explanation which defines something that is. The fact or the facts are basic, but the explanation is decisive. Every event, every word, every act, in short, everything, can be explained in numerous ways. As we say, clothes make the man. **Likewise one can truly say that the explanation makes the object of explanation what it is.** With regard to another man's words, acts, and ways of thought there is no certainty, and to suppose it means to choose. Conceptions and explanations therefore exist, **simply because a variation in explanation is possible—a choice.** But if it is a choice, it is continually in my power, if I am a lover, to choose the most mitigating explanation. When, therefore, this milder or mitigating explanation explains what others frivolously, hastily, rigorously, hard-heartedly, enviously, maliciously, in short, unlovingly, declare straightway to be guilt, when the mitigating explanation explains this in another way, it takes now one and then another guilt away and thereby makes the multiplicity of sins less or hides it. **O, if men would rightly understand what splendid use they could make of their imaginative powers,** their acuteness, their inventiveness, and their ability to relate by using them to find if possible a mitigating explanation—**then they would gain more and more a taste for one of the most**

beautiful joys in life; it would become for them a passionate desire and need which could lead them to forget everything else. Do we not observe this in other ways, how, for example, the hunter year by year becomes more and more passionately given to hunting? We do not admire his choice, but shall say nothing about this; we speak only of how year by year he devotes himself more and more passionately to this activity. And why does he do this? Because with each year he acquires experience, becomes more and more inventive, overcomes more and more difficulties, so that he, the old experienced hunter, now knows alternatives when others know none, knows how to track game where others do not, discerns signs which no one else understands, and has discovered a better way of setting traps, so that he is always rather sure of always having good hunting even when all others fail. We regard it as a burdensome task, yet in another respect satisfying and engaging to be a detective, one who discovers guilt and crime. We are amazed at such a person's knowledge of the human heart, of all its evasions and devices, even the most subtle, how he can remember from year to year the most insignificant things just to establish, if possible, a clue, how by merely glancing at the circumstances he can, as it were, exorcise out of them an explanation detrimental to the guilty one, how nothing is too trivial for his attention insofar as it could contribute to illuminate his grasp of the crime. We admire such an official servant when by keeping after what he calls a thoroughly hardened hypocrite he succeeds in tearing the cloak away from him and making the guilt transparent. Should it not be just as satisfying and just as engaging, through perseverance with what would be called exceptionally base conduct, to discover that it was something quite different, something well-intentioned! **Let the judges appointed by the state, let the detectives labour to discover guilt and crime; the rest of us are enjoined to be neither judges nor detectives—God has rather called us to love, consequently, to the hiding of the multiplicity of sins with the help of a mitigating explanation. Imagine this kind of lover, endowed by nature with such magnificent capacities that every judge must envy him, but all these capacities are employed with a zeal and rigour such as a judge would have to admire in the service of love, for the purpose of getting practice in the art and practicing the art, the art of interpretation, which, with the help of a mitigating explanation, hides the multiplicity of sins. Imag-**

ine his rich experience, blessed in the noblest sense: what knowledge he possesses of the human heart, how many remarkable and
moving instances he knows about, in which he nevertheless suc-
ceeded, however complicated the matter may have seemed, in
discovering the good or even the better, because for a long, long
time he had kept his judgment suspended, until at just the right
time a little circumstance came to light which helped him on the
track, and then by quickly and boldly concentrating all his attention upon a completely different conception of the matter he
had the fortune of discovering what he sought, by losing himself
in a man's life-relationships, and by securing the most accurate
information about his circumstances he was finally victorious in
his explanation! Consequently "He found the clue." "He had the
good fortune of finding what he sought." "He conquered with his
explanation!"—Alas, is it not strange that when these words are
read out of context almost every man will involuntarily think
they concern the discovery of a crime—most of us are far more
inclined to think of discovering evil than of discovering the
good. The state appoints judges and detectives to discover and
punish evil. Moreover, men unite for obviously praiseworthy
causes to alleviate poverty, to bring up orphan children, to rescue
the fallen—but for this splendid venture, with the aid of a mitigating explanation to secure, were it ever so little, yet a little
power over the multiplicity of sins—for this no association has
yet been organised.[1]

As a hermeneutic construal, all that's lacking here is the word
"scripture." Its absence presents us with a significant methodological
hitch. Kierkegaard is speaking—parabolically, imaginatively—about
how we might lovingly hide the sin of a "guilty one" by explaining it
away. I shall be taking his parable of love-sleuthing as an allegory of
biblical interpretation: scripture is the "**guilty one**" to be explained,
a rich repository of oppression freighted with the hypocrisy of easy
wisdom, patriarchy, ethnic prejudice, etc. Kierkegaard would have us
read this guilty text with suspended judgment until, lovingly, forgiv-
ingly, we find the "**mitigating explanation**." But how can I switch
his referent from actual person to biblical text without contrivance?
That is, do I have any warrant for reading the *Kierkegaard* text this
way? Can my allegory be justified? Before we talk about forgiving the
sins of scripture (in subsequent chapters), I need to show that Kierke-

---

[1]*WL*, 271-73.

gaard would endorse this analogy between scripture and the "guilty person."

II. WARRANTING THE FOCUS TEXT

Kierkegaard supplies a three-tiered warrant for my allegorical reading of our focus text. At the first tier he imagines scripture as a mirror. At the second he presents it under the metaphor of a love letter. At the third he literalizes the second tier's metaphor by reference to soteriology and the atonement.

1. *The Mirror*

In the opening section of *For Self-Examination*, titled "How to Derive True Benediction from Beholding Oneself in the Mirror of the Word," Kierkegaard takes up a favorite text, the ethical admonition of James 1:22-27 that Christians practice their faith by matching deeds to words. The "words" in question are the paradigmatic Christian faith statement, the "Word of God" in scripture, and the issue at stake is precisely how Christians ought to regard that Word. The answer: as a mirror in which one beholds one's true self.

What we have at this first tier is Kierkegaard's socratic conception of ethics applied explicitly to the Bible. Since, according to the socratic view, self-knowledge is the height of ethical seriousness and coming to know oneself is the essential ethical task, and since, according to Christian tradition, scripture is a privileged occasion for such knowledge, then seriously reading scripture is essential to the task.[2] This means that reading scripture is itself an ethical operation—an activity informed by basic values, dispositions, and purposes—and that what ethical content the reading reveals should, by

---

[2]Kierkegaard's view of the "stages of existence" is pertinent here, specifically the notion that versions of the aesthetic and ethical stages get taken up into the religious. John Elrod states the case this way concerning the relation between the ethical and the religious: "To know oneself as one is known by God is to discover oneself in a relationship in which one is required by God to keep the law. Obedience to the law is the existential content of the religious relationship with God. Thus, to know oneself as one is known by God is existentially transforming in the sense that it is a knowledge that entails the ethical act of loving one's neighbor as one loves oneself" (*Kierkegaard and Christendom*, 191f.). To draw the immediate point, while scripture is indeed religious literature, it is certainly nothing less than ethically serious.

the biblical principle that faith be practiced in all activities, recipro-
cally inform the manner in which the reading is done. In other words,
scripture's admonitions of how to live pertain directly to how we are
to read—unless we prefer to read as amoral abstractions. What is at
stake in both the how and the what of our reading is the very substance of our human nature, our character as moral agents and religious subjects, what Kierkegaard called our "subjectivity."[3] That kind
of reading makes of scripture a mirror in which one beholds one's true
self. With this image of the mirror, then, one piece of Kierkegaard's
"imaginative construal" of scripture is in place.

2. *The Love Letter*

It follows that if Kierkegaard finds scripture saying we should
love the neighbor's sin into concealment (1 Peter), he would conclude
that we ought to apply the same love, with its willing suspension of
judgment, to our reading of scripture. We are not left with just the
loose inference to go on. At the second tier of warranty Kierkegaard
reinforces the analogy between the guilty one and scripture by imaging the whole content of scripture as love. The mirror, it turns out,
must also be seen as a "love letter."

One could miss the point about the mirror, after all, and get
caught up in looking *at* it instead of *into* it, as if the point were to
render a prolix scholarly account of the mirror rather than to see
oneself through it.

But oh—oh, the limitless horizons of prolixity! [For example,] how much belongs in a stricter sense to God's Word?

---

[3]This word is one of the key terms in the Kierkegaard lexicon, most famous in the
slogan "truth is subjectivity" in the *Concluding Unscientific Postscript*. Its polemical use was targeted at the increasing tendency within philosophy and the culture at large to privilege objective (in the sense of "impersonal") forms of thought
and knowledge, which Kierkegaard believed to have demoralizing and dehumanizing effects when applied to ethics and religion. In particular he believed it to be utter
anathema to Christian faith. What needs to be stressed here is Kierkegaard's express
warning not to equate subjectivity with subjectivism, or in his words with "the
selfish, the eccentric,...[with] loutishness" (*CUP*, 117).

Kierkegaard's conviction that religious truth is a matter of subjectivity is theologically grounded in his understanding of the nature of God. The crucial statement
is in *CUP*, 178: "God is a subject." The importance of this statement can hardly be
overestimated, and I shall have repeated occasion to revert to it (e.g., 84f. and nn. 4, 6,
and 71 below).

which books are genuine? are they also Apostolic? and are these also authentic? have the authors themselves seen everything? or in some instances perhaps have they merely reported what they heard from others? And then the various readings—30,000 various readings. And then this throng or crowd of scholars and opinions, learned opinions and unlearned opinions, about how the particular passage is to be interpreted ... you must confess that this seems rather prolix. God's Word is the mirror—by reading or hearing it I am to see myself in the mirror; but, lo, all this about the mirror is so confusing that I never come to the point of seeing my own reflection—at least not if I take that path. One might be tempted almost to suppose...that this is craftiness, that we men are far from willing to see ourselves in that mirror, and that it is for this reason we have hit upon all this which threatens to make reflection from the mirror impossible, all this which we glorify by the laudatory name of learned and profound and serious research and investigation.

...[Therefore] think of a lover who has now received a letter from his beloved—as precious as this letter is to the lover, just so precious to thee, I assume, is God's Word; in the way the lover reads this letter, just so, I assume, dost thou read God's Word and conceive that God's Word ought to be read. (*FSE*, 51)

Kierkegaard insists that it is only when read as a word of love, from God to humans, that scripture can accurately reveal who we truly are. Without the subjectivity of love, by which he means the interestedness, the care—all the life-giving personal qualities that distinguish people and God[4] from inanimate things—scripture could only

---

[4] Recall the statement cited in n. 3 above: "God is a subject" (*CUP*, 178). The point should not be taken to imply that God cannot be an object of God's own knowing—or, thereby, an object of human knowing—in the purely grammatical sense of "object." Neither does it imply that God doesn't "really" exist. That is, it does not imply that God cannot exist prior to and independently of his creation and human knowers. What it means is that God is fully agentic, that God acts; further, that God has chosen not to exist independently of human beings, but has chosen to make himself known to human beings only in and through personal relationship. It means that God does not exist disinterestedly, and cannot be known by us disinterestedly. This point will need to be reiterated in chapter 5 when I make the heavily rhetorical remark that "objectively, God does not exist." The issue is not the "what" of God's existence, but the "how"—i.e., the manner in which God chooses to exist.

be opaque in its objectivity, certainly nothing in which a subject could see herself reflected (pp. 67-68).[5] Scripture must be lively with love to be a mirror.

Note again something of a reciprocity principle: the love that is the content of scripture, in order to be "seen," demands love from the subject who reads it. This is the like-for-like logic we observed in the first chapter and shall see repeatedly again.[6] We should note here that it is at the heart of the ocular metaphor (that what we see in scripture will depend upon the imaginative construal under which we view it) and belongs to the very nature of ethico-religious thought and discourse.

3. *Literalizing the Letter*

In "The Mirror of the Word" the idea of the love letter has subordinate status; Kierkegaard cites it as an *analogy* to the Bible, almost offhandedly.[7] To clinch our warrant, the analogy must be en-

---

If my point is correct, then it would seem that Kierkegaard is much closer to Barth on this issue than Barth himself thought. That Kierkegaard polemically overstated the "how" of revelation in relation to the (objective) "what" of it may indeed be the case. That he gave *no* place to the "what" of it is another matter. See David Gouwens, "Kierkegaard's Understanding of Doctrine," *Modern Theology*, 5 (1988): 13-22.

[5]Kierkegaard's point is a specific instance of the principle made famous by the pseudonym Johannes Climacus. Just as "Christianity is not a doctrine" (*CUP*, 290-91, 337-40), neither can "God's Word [be] merely a doctrine, an objective, impersonal something" (*FSE*, 68). A grasp of scripture's performative and self-involving logic requires reading it as more than a set of cognitive propositions. It may entail such propositions, but they are not the extent of its religious force. Further on this point, see the section on "Instruction" in this chapter. The following quotation from John Elrod also relates the point to the idea of self-knowledge:

The character of this self-knowledge is not strictly propositional, for knowing oneself as a synthesis of particularity and universality is commensurate with existentially striving to become that self. The knowledge of which Kierkegaard speaks is a *transformative* knowledge in the sense that it is not possible to separate knowing and being (*Kierkegaard and Christendom*, 191; my emphasis).

On Kierkegaard's understanding of the positive role of doctrine, see again Gouwens, "Kierkegaard's Understanding of Doctrine."

[6] Again, the conviction that "God is a subject" (see above, nn. 3 and 4) is foundational—as an item of faith, not epistemological certainty—to the idea that the reading subject needs love to see God's love as the subject matter of scripture. For the (brief) reference to "like for like" in chapter 1, see p. 38 (citing *WL*, 33).

[7]Kierkegaard develops the image less to make claims about scripture's content than to highlight two specific forms of subjectivity with which scripture should be

hanced at a third tier. The clincher comes with the second of the "Two Discourses at the Communion on Fridays" that serve to preface *FSE*. Kierkegaard liked to accompany the polemical works with shorter, more irenic religious discourses.[8] These provided a kind of indirect commentary on the larger works by placing them in the framework of first-order religious reflection. What is striking is that the second Discourse that frames *FSE* just happens to be on the very same Petrine text as that which provides our hermeneutic focus text (1 Pet 4:8). Apparently, like the Letter of James to which he returned repeatedly and into relation with which he now brings 1 Peter, Kierkegaard deemed "Love Hides the Multiplicity of Sins" a passage important enough to ponder more than once.

The Discourses yield more than one refraction of 1 Peter 4:8, however. In the version composed for the ethically oriented *WL*, Kierkegaard stresses the *human* task of loving away the sins of the neighbor; in the version for *FSE*, the subject is the soteriological paradigm for that sort of loving: *Christ's* love, which takes away the sins of the world. Kierkegaard has placed his most programmatic statement about the Bible, *FSE*'s opening chapter, "The Mirror of the Word," in the context of one of his most direct reflections on the atonement. The effect of the framing device is clear: one comes to scripture-qua-mirror via the Divine Love, a love that hides the multiplicity of sins on a cosmic scale. To do its mirroring work, in other words, scripture is not just analogous to a letter of love, it literally *is* one—God's love letter to all humanity—and is to be approached as such.[9]

---

read. These are: first, an eagerness to discover and do whatever scripture asks of one (such eagerness as a lover would feel when reading a letter from the beloved, *FSE*, 51-55), and second, a non-defensive honesty and vulnerability that Kierkegaard sums up under the metaphor of "being alone with God's Word" (as the lover would want to be with the beloved's letter, 55-58). Of course, such forms of subjectivity are appropriate because the analogy works at the level of content, too. The Bible is a kind of divine love-letter, for Kierkegaard, and the analogy is not so offhanded as it first appears. The textual clue is his caution: "Let us not dismiss this picture too soon," and again, "Let us not even yet dismiss this picture of the lover and his letter" (52, 55).

[8]See Walter Lowrie's "Preface" to *FSE* and *Judge for Yourselves*, v-vii.

[9]One might even say that the approach, indeed the construal of scripture as love, makes it such—as if scripture's meaning were in its use, and its **explanation defined** what it is. This Wittgensteinian maxim will be repeatedly demonstrated. With regard to "The Mirror of the Word," Kierkegaard's point (repeated six times, 53-58) is that the way God's Word is read in Christendom means that it is not God's Word that is being read. As he says, there is "a distinction between reading and reading" (52),

Already several broad implications have surfaced that will continue to occupy our attention. First is the way an analogy has become the Bible's "literal sense." If Kierkegaard elsewhere remarks that he takes scripture at "face value," an expression whose very innocuousness ought to alert us to ironic depths, we glimpse now how deep the expression runs. Construing the mirror-scripture as a letter of love, Kierkegaard takes its sense from the "face" he sees through its surface, namely Christ's. He is convinced that only as he strives to see Christ's face does scripture take on religious "value," and that only by seeing that face through scripture can he clearly see his own— remarkable mirror indeed!—both what he has made of himself and what in Christ, through the love of God, he is and eschatologically will become.[10] This is a complex feat of reading. Yet it is simply obvious to Kierkegaard, as the framing Discourse proves, that the words of James should be thus referred continually to Christ and that Christian scripture should be explained christologically.[11] This attests a notion of "literal sense" far removed from any objectivist, non-contextual literal*ism*.

Moreover, this notion of the literal sense of the text is deeply social in character. The social component of Kierkegaard's exegetical practice is a second implication to be drawn from the framing Discourse in *FSE*. SK's infamous individualism notwithstanding, the plain sense effected by this christological construal is hardly an individual

---

i.e., between various uses of the text, and the different uses construct different texts— or we might say, different literal senses (cf. n. 13).

Kierkegaard would of course acknowledge Barth's point, that from God's point of view—and that of faith—God's Word is always God's Word. Or so I would argue on the basis of Climacus's acknowledgement that, while there can be no "System" from any human point of view, there is from God's.

[10]For the reference to the expression "face value" (found in the *Edifying Discourses*, vol. 4, 66), I am grateful to Elaine Peterson, "Kierkegaard's Exegetical Methodology," (unpublished paper read at the Kierkegaard Conference, St. Olaf College, Northfield, MN, June, 1988). Peterson recognizes the "depth" dimension in the expression: one looks through scripture in the hope of gaining kno*WL*edge of God. We differ, however, on how to relate that to the text's "literal sense." I do not wish to apply the pejorative "literalism" to any and every concern to heed the text's literal sense.

[11]It is not so obvious to a host of commentators, Luther included, either that the Epistle as a whole "proclaims Christ," or that its specific phrases—"word of truth" (1:18), "implanted word...able to save your souls" (1:21), "doers of the word" (1:22), "the perfect law, the law of liberty" (1:25)—refer christologically. Of course, the act of referring is not something done by words themselves, but by people using the words. For more on this issue, see chapter 4, "'Heart Enough to be Confident': Doubt, Receptivity, and the Epistle of James."

production. The framing device that literalizes the analogy of the love letter *de*-literalizes (and so qualifies) the ostensibly privatistic point Kierkegaard seems to make of it. In "The Mirror of the Word" the analogy served to emphasize what he called the need "to be alone with God's Word" (55-57). In that context "alone" denotes physical isolation and solitude. But in light of the Discourse's setting "at the Communion on Fridays," "alone" turns metaphorical. In the broadened context it becomes a metaphor for "inwardness"—that is, for a kind of non-speculative, even non-introspective self-presentation before God—the inwardness that all Christians share "in the humble service of *worship*," as Louis Mackey says. And in Kierkegaard's own words, such worship is "the glory of our *common humanity*."[12] Approaching the Mirror of the Word through Divine Love includes approaching it via the Eucharist, the public liturgy of the people of God. The framework for the Bible's literal sense, Christianly construed, takes the shape of the communion table, and the Christian explanation of scripture is a work of community, even for Kierkegaard.[13]

---

[12]Louis Mackey, *Kierkegaard: A Kind of Poet* (Philadelphia: University of Pennsylvania Press, 1971), 122, quoting Kierkegaard from *The Gospel of Suffering*, D. F. and L. M. Swenson, trans. (Minneapolis: Augsburg Publishing House, 1948), 212. My emphasis.

[13]The notion of "literal sense" that Kierkegaard's practice evinces, and that his term "face value" seems to imply, differs considerably from the notion still current in much historical criticism whereby "literal sense" refers to the "historical" or "original" meaning of an expression, which has often to be speculatively reconstructed without benefit of clear data. The different notions have been charted in the formative essay by Childs, "The Sensus Literalis of Scripture," and in Hans Frei's *The Eclipse of Biblical Narrative* (see my Introduction, n. 14).

Both Childs's canon-contextual approach to scripture and the narrative-theology movement spearheaded by Frei have sought to recover and develop a conception of literal sense more like that implicit in Kierkegaard, and their efforts, notable for the role they assign the community, is part of what might characterize both scholars (and Kierkegaard, anachronistically) as "postmodern." Their position is succinctly reflected in this definition from Charles Wood, *The Formation of Christian Understanding: An Essay in Theological Hermeneutics* (Philadelphia: Westminster Press, 1981), 40:

"Literal Sense" is intimately bound up with the conventions of reading, with the capacities and dispositions, linguistic and personal, which the reader brings to the text, by virtue of having been formed in a community with a fairly secure style of interaction with this material."

When one considers that an expression or text's context will include everything from the linguistic "conventions" to the "secure style" of the community, as well as other proximate texts and expressions and activities, it becomes clear why literary theorist Stanley Fish can say that, depending on context, any given expression/text might have many literal senses, though only one at a time (*Is There a Text in This*

I would note a final implication by way of transition to the next section. The task of warranting the focus text has led us along an abbreviated version of the path Kierkegaard's own authorship takes: from the abundant aesthetic and ethical works to which our focus text bears obvious resemblances,[14] to a rare piece on the atonement. On the way we have seen that the latter, though chronologically later (*FSE* was published in 1851, *WL* in 1847), is the logical presupposition for the former. The ethical imitation of Christ in *WL* depends on Christ's being the Savior confessed in *For Self Examination*. The theological confession turns out to be the quiet heart of the whole corpus. The rest of the literature serves to draw the readership toward this shy center, while the center secretly gives life to all the rest. The confession is foundational. I want now to explore that foundation's intricate depths, viewing the confession as a community work prescriptive of interpretation.

III. THE RULE OF FAITH[15]

To say that a confession is foundational is to say that it has the force of a rule, or in the language of our focus text, of a **defining explanation**. And part of the hermeneutical significance of our focus text is precisely its witness to and dependence upon a theological confession that would define and govern as ostensibly mental and disinterestedly rational an activity as textual interpretation has often been

---

Class? The Authority of Interpretive Communities [Cambridge, MA: Harvard University Press, 1980], 275-77).

[14]The resemblances come via the emphasis on the imagination, the ethics of love that the text attests, and the image of the love-sleuth so suggestive of the "spies" posited by the pseudonyms (e.g., *CUP*, 417-29).

[15]For all the weight I place on this term, I have to admit to a certain vagueness in my use of it. In the words of Jaroslav Pelikan, "The term 'rule of faith' or 'rule of truth' did not always refer to...creeds and confessions, and seems sometimes to have meant the 'tradition,' sometimes the Scriptures, sometimes the message of the gospel" (*The Christian Tradition, 1: The Emergence of the Catholic Tradition* [Chicago: The University of Chicago, 1971], 117).

For present purposes I want not just to admit this vagueness but to insist on it. I would hope to avoid some of the overly precise denotations that the term took on in the post-Augustinian period. The degree of elasticity in the Rule is its virtue, a sign of its intent to be faithful to the translinguistic sovereignty of God. Or so Kierkegaard might read it, since he would want to stress that the point of the Rule is not to sponsor mere talk about loving, but actual loving. This is the burden of his famous remarks that "truth is subjectivity" and again "Christianity is not a doctrine" (*CUP*, 169, 339, *et passim*).

supposed to be. This confessional, "subjective" basis may pose something of an embarrassment. That interpreting scripture should be like interpreting the neighbor, a work of imagination in the service of love, covering the multiplicity of scripture's sins—surely that goes too far, verging on subjectivism, new-age aestheticism, or good old-fashioned, text-distorting pietism. But as I have said, for Kierkegaard interpreting scripture by love has the force of a rule. As such, it has roots deep in tradition. Moreover, it has a logic, a form of rationality proper to its function, for rules are not the idiosyncratic inventions of private individuals, particularly in matters of social communication like interpretation. Let us turn then to a discussion of the primal rule for Kierkegaard, the Rule of faith.

Formulating the Rule of faith was a lengthy preoccupation of the early church and the product of a centuries-long development before that. If we summarize the Rule's gist as Augustine did, in terms of charity, the similarity with Kierkegaard's imaginative construal becomes obvious. For Augustine, the Rule affirms that everything in scripture and the world is a sign that is only properly read in light of the love of God and that points to the love of God when properly read.[16] This formulation has only provisional adequacy, of course. Complex and protean as faith itself, "the Rule" represents both faith's fact-assertive, cognitive character (the fact that we do state what we believe) and faith's character as a dynamic principle or form of life never exhausted by the efforts to state it. Bearing therefore on both the what and the how of reading, both the content of scripture and the manner in which one reads it, the Rule presents a host of issues, and potential embarrassments, pertinent to Kierkegaard. No doubt it is because the embarrassments of the Rule of faith ultimately belong to the Paradox—and "scandal"[17]—of the Incarnation, which

---

[16]My saying "everything in the world [is] a sign" might seem to be contradicted by a distinction Augustine draws between "signs" and "things" early in *On Christian Doctrine* (D.W. Robertson, Jr., trans. [New York: Macmillan, 1958], Book One, II, 2, 8f.). Whereas "signs" are things which invariably signify something else, some "things" may have no signifying function. Thus, all signs are things, but not all things are signs. Later, however, in summarizing the discussion of Book One, Augustine observes that "the whole dispensation was made by divine providence for our salvation" and we therefore "should use it...with a transitory love and delight like that in a road or in vehicles or in other instruments...for the sake of that toward which we are carried" (XXXV, 39, 30). In effect, Augustine has assigned the world a signifying status in our quest for knowing and loving God.

[17]Kierkegaard's notion of paradox entailed that of "offense," a term we began to illustrate in chapter 1. A New Testament synonym for offense is "scandal" (Gr. *scandalon*). The idea is that the form of God's enfleshment—in weakness, frailty, mortal-

Kierkegaard was jealous to guard, that he was so traditional as to follow it.[18]

1. *Embarrassments of the Rule of Faith*

Circularity is the initial embarrassment. Hermeneutically, the Rule of faith reflects a recognition, more often tacit than confessed, that the Bible is not strictly self-interpreting—no more than any other text. No text can fully prescribe its own meaning and use, as if simply by following its signs one will be led to the right destination. Instead, the act of following requires decisions, and texts with their signs remain ever context- and community-dependent for whatever uses and senses get made of them. The fact that the decisions, contexts and communities then prove to be somehow dependent on the texts they help interpret frustrates any effort to determine a meaning that can be rationally justified without begging the question. What we have here is a version of the reciprocity principle mentioned earlier in this chapter, and of the hermeneutic circle that we met in chapter 1. What we make of texts seems to presuppose our identity and our projects, who we are and what we are about. And our identity and projects are mediated to us by texts, in the case of Christians by the canonical texts of scripture. In this respect, the circle the Rule traces of text and context is a tight one. It is precisely this same circle that Kelsey finds implicated in the theologian's imaginative construal.[19]

However, with the Rule, as with further imaginative construals and their *discrimen*, the church confesses that the circle admits openings of a sort, while harboring a corresponding hope that discriminations might be possible among rival readings: that some readings, like lives, may be found truer or more faithful than others, which may seem by comparison conspicuously hateful and senseless, or in other ways urgently needing correction. Naturally, immanent certainty in these discriminations will be unavailable—and by the logic of the Rule, the discriminations are to be applied less to the neighbor than to oneself. Still, we would have to ask, apart from the possibility

---

ity, etc.—so confounds our worldly preconceptions of how God ought to appear when he appears that we do not recognize him when he does. In fact, we are repelled. Hermeneutically, following Kierkegaard, I want to apply this principle to scripture. In chapter 3 the concept "offense"/"scandal" is developed programmatically.

[18]The use is implicit. As noted in the Introduction (n. 15), Kierkegaard never names the Rule of faith as such in *WL*. Further on this point, see below, n. 41.

[19]Kelsey, *The Uses of Scripture*, 205.

of discriminating among rival readings, what is theology for?[20] In any event, the need is often felt for recourse to some extra-textual reality transcendent of language if the circle is not to be vicious, if the language-game of interpretation is not to be hopelessly self-referential.

For the church, the circle opens to God. Thus the Rule invokes God as the transcendent basis of the hope and the standard for the truth and faithfulness of one's reading.[21] However, the idea of transcendence introduces an element of radical heterogeneity such that the very notions of hope and truth and faith and love may, as we saw in chapter 1, undergo a transformation from the way they are often conceived by the larger culture, while the fact that God is not a neutrally established and publicly verifiable "ground" will mean that, empirically speaking, the hermeneutic circle *appears* to remain closed ...and interpretation baseless.

Here we seem to have compounded the embarrassment of circularity with that of a "Transcendental Signified." Because of the latter, Christian norms are counter-cultural and their truth claims are faith-based. This situation has often led to efforts to ground theological hermeneutics by the same measures more decidedly empirical or purely analytic disciplines employ. However, such efforts do not reckon seriously enough with just how radical an element of heterogeneity the Bible's Transcendental Signified really is. Having God as subject effects a bigger shift than usually supposed. Indeed, one effect of the transformation of concepts is that the very status of the Rule will be shifted from the way it might have first appeared in this discussion. It looked as if it might be the (rather desperate) solution to an epistemological problem: How do we avoid vicious circularity in our truth claims? How do we know our claims about God and the world are warranted? (Desperate answer: God "tells" us.) But once in the language games of faith (in those activities of praise and prayer and ethi-

---

[20]Kelsey defines theology as a reflective, intellectual, reformist activity by which the church "self-consciously criticizes her own faithfulness to her mission" (*The Uses of Scripture*, 98-100, 159-60). See also his essay, "The Bible and Christian Theology," *The Journal of the American Academy of Religion*, 48 (1980), 390-93.

[21]According to Kelsey and Wood, it is virtually part of the grammar of the Christian concept of scripture that God makes use of the church's reading of it, that God in effect "speaks through" scripture as its "author" so as to shape Christian understanding and life. (See Kelsey, *The Uses of Scripture*, 93; "Bible and Theology," 396; and Wood, 39-41, 67.) Such a claim must not be taken to mean that the believer therefore fully knows God or has the full "truth" in his interpretation. On the other hand, it is equally wrongheaded for the Christian to say she can know nothing of God—or that the metaphors we necessarily employ in referring to God have no propositional force. See further in this chapter, pp 79 and nn. 59f.

cal witness that Kierkegaard calls the "religious stage" of existence), what we know of God (mediated by the biblical text, of course) rules this epistemological orientation inappropriate. The demand for intellectual certainty in our propositions follows from what the dominant culture, arrested in its "aesthetic stage," counts as "knowledge," and this demand gets displaced by God's demand to love God above all and one's neighbor as oneself. The criterion of truthfulness proper to *that* demand is not propositional correspondence to a neutrally ascertainable set of facts or state of affairs, but obedience, a personal fidelity presupposing commitment, loyalty, and trust. In this sense, truthfulness is primarily a relational category, a quality of "being true to another" in the terms appropriate to the given relationship, as when we say that someone has shown him/herself a "true" son or daughter to the parent, or that the lover has proved "true" to the beloved. Now, as the criterion for truthfulness changes, so does the concept of knowledge, from an "aesthetic" to an "ethico-religious" (Kierkegaard would add, "subjective") conception, where knowing God means lovingly obeying God.[22]

Thus, with obedience as its purpose, the church's "recourse" to God in the Rule does not normatively aim at buttressing the reliability of impersonal information that it disinterestedly abstracts from scripture (in order to construct doctrines that it self-interestedly wields against its adversaries). The recourse is instead an appeal for God's aid in listening and responding faithfully to God's demand and promise. From this perspective, "vicious" circularity means the illusion of self-sufficiency and of the finite instruments one works with, and the primary problem is not the hermeneutic one of how we understand or the epistemological one of how we gain certainty, but, as Kierkegaard insisted, the moral-existential one of how to obey.

This is not to say that no hermeneutic problem remains or that obedience does not entail testing one's "knowledge," only that the context and terms of the test participate in mystery, the mystery of the divine life attested by the text and of the human life lived in its presence. By thus defining the context and terms *theologically*, the Rule means to underscore, not annul, the highly mysterious and strenuous business that Christian sense-making remains.

Again, none of this vitiates the fact of circularity, which is nowhere clearer than when the church refers to scripture itself to support the appeal to God as an unconditioned source and norm for in-

---

[22]On this notion of knowing God, see chapter 4, "'Heart Enough to be Confident,'" 213.

terpretation and to name love as a governing category. Axiomatic in the Rule, after all, is that a continuity exists between the Rule and the text it governs. It is not surprising, then, that the same appeal to God can be traced in the Bible itself where it belongs to an inner-biblical development of the very concept "scripture." Tracing that development will underscore some ingredients of the mystery most relevant to our focus text and Kierkegaard's exegetical practice.

2. Interpretation As Inspiration: The Development of the Rule

Israel's prophets took the lead in conceptualizing, with considerable "**imaginative powers**," God's agency and initiative in divine-human communication. From Jeremiah's image of the divine "word" placed in his mouth by God (1:9, 5:14, 15:16), through Ezekiel's refiguring the word into a "scroll," a *text* which he must eat (2:8-3:3), on to Zechariah's vision of the now "flying scroll" which, like the angel of the Lord in the Pentateuch, visits judgment upon those who resist it (5:1-4), we have a trajectory charting scripture as Actor, the active and effective Word of God.[23] For the future development of the Rule, this means that the concept "Word of God" will be analytic in the Rule's "love of God": each fully entails the other.

The concept is further developed as sages and apocalyptic seers of a later period, persuaded of the continuing vitality of the divine word, no less its mysteriousness, seek to interpret older prophetic literature for their own day. In the Book of Daniel the idea of interpretation is thus thematized. Honoring both the efficacy and sovereignty of the Word, Daniel shows interpretation beginning, as James Kugel says, "by the interpreter reproducing the *text itself*, for the latter...is itself a gift from God *granted afresh to the interpreter*; proper understanding is akin to prophecy itself."[24] Apparently, proper understanding involves the ability not just to explicate the text but to *apprehend* it in the first place, and this must be from God.[25] It is rather like the fact that explaining away the neighbor's sins in love depends on loving him enough to see him as neighbor in the first place. In the

---

[23]James Kugel, in Kugel and Greer, *Early Biblical Interpretation* (Philadelphia: Westminster, 1986), Part One: "The Common Background of Later Forms of Biblical Exegesis," 19.

[24]Kugel, 58 (his emphasis). Cf. Daniel 2 and 5.

[25]This is to suggest, first, that one might not "see" a text as a text; second, that to see it as such is already to be interpreting, i.e., reading, it; and third, that if one does see it as such, just what text one sees it to be—what one sees in it—is conditioned by various surrounding factors. See also nn. 9 and 13 above.

first place is a capacity for imaginative construal with which humans find themselves marvelously "**endowed**," as our focus text puts it.

It is only a short step from Daniel to a full-blown notion of inspired interpretation. Whether the task is studying the law or writing biblical commentary, God is the agent of insight.[26] It remains only for the Qumran literature and the New Testament to specify that agency in terms of the "Spirit." And here what Kugel says of Qumran exegesis holds also for its Christian counterpart: "It is the gift of the `spirit of knowledge' from God, or the 'spirit of holiness,' that allows the Qumran interpreter to penetrate the 'secrets,' 'mysteries,' or `hidden things' in ancient Scripture and *read aright* their message for himself and his contemporaries."[27] One difference from Qumran is that the NT writers tend to avoid the expression "spirit of knowledge," preferring the predicates "truth" or "wisdom."[28]

The first-century evidence thus attests two striking principles: that there *is* right reading (which does not imply that there is only *one* right reading),[29] and that such reading occurs in conformity with and through the mediation of God's love-working Spirit. Here then we have a biblical prototype of the Rule of faith, though so far it applies only to the Hebrew scriptures.

Moreover, the prototype already displays a characteristic circularity. For insofar as the community finds *in scripture* the decisive attestation of the "extra-textual reality" (God) to which it takes recourse in order to legitimate its rules and readings, to the same degree it tacitly acknowledges its extra-textual reality to be a *textual construct*, which to the natural eye, unschooled in the practices and norms of the Christian community, will appear to be a *merely* textual construct, to the extent that it appears at all.

The point is hardly fatuous. The non-believing reader will surely be able to see the word "God" in the text, but his non-belief usually entails that the interests governing his reading and the practices surrounding it are different from the believer's. For example, it is unlikely either that his interest would be in trying to discern how to obey God in a moral crisis, or that the surrounding practice would be

---

[26]Kugel, 60-61, citing Ps 119:12, 18, 27, 33-35 and The Book of Jubilees, an expansionist retelling of Genesis and Exod 1-14 presented in the form of a revelation.

[27]On Qumran, see Kugel, 61-62. For the NT, see Lk 4:14, 18; Jn 15:25-27; Rom 1:4, 2:29; 1 Cor 2:7-16; 2 Cor 3:15-17; and Eph 1:17-18. (My emphasis.)

[28]Kugel, 62.

[29]The number and kinds of right reading possible are indefinite, as are the contextual situations in and for which they are produced. Indeed, depending on the circumstances, some may not even be verbal.

first-person activities of direct address, like prayer and praise. For believers and non-believers, the text is put to different uses. Accordingly, the concept "God" will function differently in their readings. In
other words, it will be a different *concept*. In that sense, one might
say that the Christian concept of God does not appear to the non-
believer at all. The complicating factor in this scenario of course, as
Kierkegaard would be quick to point out, is that the Christian is subject to non-belief too, so that God may not appear in her reading either.[30] But the immediate point is this: the principles that constitute
the Rule are like all axioms—grammatical, definitional, pre-empirical,
confessional.

The situation does not change in the second century when the
Rule receives its definitive formulation and gets applied to the whole
Christian canon. As a first step, the earlier circle gets retraced when
Marcion challenges the authority of the "Old Testament." Ignatius
had already anticipated the challenge and affirmed that the OT *does*
have authority—when read in light of the oral gospel: i.e., the early
Christian preaching and its message, out of which the NT was to
grow.[31] But if Ignatius thus claims for Christian preaching a prior
authority in determining the meaning of Hebrew scripture, surely the
preaching can have such authority only by virtue of first having been
shaped, largely, by the ancient material it now presumes to rule.[32] The

---

[30]The analogous situations of the non-believer and the Christian are illustrated
by the following two grammatical remarks from *CUP*. The first applies to the modern
discipline of history, the second to the claim that "subjectivity is truth":

> In the world-historical process as this is viewed by human beings, God does
> not play the role of sovereign; just as the ethical fails to appear in it, so God
> also fails to appear, for if he is not seen as sovereign he is not seen at all (139-
> 40).

> If one who lives in the midst of Christendom goes up to the house of God, the
> house of the true God, with the true conception of God in his knowledge, and
> prays, but prays in a false spirit; and one who lives in an idolatrous community
> prays with the entire passion of the infinite, although his eyes rest upon an
> idol: where is there most truth? The one prays in truth to God though he wor-
> ships an idol; the other prays falsely to the true God, and hence worships in
> fact an idol (179-80).

[31]Rowan Greer, "Part Two: The Christian Bible and its Interpretation," in *Early
Biblical Interpretation*, 114.

[32]One need name but a few key Christian concepts—"prophet," "priest," "king,"
"messiah," "Lord," "repentance," "forgiveness," "salvation," "resurrection," etc.—
to be reminded of the gospel's essential dependence on the OT and its symbolic
world, a dependence explicitly affirmed by Paul (Rom 1:1-4, chaps. 9-11) and illustrated by Peter's Pentecost sermon in Acts, which begins by citing the prophet Joel
(Acts 2:14-21).

authority of Christian preaching, certainly its *sense*, is to that extent
derivative and textually mediated. To affirm the Christian message as
both true and capable of illuminating the true meaning of Hebrew
scripture is to confess both the older scriptures and the newer
preaching as the work and Word of God, as Ignatius does. But note
again: the confessional affirmation presupposes the notion of inspired
interpretation, for it is not flesh and blood that has revealed the Word
to Ignatius, as he would surely confess.

The continuing controversy with Gnosticism impels the crystal-
lization of the Rule in Irenaeus. Building on Justin Martyr, Irenaeus
insists on the continuity as well as the discontinuity of the church
with Israel, on the identity of the God of Hebrew scriptures with the
God who does a "new thing" in Jesus Christ, and on the nature of
Christ as Incarnate Word and Savior, fully human and divine.[33] The
thrust of his argument is to identify these contested elements with the
"apostolic faith" and to advance the apostolic faith as the norm for
Christian belief. Where then does one find the apostolic faith? In
scripture (now both OT and NT)—as read, interpreted and practiced
by the catholic church;[34] that is to say, in scripture and the Rule of
faith, the latter now taking on determinate content as it articulates in
summary, credal fashion the crucial elements mentioned above: the
identity of the Creator and Redeemer God, the incarnate nature of
Christ, and the complex relation of the church to Israel.

Further, with Irenaeus, the Rule now posits a narrative structure
that holds these features together. It **explains/defines** scripture as a
complex, composite kind of story that tells of God's dealings with
humankind in a "salvation history," if you will, pregnant with meaning for one's own moment. The narrative structure thus serves not
only to display the interrelatedness of the contested features more
precisely; it imputes a broad coherence to scripture among all its varied parts, bringing it all to bear upon its readers.

As for the coherence of Rule to scripture, certainly as conceived
by Irenaeus the Rule has a thoroughly biblical physiognomy. Naturally, as the authoritative *summary* of the sacred writings, the Rule is
drawn *from* them and so bears their indelible marks, so much so that
Rowan Greer observes, "text and interpretation are like twin brothers;
one can scarcely tell the one from the other"[35]—although various

---

[33]Greer, 123-24, 153-57, 163-71.
[34]According to Greer (110), Irenaeus's New Testament would be ours minus
James, Jude, 2 Peter, and Hebrews.
[35]Greer, 157.

Gnostics apparently could. Yet, against the Gnostics Irenaeus had insisted on the *identity* of scripture and the Rule, and in describing the narrative framework that constitutes the "right order" of scripture, he claimed only to be making explicit what is already implicit within it.[36]

See how the essential problematic has surfaced again. The Rule being a normative summary, what normed the summary's construction in the first place? Itself an interpretation, how could it be drawn up prior to there being a norm for interpretation, without the logically odd, indeed circular postulate that it normed itself?[37] Clearly, the interpretive process of explicating the implicit can only produce an identity-with-a-difference. The difference between the brothers Text and Interpretation, Scripture and Rule, is likely to be more noticeable to people *outside* the family than to those within; i.e., it will be more readily seen by those who do not already believe that the difference does not really count. The principle of identity, it would seem, cannot be established independently of a belief in the identity it asserts, therefore independently of a belief about the substance of the "apostolic faith," which is one of the terms of the identity.

The grooves of our circuit are by now well worn, and the upshot is predictable. As with Ignatius, Irenaeus's logic does not begin with flesh and blood. Or as Greer says, "The proper order of the Rule of faith, though implicit in Scripture, is made explicit *only by revelation*."[38] The ultimate Author of authoritative interpretation, as of the text itself, is the Word itself, and to assert the principle of their identity can only be an act of faith. Shared understandings in this regard would entail sharing a faith and, concomitantly, would constitute an interpretive community. If that seems to place certain limits on the scope of human communication and intelligibility, we might at least take comfort in that bit of clarity about our local limitations—and note that Kierkegaard made "*indirect* communication" one of the central themes of his authorship.[39]

---

[36]Greer, 124 (Irenaeus, *Against Heresies*, 1.8), 175.

[37]To answer by resorting to the oral tradition is of course only to pose the problem again at that level, discussed several paragraphs above (re: Ignatius).

[38]Greer, 175 (my emphasis).

[39]Here is one of several points where Kierkegaard and deconstruction converge. For both Kierkegaqard and Derrida, for instance, language can directly convey neither "meaning" nor "truth" from one mind to another. For Kierkegaard, the most one person can do for another is prod her toward a sense she must make for herself. The demand for "indirection" makes Kierkegaard a rhetorician in principle; his practice, like Derrida's, confirms it—including his denunciations of rhetoric (e.g., *CUP*, 16-20). On Derrida, see *Positions*, Alan Bass, trans. (Chicago: University of Chicago Press, 1981), 23.

The issue of communication and community marks the most complex of three points where Kierkegaard's practice intersects with our historical review of the Rule. Let me comment on each point, in ascending order of complexity.

First, Kierkegaard conforms to the broad biblical tradition in conceiving of God's agency in interpretation in terms of inspiration, i.e., as the work of the Holy Spirit. In particular, he follows the New Testament writers, Paul and John,[40] in stressing that the primary work of the Spirit is not knowledge but love. Thus, the Rule's rootage in early-Christian polemic against Gnosticism and its precursors gets reiterated in Kierkegaard's polemic against Hegelianism, the gnosticism of his own day. For both the early church and Kierkegaard, the subjectivity of love is privileged over the objectivity of knowledge.

Second, Kierkegaard shows a ready reliance on Irenaeus's conception of the Rule in terms of a narrative structure that imputes a broad coherence to all of scripture. Emboldened by a Rule he has so internalized that he does not bother to cite it, Kierkegaard will not be afraid to use 1 Peter with Paul one moment and with James the next; nor will he think that doing so violates the sense of any. Indeed, the Rule makes it part of the grammar[41] of scripture that the various writings make their *best* sense as ethico-religious instruction in relation to each other.[42]

---

[40]See 1 Cor 12-14, Gal 5:22 and 1 Jn 4.

[41]On this use of the term "grammar," developed largely from Wittgenstein, see Paul L. Holmer, *The Grammar of Faith* (San Francisco: Harper & Row, 1978), ix-xi, 17-23. Kierkegaard's failure to cite the Rule explicitly (see n. 18 above) is at least partly to be explained by its "grammatical" nature. To illustrate from ordinary usage, the rules of grammar typically remain implicit in our discourse. We need not always be able to cite the rules, or even be conscious of them, in order to speak correctly. Especially in discourse among native speakers, people do not speak about grammar so much as simply use it. They speak about it only when misunderstandings or disagreements have arisen as to what correct speech really is. In this respect, Kierkegaard's "failure" to cite the Rule by name may be no failure at all, given that he is consistently addressing "Christendom," that is, other native speakers of the Christian language game. He assumes that they will recognize the propriety of his utterances about scripture, *qua* Christian utterances, when they hear or see them. On the other hand, the fact that the crisis within Christianity over its scripture seems to have continued unabated since the mid-nineteenth century suggests that perhaps his judgment was mistaken and that he needed to explicate more deeply the grammar of our use of scripture.

[42]My reflections on the Rule converge here with Brevard Childs's idea of "canon." Kierkegaard's practice of bringing diverse voices of scripture into immediate relationship illustrates several of Childs's themes, not least his appreciation of

Of course, the claim to coherence (like the claims for "narrative" *per se*) should not be exaggerated, and Kierkegaard never did. The content articulated by the narrative structure posited by the Rule must not be imagined to be *fully* determinate, specifiable in every detail, as it might exist in the mind of God. From Kierkegaard's perspective, it is a hopelessly idealist metaphysics that conceives "meaning" univocally and assumes it to be either totally determinate or indeterminate, either fully coherent or entirely lacking in coherence. Clearly, both Rule and narrative provide sufficient areas of ambiguity to fuel inner-Christian differences till the end of time. In addition, and more salient for Kierkegaard, instruction of a perfectly *un*-ambiguous sort would hardly be fitting to our subjective development as ethico-religious creatures. Only the open-ended instruction that requires readers' creative and personal engagement for its completion would be suitable. For someone like Kierkegaard, therefore, the effect of scripture's being ruled story-like is to enhance its instructional value, an element explicitly emphasized by Irenaeus and always crucial to scripture's religious use.[43]

The third point for comment is sufficiently complex to require a section of its own. At the end of part II ("Warranting the Focus Text"), we saw that Kierkegaard's choice of a framing discourse for *FSE* attests the social character of interpretation, even for him. Four paragraphs above, we saw that the Rule of faith logically entails the idea of community. Here we pursue that entailment in relation to the peculiar spin it receives at Kierkegaard's hands, as epitomized in our focus text.

3. *Kierkegaard and Community:*
The Social Context of Interpretation[44]

To recall Greer's analogy of the twins, one reason Text and Interpretation (Bible and Rule of faith), might look like twins to the observing scholar would be that the scholar is a member of the family, or at least a friend. Even in his capacity as historical critic who can tell the twins apart, he surely belongs to an interpretive community

the theological vigor of much pre-critical exegesis that operated within the canon, as well as the logic of the Rule that informed such exegesis.

[43]Greer, 172-74.

[44]The following discussion owes much to George Lindbeck's *The Nature of Doctrine: Religion and Theology in a Postliberal Age* (Philadelphia: Westminster, 1984), particularly the section "Faithfulness as Intratextuality," 113-24.

whose reading conventions have been so decisively influenced by a Christian style of reading that it takes a conscious effort, perhaps years of training, *not* to see the Bible as an overarching narrative, a comprehensive and reasonably coherent story of the world. Yet other communities exist, and there have always been other ways of reading the Bible. **"A variation in explanation is possible,"** Kierkegaard says.

The presence of other communities raises the issue of apologetics, an item crucial for understanding Kierkegaard's relation to his audience. So we are led to ask how Kierkegaard and the Rule of faith interface in the pluralistic situation. Ironically, the question is intensified when the pluralism exists within what is already ostensibly Christian—and where family membership is increasingly voluntary. **"Variation in explanation is possible—a** *choice.*"

Rules are definitional, we have said. They define the game to be played, if one is interested in playing. Or to use another image, rules chart the territory in which one chooses to travel; they provide the horizon and perspective of our vision. Thus the faith that the Rule of faith stipulates belongs to a unique game of religious seeing and reading, and precisely as it specifies the decisive content, the Rule inscribes a kind of boundary. Or, like the legend for a tourist map, the Rule indicates the crucial landmarks and access routes for the labyrinthine terrain in which the community's sacred texts, convictions, and practices overlap and criss-cross to shape specifically Christian forms of life.[45] Hence the Rule's peculiar role in Christian apologetics: given its confessional basis, it does more to edify "insiders" than to convince "outsiders." It is more *constitutive of* Christian identity and community than an argument for them, except insofar as what it constitutes proves somehow—evangelically by the grace of God and indirectly by appeal to the imagination of the needy—inviting.

So as an argument of orthodox apologetics, meant to compel unbelievers by dint of logic and evidence, i.e., directly, the Rule proves singularly ineffective, since it is not adducible from anything to which the uncommitted has immanent access. And whatever common ground of rationality it might attest would be so banal as hardly to

---

[45]A limitation of the cartographic simile is that the "boundaries" provided by the Rule get fuzzier the closer one gets to them. As noted before (n. 29), the Rule permits abundant room for argument over borderline cases, and there is extensive territory for different readings of (and behavioral responses to) the same texts. With respect to the Rule's latitude for interpretation, Jesus' remark surely applies, "In my Father's house are many rooms" (Jn 14:2). On the other hand, Kierkegaard would assert, the Rule permits only one interpretation: that in reading and living, "thou shalt love."

coerce belief.[46] But in articulating the Christian categories and distinctive forms of life, the Rule instructs the already converted, or those who think they are, in who they really are. It should at least figure in argument *over* that identity and over the uses of scripture in which that identity is at stake. Thus, in Rule-governed exegesis one can expect to find everything from gentle consolation to stern prophetic challenge—in other words, a rhetoric of faith, or indirect communication, addressed mainly to the confessing community.

This of course is the strategy in *WL*. In his deployment of scripture, as in all else, Kierkegaard aims to "build up" readers insofar as they are Christian; but, insofar as they are also members of "Christendom," the aim is to "wound from behind."[47] As for others, Kierkegaard has no interest or competence in saying how a biblical text should play, for other rules than that of faith would presumably pertain.[48] Consider this portion of our focus text:

Let the judges appointed by the state, let the detectives labour to discover guilt and crime; the rest of us are enjoined to be neither judges nor detectives—God has rather called us to love, consequently to the hiding of

---

[46]I would say the same of any hermeneutic substitute offered for the Rule, whether it fly under the flag of "history," "narrativity," "experience," "liberation," "process," or "magisterium." All deconstruct under the pressure of their own logic.

[47]*The Point of View for My Work as an Author: A Report to History*, Walter Lowrie, trans. (New York: Harper & Brothers, 1962), 24-25, 97. Kierkegaard was strongly averse to Christian apologetics because of the tendency, motivated by our dread of self-renunciation, to whittle the "offense" given by the Paradox down to human notions of self-sufficiency. He makes the point squarely in *WL*:

We have too earnest a conception of Christianity to entice anyone; we wish rather almost to give warning...If what is needed is to be done, we should not hesitate...to preach in Christian sermons—yes, precisely in Christian sermons—AGAINST Christianity. For we know full well where disaster strikes these days—namely, that by foolish and ingratiating Sunday-talk Christianity has been deceptively transformed into an illusion and we have been tricked into the fancy that we, just as we are, are Christians (190f.).

[48]Kierkegaard apparently did not object to a biblical exposition done under rules other than, or as we might say these days, under a paradigm different from, the Christian one. What he objected to was the careless assimilation of one kind of exposition to another, or as he said in another context, the "category confusion." Demanding only honest clarity, he could appreciate expositors who had the courage to follow their rival rules to avowedly non-Christian readings, like Feuerbach and Strauss. See, for example, Soren Kierkegaard's *Journals and Papers*, 7 vols., Howard V. Hong and Edna H. Hong, trans. and ed. (Bloomington: Indiana University Press, 1967-78), VI, #6523, 243f.; also Elrod, 71.

the multiplicity of sins with the help of a mitigating
explanation. Imagine this kind of lover...!

A logic of governance proper to "the state" is tacitly acknowledged. Kierkegaard knows there to be a rule of institutionalized guilt-
finding that is normal, perhaps even necessary, to ordered social existence. No matter, with the invocation of 1 Peter as the Word of God
("**God has rather called us to love**"), a wedge is driven between the
normal cultural logic and another sort, one proper to "**the rest of
us.**" The self-involving first-person plural "us" attests the community identified by this other logic. This other logic is of course the
Rule of faith. And, characteristic of the Rule, the community of "us"
is defined not by the privileges of superiority but by the obligations of
a holy commission to love. How judges and detectives who happen to
belong to the same community should negotiate the rival logics is left
painfully unclear. What is clear is that the logics, the reality definitions they assert and the forms of life they appoint, finding guilt vs.
mitigating guilt, *are* rival and are not to be casually harmonized.

Ironically, one way to have harmonized them would have been
to try to justify the authority of scripture that Kierkegaard here so
matter-of-factly assumes in his extravagant claim, "**God has called
us to love.**" Such justification could take numerous forms, each with
its own culture-legitimating, ideological force. The route taken by the
orthodox apologetics of his own day was flatly to assert scripture's
authority *because* it is the Word of God. This simply assumed a cultural status-quo in which hierarchic structures (logics) of state and
church were already so assimilated as to be practically indistinguishable, and the apologetes apparently liked it that way. A more elaborate apologetic with an eye for modernity and a stake in the shifting
social landscape would want to show how it is *possible* for scripture to
be the Word of God, with certain adjustments in one's thinking (and
in institutional power structures). This route tacitly assumed the adequacy of the contemporary metaphysical and epistemological criteria
for judging what is possible. Finally, a branch of the latter route, in
which the tacit assumption has now become a self-conscious conviction thoroughly historical in orientation, would show how it *was* possible for earlier generations to have believed scripture to be the Word
of God but how now the modern understanding of the world has advanced so far beyond that primitive level of conceptualization as to
render it obsolete, though modernity might still appreciate the earlier
level's indispensable contributions to the current superior state of af-

fairs, or the future state imminently to be achieved—or violently to be imposed.

Kierkegaard rejects these routes. As we have seen, the claim that scripture is the Word of God is analytic in the Rule that scripture "speaks" the Love of God. And Kierkegaard takes the Rule *on faith*, which, given its circularity and empirical non-verifiabilty, is the only way it can be taken. Apologetic moves only obscure the issue. He does not therefore try to *establish* scripture's authority but to *realize* it: by recalling it (**"God has called"**), by standing under it (**"God has called us"**), and by setting it to the work of authoring the life it aims at (**"Imagine this kind of lover"**).[49] This is what Kelsey calls a "functionalist" view of authority, inextricably linking the concepts "scripture" and "community."[50] And in Kierkegaard's hands it func-

---

[49]The attempt to establish scripture's authority only proves that it is gone (at least for the humans attempting to establish it). Genuine authority cannot be established, only attested. As Kierkegaard elsewhere remarks, "...what is needed is not professors but witnesses" (*JP*, I, #106, 44; cf. *JP* I, #186, 74, and #191, 77f). Or as Kelsey says, "'Authority' is not conferred on scripture by our decision to treat it as authority. 'Authority' is acknowledged by scripture's readers or hearers" (*The Uses of Scripture*, 152). I.e., the authority is conferred by (or simply is) God.

[50]According to Kelsey, the authority of scripture is understood in functional terms when "the texts are authoritative not in virtue of any inherent property they may have, such as being inerrant or inspired, but in virtue of a function they fill in the life of the Christian community" (*The Uses of Scripture*, 47).

The point is amplified, and the analytic linkage among concepts made especially clear, in the following:

Writings are not declared "scripture" and hence "authoritative" because as a matter of contingent fact they exhibit certain properties or characteristics (e.g., "inerrancy" or "inspiredness") that meet some pre-established criteria for inclusion in a class called "Christianly authoritative writings." Rather, they are declared "scripture of the church" and hence "authority for church life" because it is part of relevant concepts "church" to do so. "Scripture" and certain concepts of "church" are dialectically related concepts. Part of what it means to call a community of persons "church," according to some concepts "church," is that use of "scriptures" is essential to the preservation and shaping of their self-identity; part of what it means to call certain writings "scripture" is that according to certain concepts "church" they ought to be used in the common life of the church to nourish and reform it (*Uses*, 98).

Brevard Childs strongly objects to this functionalist view on the grounds that it tends to evacuate scripture of "a determinate meaning" (*The New Testament as Canon*, 545f.). To attempt to mediate, I would want to distinguish between inherent "properties" or "characteristics" that might be claimed for the writings (like inerrancy) and their inherent subject matter or content. The scriptures are scripture, I think the church wants to be able to say, because they speak of Christ, are a unique witness to Christ. But as I have been arguing, this subject matter can only be said to "inhere" in scripture insofar as the reader is equipped to "see" it there in a way that

tions not by the direct modes of mathematical inference, discursive reasoning, and empirical demonstration favored by so much apologetics, but by the indirect communication that appeals to readers to exercise their own imaginations to enter a world counter to the current one.

This might seem a backdoor way of reconciling Kierkegaard with the idea of community, moreover a way that still exacts a cost. Granted the Rule implies the social character of scripture's *reception*. Still, one might argue, in ruling that the community receive scripture as divine speech, the Rule, at least as practiced by Kierkegaard, seems to suppress the fact of the community's role in the text's historical *production*. One would think the historical-critical facts should have their say lest the Rule itself become (remain?) just another ideological ploy. After all, *"the facts are basic."*

True, *"but the explanation is decisive."* "The facts" did not speak for themselves in 1847 any more than now. How to speak of scripture in any moment calls for prophetic discernment into the character of both the factfinders and their times.[51] Prophetically, Kierkegaard believed God's love to be the only weapon ever sufficient to combat ideology.[52] The danger he perceived was from a historical critica*lism* that would legitimate scripture's authority by resolving it into the community's. The question was whether historical facts would not be marshaled against theological facts and end up in a monstrous category confusion, serving a different god.

---

seems to him or her virtually self-evidential, indeed, to see it as the literal sense of the text. As I have been saying, when it comes to meaning, "inherent" is a highly ambiguous concept. (I return to Childs's objection in chapter 6 below, pp. 202f.)

[51]Because Kierkegaard's anti-apologetic stance was based on an historically informed view of human reason as an interest-laden social enterprise, Merold Westphal is able to call it prophetic:

This is where the genuinely prophetic element becomes apparent. When the finitude and sinfulness of human reason are included in reason's historicity, the critique of reason becomes a critique of ideology and Kierkegaard becomes more than just another skeptic, doubtful about the soundness of apologetic arguments. He is persuaded that the final result will be corrupted Christianity, that the failure of apologetics lies not so much in an inability to provide the demonstrations or plausibilities it promises as in making promises that lead in the wrong direction altogether (Kierkegaard's *Critique of Reason and Society*, 22).

For a stunning example in *WL*, see the prophetically-styled "woe sayings" against Christian apologetics on 192f.

[52]By definition, ideology is self-interested. For historical reasons (i.e., human sin), the love of God is self-sacrificial. The two are therefore often in conflict, if not flatly antithetical.

Certainly, part of the mystery of scripture that the Rule would enforce is that speech—*obviously* human, attributed to human writers, and identified by those writers as their frail human witness to a greater reality—can nevertheless be used by God for God's purposes of authoring among humans new life, community, and identity. And when Kierkegaard elsewhere makes use of the canonical appellations in referring to "apostolic" authors, he expresses, theologically, something of the wide scope the Rule gives for speaking of scripture as historically, humanly produced.[53] In fact, speaking as Climacus, he implies that Christians have not just a theological warrant but a veritable need for historical research, a need rooted in the passion of faith itself. The need follows from the Paradox of the Incarnation, the infinite God's taking mortal flesh. It is inevitable, Climacus reasons, that we "be interested in the least detail" concerning the historical figure, Jesus of Nazareth, since he is the source of our eternal happiness. The passion's irony, of course, is that our historical research can provide no certainty about Jesus commensurate with our need.[54] It would be a category confusion, therefore, to assign the results of historical research direct and decisive theological significance. In its most transparent form, this would be the mistake of concluding about God what with only approximate accuracy has been discovered about humans. It takes more insidious form when humans, recognizing their inability to reach more than approximate results, disqualify talk about God while usurping God's sovereignty.

This is what Kierkegaard saw in the Hegelian-dominated historical criticism of his day. Apologetically inclined, it was worse than a distraction to religious seriousness, because it tended to accommodate scripture to the reality presuppositions of the modern industrial state.[55] To that degree ideologically driven, it was part of Christendom's adventure in community self-deification.[56]

---

[53]See the discussion of Kierkegaard's reference to "the Apostle James" as author in chapter 4 below.

[54]*CUP*, 508-12.

[55]It was Kierkegaard himself who spoke of the danger of historical criticism as a "distraction" (for example, in the Journal passage previously quoted, n. 49: *JP*, I, #106). Both Elrod (61-63) and Westphal (22), however, describe the perceived danger in the context of his larger critique of culture, including that of a scholarship falling increasingly under a scientific paradigm. The real danger, then, was of deception as to what Christianity really is and transformation of the Bible from religious literature to aesthetic artifact. Kierkegaard's own remarks about scholars and scholarship thoroughly bear out the assessment. Note, for example, how the terms "illusion," "deception," "self-deception," "evasion," "vanity," "cunning," "craftiness," even

Kierkegaard's non-apologetic reading by the Rule, therefore, is at least as polemical, and prophetic, as pious. By polemically hearing *God's* voice speaking through scripture, rather than the *vox populi*, he heads off self-serving bids for popular authority by which scripture might be summoned or dismissed at convenience. Rather than concede Christendom's right to pass judgment on scripture, he positions readers to hear scripture's judgment on Christendom. All in all, he allows that scripture has a *negative* normative role to play and a *critical* authority, that of articulating the standards against which the present life of the community is to be measured.[57]

Once one begins to sense the polemical thrust of Kierkegaard's biblical rhetoric, its "orthodoxy" turns ironic. Then it becomes difficult not to feel the Rule's critical edge cutting everywhere. But the negative note merits a dialectical reminder. The *positive* relation between scripture and church, Rule and community, still has a priority, best evidenced in the socially rooted activities of prayer, worship and other "works of love" that Kierkegaard says must surround the Christian's reading and with which he surrounds his own.[58]

4. *Summary Themes in Kierkegaard's Practice of the Rule*

We have been considering the way the analytic relations between Rule and community get spun out in the Kierkegaard text. Four related themes now round out our circuit of the Rule and allow us to regroup our observations. The first pertains to those standards against which the church is measured and to which we shall refer as scripture's "distinctive categories." The others come under the headings "intratextuality," "instruction/edification," and finally, "vision." Each is integral to both the Rule of faith and Kierkegaard's exegetical practice.

"conspiracy" abound in these remarks: see *FSE*, 50-67; and *JP* III, #'s 2872, 2874, 2890.

[56]Westphal, 23f., *et passim*. It has also been argued that, while historical criticism was often wielded against "tradition" in behalf of the freedom of individual conscience, it ironically contributed to a demoralizing conformism by its abstract conception of human being. See Elrod, 42f., 64-70.

[57]This idea is what Kelsey could call scripture's authority "for doing theology," which as we have seen he distinguished from its existential authority for personal life. To the degree that the distinction can be made, I am arguing (in the next paragraph) that for Kierkegaard the latter ranks higher. (Cf. chapter 1 above, and n. 38.)

[58]The prayers that begin all the works of the second literature are not just displays of piety; they are hermeneutic signifiers.

a. *Distinctive Categories.* Standards imply distinctions. To the degree that the Rule of faith identifies, defines, explains, prescribes, or measures anything (e.g., scripture-church), it does so by drawing on and generating distinctive scriptural categories and concepts.[59] We have had occasion to observe several key ones in connection with the radical heterogeneity invoked when the Rule refers to God as the source and subject of scripture. The concepts of faith, truth, and hope, it was noted, are dramatically qualified, in fact "transformed," when set in relation to God. Now we should consider that same transformation in relation to the narrative shape and content that Irenaeus imputes to the Bible. The upshot of Irenaeus's move will be that, for ethico-religious purposes,[60] scripture defines the world, not the other way around.[61] As a consequence, the shape and sense of scripture's

---

[59]This is tricky territory. The awkward formulation is meant to maintain the element of circularity in the Rule-church-scripture complex, and to highlight the element of use relevant to this social matrix and requisite to the concepts' distinctiveness. The point is to avoid the criticism justly leveled at those who try to hang the authority of scripture on its "distinctive concepts" when these are conceived as "intrinsic properties" of the text (cf. Kelsey, *Uses of Scripture*, 24-30). In a more functionalist vein one might argue that scripture's authority, while not deriving from distinctive concepts, would still entail and sponsor them.

[60]The qualification "ethico-religious purposes" is just one of Kierkegaard's hedges against fundamentalism, which he would have regarded as a form of disoriented aestheticism: while "objectifying" scripture and flattening it into essentially propositional knowledge, thus repressing the "objective uncertainty" that provides the ethico-religious tension constitutive of authentic faith (*CUP*, 182f., 407), fundamentalism denies the autonomy of non-religious language games like the natural sciences to speak of the world in ways that do not entail ethical and religious judgments. In other words, it is an enormous and compound category confusion. (Admittedly, the qualification leaves plenty of room for questions like, "What count as ethico-religious purposes?")

[61]In contemporary hermeneutics the seminal statement of this position was Hans Frei's *The Eclipse of Biblical Narrative.* The following remarks by George Lindbeck, however, provide a tidy summary:

> For those who are steeped in [the canonical writings], no world is more real than the ones they create. A scriptural world is thus able to absorb the universe. It supplies the interpretive framework within which believers seek to live their lives and understand reality...It is important to note the direction of interpretation. [It is not] that believers find their stories in the Bible, but rather that they make the story of the Bible their story. ...More generally stated, it is the religion instantiated in Scripture which defines being, truth, goodness, and beauty, and the nonscriptural exemplifications of these realities need to be transformed into figures of the scriptural ones. Intratextual theology redescribes reality within the scriptural framework rather than translating Scripture into extrascriptural categories. It is the text, so to speak, which absorbs the world, rather than the world the text (*The Nature of Doctrine*, 117f.).

terms will depend principally on their use within the canonical narrative context.

When the Rule describes scripture as the story of the world from Creation to Apocalypse, and thereby defines the world as *God's* world, it fixes the God-world relation along a certain line of authority. Fish's version of the Augustinian formula, "Everything in scripture and the world is to be read in light of the love of God and points to God's love when so read," now proves too loose. It can make scripture and world seem like independent realities, parallel but separate means of Christian understanding. But now a connection has been established between them that places them in an epistemological hierarchy. This is not to deny the dialectical relation between sacred text and readers' experience of the world, only their symmetry. Having learned a common language with the world, Christians have it qualified by scripture. According to the Rule of faith, it is the Bible that instructs believers in the truth about the world, and its categories become decisive.[62]

The lesson usually differs from those taught in and by "the world." This is only to admit the obvious, that the prophetic edge by which the Rule cuts against the cultural grain has a cognitive component. The conceptual stuff of scripture includes the conceptual equipment its students learn to think by, and the tasks the equipment is geared to perform are specific to that stuff. Or, to mix the metaphor, the concepts are native to scripture's soil and do not suffer transplantation without change. Thus, the very concepts "world," "freedom," "justice," "faith," "truth," and "hope," let alone the no-

---

For an important qualification of this position, however, see Terence Tilley's remarks about "dirty intratextuality" in his essay, "Incommen-surability, Intratextuality, and Fideism," *Modern Theology*, 5 (1989): 87-111. See also nn. 62 and 68 below.

[62]It may be that our experience of the world, in and through secular events, can awaken us to the peculiar qualifications scripture puts on key concepts and categories, which then serve to distinguish a Christian understanding from a worldly one (i.e., an understanding typical of the dominant culture). That is, the world can sometimes instruct us in the meaning of the gospel. Thus, I want to acknowledge just how complex the dialectical relation between sacred text and reader's experience can be. This seems to be the burden of the criticism Rowan Williams makes of Lindbeck's position. When Lindbeck describes the privileged biblical understanding of reality as transpiring in the church qua "communal enclave," he threatens to ghettoize the church and oversimplify the hermeneutic relation. See Williams, "Postmodern Theology and the Judgment of the World," in *Postmodern Theology: Christian Faith in a Pluralist World*, Frederic B. Burnham, ed. (San Francisco: Harper, 1989), 92-112; see especially, 101. Another word for the problem of ghettoizing the church is "sectarianism," which is the charge frequently levelled against Stanley Hauerwas.

tion of what is possible, are different when God is part of their gram-mar—when they belong to scripture's complex rendering of peculiar agents, events and activities, including those linguistic activities of speaking to and about God that make up scripture—than when they are defined with reference to other contexts.[63]

Of course, in *WL* as in the Rule, love is the distinctive concept *par excellence*. Kierkegaard, scrupulous grammarian that he is, takes care to cultivate it in its native soil; the framework for the explica-tion is consistently biblical. Despite the tendency of commentators to think otherwise, it is neither accident nor pious guise that *WL* is struc-tured as a series of biblical exegeses.[64] It is the Bible that has supplied his singular conception of love—a conception so singular, we ob-served in chapter 1, it seems to contradict nearly everything in the common experience of Christendom that goes by the name. To keep *that* love in focus, Kierkegaard has to keep his eye on scripture. Now, keeping one's eye on scripture, while construing it as a vast and com-plex whole, is an intratextual operation. Scripture's distinctive cate-

---

[63]*WL* abounds in examples of what Kierkegaard calls "the secret of transferred language" (199). These include his descriptions of Christian "hope" (244), "victory" (311, "win"), and, perhaps most brilliantly, "feast" (90f.).

Naturally, the structural complexity of scripture and the kind of wholeness it rep-resents means that the categories are not systematically arranged or schematized into a technical jargon. Just as scripture as a whole works as indirect, parabolic communi-cation rather than as a system of doctrines—by virtue of the Rule that construes it as a narrative (story-like) whole—so its terms tend to have all the tensiveness that metaphors have in literary or ordinary discourse. The well-known differences be-tween the Pauline and Johannine concepts of love, for instance, give rise to a friction inhospitable to systematic conceptual unity. Add to them something like Song of Songs, and the canonical profile becomes so ornate it seems hardly possible to speak of a singular biblical concept of love at all. The Rule, however, legislates a canonical wholeness to the literature in which the manifold uses (concepts) interrelate one way or another, not always neatly. They will play off or against each other so as to shade, qualify, and even correct some uses, restricting certain uses to specific contexts, sug-gesting certain contexts appropriate for others—again, charting not a tight "system" of denotations but a field of play for the creative language games collectively known as love.

[64]E.g., Elrod, 296: "By presenting his works in the *guise* of exegeses of biblical passages, he leads the reader to reflect on the divine word, which in turn facilitates his purpose of cultivating the divine-human relationship." (My emphasis.) Elrod's major point is right on target. No doubt it is the standard picture of exegesis as di-rect, objective discourse that inclines him to see Kierkegaard's style of maieutic re-flection as exegetical "guise," whereas from Kierkegaard's point of view, given the Bible's character as ethico-religious literature, only a maieutic style would be exe-getically fitting.

gories lead to *intratextuality* as the second theme recurrent in our circuit of the Rule.

b. *Intratextuality*. In technical parlance, "intratextuality" refers to a conception of scripture as a "semiotic code," a network of mutually conditioning signifiers the sense of any one of which depends on its place in the overall "system."[65] The term is closely associated with a view of scripture as *canon*, which denotes the normative and paradigmatic status of the textual system. The common factor is the emphasis on scripture as somehow whole, and there we see the clear influence of the Rule. Thus both "intratextuality" and "canon" apply to the point made earlier when I spoke of the exegete's being able to interrelate scripture's diverse parts under the Rule (p. 70). Because ruled to be a canonical whole, all of it oriented to God's plan of salvation, the Bible *can* be read intratextually, and for theological purposes *should* be. This means interpreting the various canonical voices in light of each other, no matter how different they may be genetically.[66] As already suggested, for Kierkegaard the different tradition histories of Pauline, Petrine, and Jamesian materials do not disqualify the diverse materials' being heard *ensemble* once established within the canon.

A vigorous intratextualism thus corresponds to Kierkegaard's polemic against the ideological tendencies of historical criticism (pp. 76-78, above). In the face of historical criticism's atomistic and rela-

---

[65]Lindbeck, 33f., 62, 113-15.

[66]The genetic (historical) account typically explains how and with whom a literary unit originated and was transmitted. My point is that the description of origins is not necessarily the same as an (intratextual) account of the material's function in its canonical context where its earlier uses may be significantly altered. The distinction should not be taken as anti-historical prejudice, however. An historical-critical perspective can be hugely helpful for discerning the material's canonical profile. Insofar as it allows one to measure the differences among earlier and later uses, it enhances one's sense of the canonical editors' intentions with the material, and of how one voice harmonizes or plays counterpoint with others in the canonical ensemble.

Kierkegaard himself did not take issue with critical findings or deny the scholar's right to pursue them, only with the prescriptive claim that understanding scripture was impossible without them (see Elrod, 61f.; *JP*, III, #'s 2872, 2874; IV, #3860). Indeed, one of the impressive things about Kierkegaard's use of scripture is the precision with which he could hear subtle differences among the canonical voices without historical-critical aids—though indeed the nuances he heard were often different from those heard by historical-critically aided ears, especially ears aided only historical-critically.

Chapters 4 and 5 below provide specific examples of how Kierkegaard's intratextual, canonical approach compares with a historical-critical approach.

tivizing influence, Kierkegaard presents a holistic view of scripture that affirms its integrity as a theological construal and preserves its ethico-religious function. At the same time, his intratextual approach serves to check the tendentious eclecticism of promoting congenial texts and dismissing uncomfortable ones. It is in this light we should understand his fondness for the hard sayings, what he calls "the existentially strenuous passages," of scripture and his emphasis on the "requirement" of Christianity.[67] *WL*, for instance, foregrounds the royal imperative "you shall love" precisely to counterbalance the prevailing ethos that would always dissolve the Law-Grace dialectic into an abandoned law and a cheap grace.

Further, by focusing on the love command, Kierkegaard taps a central nerve in the connective tissue between Old and New Testaments. He thereby upholds the canonical shape of scripture—the Christian Bible includes *both* Testaments—against a perennial Marcionite impulse to truncate it. True, in the *Journals*, less often in the public writings, he succumbs to that impulse himself. He remains all too willing to play the second Testament off against the first, the younger religion (and community) against the elder.[68] If he thereby shares in the more demonic dimension of the Marcionite heresy, revealing his own complicity in Christendom's deep and abiding anti-Semitism, he has nevertheless left *WL* (and *Fear and Trembling*) to witness against him. In any case, anti-Semitism is not the most prominent item in his hermeneutic profile.

Far more prominent is the unrelenting insistence upon "appropriation" as the prerequisite for making religious sense of religious texts. Here Kierkegaard hears the two Testaments speaking in perfect unison. The operative principle behind appropriation is that, where God is concerned, knowing entails doing.[69] Kierkegaard never tires of making the point that unless one takes scripture to heart,

---

[67]*JP*, III, #2881, 277.

[68]It would be correct to point out that such "playing off against" is a form of intratextual reading, too. "Intratextuality" taken by itself implies neither a positive nor a negative relation among the parts of the larger text one reads, only that some relation exists among them, even one of pure contradiction. That is why for Christian hermeneutical purposes the term "intratextuality" has to be qualified by "canon." The decision of the early church in the formation of the Christian canon was that intratextual readings which allow the tensions between the Testaments to become unbridgeable chasms, to the point that the authority of the first is simply denied, violate the apostolic faith. Part of what it means to be Christian, normatively speaking, is to live and read within that decision.

[69]This point is pervasive throughout both Kierkegaard and this book. Its biblical basis will be developed in chapter 4 below.

which means putting it to practice, one hasn't taken it as scripture. The force of his insight extends our contemporary understanding of the term "intratextual." Just as the biblical imperatives direct the reader into life (consider the depth grammar of "**God has rather called us to love**"), a Rule-governed intratextuality incorporates the social practice of its believing readers. As we saw above in part II, the life of the church—its prayer, worship, ethical striving, even its theologizing—becomes part of the text intratextually interpreted, and the life becomes part of the interpretation. The theme of intratextuality belongs to the circle connecting Rule and community, text and context, reading and practice.

c. *Instruction/Edification*. The insistence on appropriation forges the link between intratextuality, defined so as to "textualize" life, and our third theme, instruction or edification.[70] That scripture is read for instruction seems too obvious to say. By definition of appropriation, instruction would be precisely whatever one appropriates—whatever one consumes and digests in order to live. Of course, the obviousness only indicates how grammatical a feature of religious reading, how integral to the Rule and definitive of scripture, scripture's instructional character is. Things most self-evidential are typically among the most essential. As noted earlier, instruction was one of the essentials of scripture singled out for emphasis by Irenaeus and everywhere implicit in scripture's use before him, and our discussions of scripture's narrative shape and distinctive categories presupposed it.

What Kierkegaard had to stress in the post-Enlightenment context was the *personal* quality of the learning that takes place when scripture gets woven into life. It is a far different kind of learning, he believed, from what was being produced by most biblical scholarship. In contrast to the objectivity of scientific disinterestedness, scripture's instruction is in the mode of "subjectivity" (cf. above, pp. 54f., 70f.). As God's Word, and thus a medium of communication between personal agents, Subject and subject,[71] scripture must engage the intellectual, volitional, and emotional capacities constitutive of personhood. Scripture therefore requires not that human wishes, interests,

---

[70]Indeed, appropriation is the funnel through which all Kierkegaardian currents pour. If we were only trying to describe Kierkegaard's hermeneutic in his own terms, "appropriation" would be the primary candidate. (So Minear and Morimoto, *Kierkegaard and the Bible*, 3-12. Rebecca Patten, however, makes a good case for "repetition," a concept closely related to "appropriation." [Unpublished paper, "Kierkegaard's Hermeneutics," 3-7.])

[71]Recall the key statement from *CUP*, "God is a subject" (178).

commitments, beliefs, emotions, attitudes, and dispositional propensi-
ties be *bracketed*, as for an objective purview of impersonal data, but
that they be *foregrounded* as both an active ingredient of the reading
process and a target for alteration and development. Certainly, to
foreground and target them is not simply to give in to them—
uncritically, irrationally—but to order them according to one's
(reasoned) purpose. One may, like Kierkegaard's detective, "**for a
long, long time [have to keep] his judgment suspended**," having already exercised his judgment in choosing to want to detect love.
Clearly, with scripture one is probing one's faculties even while
thinking *by* them. We might go so far as to say that one has to let
scripture pry deep into one's sense of self (as creature, sinner, mini-
god) if even its literal sense—e.g., its performative sense as an invita-
tion to intimacy between creature and Creator—is ever to be
grasped.[72]

This assumes of course that one agrees to construe scripture as
divine instruction in the first place, that is, to construe it by the Rule.
But given the assumption, the Subject-Teacher clearly requires the
expansion of the subject-learner. In any event, though the term itself
tended to be restricted to the pseudonymous works, Kierkegaard's attention to the principle of "subjectivity" in *WL* paralleled his insistence upon appropriation. To take scripture as instruction is to enlist
in a regimen of training in subjectivity.[73]

Both images in Kierkegaard's construal of scripture, the "mirror"
and the "love letter," express the depth dimensions of the divine
pedagogy. Instruction taken from the mirror, we have seen, issues in a
passionate self-knowledge. One looks into scripture to learn who one
is with the sense that one's life is at stake in the learning. When the
scriptural mirror is also construed as a word of love, the accent falls
on the form of instruction Kierkegaard called edification or upbuilding. No less passional than learning about oneself, edification is more
dynamic because of its transitivity: it *creates* the self. Meant to be
appropriated and lived, scripture not just instructs but *con*structs the

---

[72]Again, my assumption is that "literal sense" is context-specific. I speak of the
literal sense the biblical text takes on when read in a religious context of particular
beliefs, commitments, purposes, practices, and expectations.

[73]The allusion is to *Training/Practice in Christianity*. Kierkegaard's titling of
that work, which like *WL* is organized as a series of biblical exegeses, shows how
prominent in his mind the instructional dimension of reading scripture truly was.

appropriating reader.[74] Belonging to the creative-redemptive agency of God, scripture forms the self who is willing to read it with a passion commensurate with God's own. As Word of Love, scripture builds up those human capacities it engages, and transforms them for closer correspondence to the Word's own image. Of course, this is exactly what love itself does, according to the testimony of scripture (e.g., 1 Cor 8:2). And by this time we hardly need reminding that the identity of function between love and scripture in Kierkegaard is also a stipulation of the Rule of faith.

We have observed a similar Rule-dependency with each of our themes. Now we see how even the pathos of instruction derives from the Rule, so that the Rule, too, is weighty with pathos. So much turns on the rulish business of stipulating and defining and explaining. So much would be lost if it were dismissed as scholastic word-play, or worse, an inhibitive legalism at odds with the freedom of the gospel. In socio-linguistic jargon, what needs stressing is the illocutionary force of the Rule and its world-constructive capacity. Theologically, one would say that taking on the yoke of the kingdom—in reading as in all else—is meant to be creative and liberating. Like the knowledge of God that scripture aims to induce, the grammar for reading scripture does not consist simply in a set of cognitive propositions, constatives that simply leave things as they are, as if the "things" and the mode of either their perception or description were unrelated. Because the Rule is "of faith," it has affective entailments, too, that influence which reality will be perceived and enable that reality's perception. Of course it is these relational, affective entailments, crucial elements of our subjectivity, that Kierkegaard believed to be the very fabric of one's God-relationship (since "God is a subject" [*CUP*, 178]).

For example, one heeds the Rule's directives only to the degree that one ventures to read in *trust*. For Christians, trusting that God will use scripture for our good is part of trusting God. Relatedly, if the stipulation "that scripture edifies like love" were not also a *promise* that animates Christian reading with *hope*, and, again, relates the reader to God, there would be little religious point to the reading, certainly no zest or urgency. And it would be arguable whether what one read were really "scripture."

This must be the burden of the optative mood in our focus text:

---

[74]In the lead chapter of Part Two of *WL*, "Love Builds Up," Kierkegaard makes an extended point of deriving the moral sense of "edification" from its architectural use (cf. "edifice"). He is very deliberate, to edify means to build a person up.

O, if men would rightly understand what splendid use they could make of their imaginative powers...then they would gain more and more a taste for one of the most beautiful joys of life...Imagine this kind of lover, endowed by nature with such magnificent capacities that every judge must envy him, but all these capacities are employed with a zeal and rigour such as a judge would have to admire in the service of love, for the purpose of getting practice in the art and practising the art, the art of interpretation, which, with the help of a mitigating explanation, hides the multiplicity of sins!

There is an anticipation of joy that belongs to the grammar of the Christian life, and Kierkegaard would have his readers taste it as they read his text. It is fundamentally the same anticipation—that the reader might become a love-sleuth of scripture, artful interpreter **"in the service of love"**—that the Rule induces with its prescriptions. "Read this and become a lover, and practice your loving in reading this," the Rule says in effect. Such anticipation would quickly evaporate were reading "liberated" from all normative definitions.[75] Of course, apart from the affective, promissory dimension of its definitions, the Rule would itself be just another dry objective doctrine, the target of Kierkegaard's polemic rather than a prize.

For all its conventionality, then, the Rule potentiates scripture's instructional efficacy—by declaring it. As a community principle that instructs as it asserts, directs as it defines, the Rule summarily indicates the form of human responsiveness to the divine initiative by which humans grant God the room to work. It is as if faith's construal of scripture as powerful allows it to be so, if it can be so at all. Only when the Rule identifies something as objectively inert as a book with something as subjectively agentic as Love can scripture be said to do the things Christians say it does, like instruct and edify, and to be what they say it is: scripture. Kierkegaard's bold remark in the focus text, **"that the explanation [the Rule] makes the object of explanation [scripture] what it is [God's Word of Love],"** is thus a clue to the cosmogonic force of the Rule of faith. Faith builds a text-

---

[75]Needless to say, the anticipation would never arise if I had no desire to become a lover, if the prospect of loving had no appeal for me. But this too is a capacity that can be learned—to want to love.

world of possibility.[76] Faith makes the Bible scripture. At least, only by faith can readers see it as such.

d. *Vision.* The vision metaphor has resurfaced, and with it our ubiquitous last theme. I have been arguing from the instructive and edifying character of scripture to the instructive and edifying character of the Rule. The explanatory definitions that constitute scripture direct and capacitate readers to see it so. And I have emphasized the pathos that the Rule entails. It is indeed a pathos-laden situation that so much rides upon the Rule, which works two ways at once, constructing as it were both its text and its readers. I set out to speak of the Rule of faith as a construal or vision of the Bible as scripture; in effect we have just witnessed the Rule's deep implication, by virtue of its reader-capacitating prowess, in the dialectic of vision and the moral life, a dialectic attested by Kierkegaard and countless exegetes before him: under the tutelage of scripture "virtue leads to vision, and vision empowers virtue."[77]

Of course, the dialectics Kierkegaard spoke of go beyond that of ethical development, for vision's highest passion is not to enhance one's own virtue, as if self-perfection were the self-sufficient goal.[78] To speak of the highest, we should recall the narrative shape the Rule appoints to scripture. We saw that according to the Rule of faith, the

---

[76]Naturally, whether the possibility faith constructs is real (i.e., "Is scripture truly the Word of God/Love?") depends on whether the God is real whom faith confesses as its source and object, and of course there is no neutral position from which to adjudicate that question since to step into neutrality is to abandon precisely the relationship, the subjective activities like trust, by which the God of scripture, the God who "is a subject" (*CUP*, 178), can be known. Apart from the context of life commitments and passional involvements, the reality question can only remain a moot point, what Kierkegaard calls a matter of "objective uncertainty."

The question of the rationality of this position is a different matter. For example, the charge of "fideism" typically levelled against Kierkegaard (and Wittgenstein) implies that the position is irrational because subjective. But this tendentiously assumes a notion of "Reason" as monolithic and univocal, the same for all orders of reality, non-context specific and occupying a neutral position to which humans somehow have access. If it is fideism to reject this sort of "foundationalism," by all means count me a fideist.

[77]Greer, 191, discussing Origen's understanding of interpretation as a moral-spiritual (Kierkegaard: ethico-religious) task.

[78]For Kierkegaard, the selfishness ingredient in all moralism can only be overcome when the striving individual has a transcendent telos, in other words is focused beyond himself on God. Indicative of this position is the next-to-last chapter of *WL*: "The Work of Love in Praising Love." Love is ultimately doxological, Other-centered first and last. This is the theme of chapter 5 below.

Bible tells the story of the world from beginning to end. With imperial sweep it would include all human experience, past, present and future, as transpiring under the cosmic governance of God, paradigmatically manifested in the story of Israel, Jesus, and the Apostolic Church. The biblical story thus becomes everyone's story. Now, by so absorbing all worlds into its own, the Bible also characterizes the course of Christian life to be in micro-cosmic imitation of its own narrative pattern of Creation to Apocalypse. For the individual, life is a lesson leading to revelation. So is the Bible.

But the focus of revelation is God. Hence Kierkegaard's phrase, "stages along life's way," with its ancient underlying metaphor of life as a journey; hence also his talk in our lead text of the discipline of agapic interpretation. Both imply the possibility of improvement, the latter suggesting that the destination is eschatological. Like salvation history as a whole, the life of faith makes indeed a kind of progress, but a mysterious, hidden kind. Similarly, the Bible, like both the neighbor and the self, exists not simply as an end in itself, but instrumentally for a transcendent *telos*: it exists, as Kierkegaard says, **"for the purpose of getting practice in the art and practicing the art of interpretation ... in the service of love."**

Scripture provides *exercises* in vision and is itself but an occasion, if a privileged one, for the moral growth, given by God, that readies one to see *beyond* both text and self. Again, the progress comes not primarily by textual transmission of discursive knowledge,[79] but by the text's inducing a kenotic, cruciform life. This will mean a continuous education of resistant but mutually reinforcing capacities, a hard schooling whose culmination can only be eschatological. As for what that culmination consists in: the better one reads/lives, according to the Rule (i.e., for and by the love of God), the more clearly might one love; and the better one loves/lives, the clearer one will read, so as to see the traces of God's love perhaps not so darkly as at first, until the vision is clear at the last and one comes to see God's very self. The goal of faithful life and reading is the *visio dei*.

The last word on vision and the Rule must be to repeat one of the first. The religious dialectics of Christian reading cannot be one of immanence that forms a closed circle by which text and reader pro-

---

[79]This concept is why love cannot be discursively formulated with ultimate adequacy, and why a specifically Christian hermeneutic—the Rule of love—cannot be the sort of rule we usually expect hermeneutics to provide. We want to solve our differences of interpretation objectively, cerebrally, neatly and tidily. For Kierkegaard, I suspect, that means unlovingly.

duce a vision of God, which must invariably reduce to a function of text and reader. That would be the dialectic of "Religiousness A." Kierkegaard goes beyond that dialectic to take a stand with Augustine, who saw and acknowledged with full force the problem of textual ambiguity and the indeterminacy of signs, and "resolved" it with a confession no less problematic, epistemologically, than the circle it opens. At the beginning of his classic statement on the Rule, Augustine remarks on the difficulty of understanding the apparently simple gesture of pointing: "Although I can lift my finger to point something out, I cannot supply the vision by means of which either this gesture or what it indicates can be seen."[80] Only God can give the vision.

---

[80]Augustine, *On Christian Doctrine*, D. W. Robertson, Jr. trans. (New York: Macmillan, 1958), 3-4.

CHAPTER 3

HERMENEUTIC SCANDAL: HIDING SIN

One of the questions posed in the Introduction was how Kierkegaard might help Christians read the Bible as scripture in the face of its manifold shortcomings: its patriarchalism, ethnocentrism, homophobia, sectarian anxieties, and other barbarisms that give us offense. In chapter 1 I argued for the inadequacy of the construal "classic" as a substitute for "scripture." For various writers, particularly feminist theologians, the substitution is motivated by a recognition of the oppression enshrined in Christian scripture and the history of abuse facilitated by scripture's "authority." The agenda in chapter 1, however, did not allow room to reflect properly on the particulars of that oppression; the primary task was to illustrate the difference between the construals "classic" and "scripture" and to delineate Kierkegaard's notion of Christian love as a key ingredient in the latter. Relying primarily on Part One of his *WL* (1847), I went on to propose that the "neighbor love" that Kierkegaard finds distinctive of Christianity is also central to his biblical hermeneutic, which turns out to be a reader-response version of the Augustinian "Rule of faith." For Kierkegaard as for Augustine, I have been arguing, it was axiomatic that scripture is to be read in light of and in response to the love of God, and that it points to the love of God when so read.

A direct response to the problem of oppression was deferred again in chapter 2. There I used an extended passage from the Discourse "Love Hides the Multiplicity of Sins" in Part Two of *WL* to illustrate the relevance of the Augustinian hermeneutic axiom to Kierkegaard's exegetical practice.[1] At the same time, I characterized the Rule as a form of imaginative construal, charted its historic

---

[1] *WL* 271-73.

development within ancient Israel and the early church, and explicated its peculiar, if characteristically hermeneutic, circularity. Motifs in that discussion—agapic imagination and vision as interpretive skills, canonical intratextuality, and edification as scripture's purpose—will circulate through the present chapter as well. Now, however, with the theoretical equipment in place, the practical task can no longer be deferred. The problem of scripture's, and Kierkegaard's, oppressive potential must be addressed head on, specifically with respect to "Love Hides the Multiplicity of Sins." If in what follows I frame the issue in feminist terms, that is because feminism is arguably the most important theological movement since the Reformation. It is also because those are the terms in which the issue has confronted me most personally.

I. The Personal Stake

The issue has confronted me in several venues. Since I am a teacher, the most immediate has been the classroom where my students and I play out variations on what must be an increasingly familiar theme in higher education. Surely the woman was not unique who announced one evening in my course on Eros and Agape that she had had a surfeit of dead males.[2] Her statement took courage; it represented a significant political act, especially before a male teacher. Unfortunately, a predisposition against the literature in someone both religiously serious and intellectually capable would likely block a fruitful reading of it. The loss would be not only hers, but the church's, even society's, as well. Multiplied throughout academia and the church, the tendency to paint "the tradition" with brush strokes so broad that one is inclined to dismiss it as a whole deprives our institutions of the disciplined critical scrutiny they require and produces debased forms of spirituality. I think this matters.

Another venue in which the issue has confronted me has been among my female colleagues. When I presented a paper for an in-house faculty seminar on the theme, "the prisonhouse of language," I

---

[2] Her protest was triggered by this chapter in *WL*, on top of the biblical literature we had looked at. However, the reading list for the course did include numerous women writers: e.g., novelists Toni Morrison and Gail Godwin, and feminist theologians Rita Brock, Linell Cady, Beverly Harrison, and Carter Heyward. Needless to say, I chafed at the protest.

included, not unprovocatively, several pages of Kierkegaard's "Love Hides the Multiplicity of Sins," ostensibly to help emphasize the measure of freedom people always have in the language they use. In the energetic debate that followed, it was not only Kierkegaard's glib references to "small-town beauties" (265) that made him an inviting target. As one colleague put it, his text is a classic instance of "the technology of Christian discourse by which women have been systematically subordinated to male authority." Here, too, the issue is as much pedagogical as personal. Apart from worrying (egocentrically) about how my commitments and interests appear to associates who are also dear friends, I have to ask what happens when I place such texts, which I obviously respect, before students who may, perhaps unduly, respect me and my institutionally vested authority. This also matters.

My colleague's charge can obviously be extended beyond Kierkegaard to include not just the biblical text of 1 Peter that Kierkegaard was expounding, but the form of love that both he and 1 Peter were promoting. Linell Cady states the case forcefully:

> Christian self-sacrificial love has been increasingly criticized, especially by feminists, for various deficiencies. Perhaps its most serious drawback is, as the literature attests, its complicity in reinforcing social inequality. By making self-sacrifice the primary criterion of the virtuous life, Christianity has given powerful religious validation to the situation of oppression. For those who lack power and status in a society, there is no motivational lever by which equality can be gained when the religious ideal is one of altruistic selflessness. Indeed, this ideal tends to foster the reverse dynamic: an inducement to remain subjugated in testimony to one's disregard for self.[3]

Whether Christianity—or Kierkegaard, or 1 Peter—has in fact made self-sacrifice *per se* the primary criterion of the virtuous life is debatable; what is important is the larger point being made. Patriarchy was and is a cultural fact—one among others—formative of and pervasive throughout Christianity. The Bible and the exegetical tradition cannot escape the influence of the patriarchal condition any more than any other literature can escape the influence of the

---

[3] Linell E. Cady, "Relational Love: A Feminist Christian Vision," *Embodied Love: Sensuality and Relationship as Feminist Values*, Paula M. Cooey, *et al.*, eds. (San Francisco: Harper & Row, 1987), 140.

conditions under which it is produced and read. This holds for the secondary "products" of the Bible as well, such as the daily life and social arrangements legitimated by scripture's ideals, like neighbor-love. This fact is part and parcel of what I referred to in chapter 2 as the "embarrassment" or "scandal" of the Incarnation.[4] When the terms and texts of Christianity seem scandalous and give offense, it matters theologically—i.e., it lies at the heart of what we take Christianity to be.

Accordingly, the aim of this chapter is, first, to clarify the offense given by Kierkegaard and his selected biblical text, and second, to consider whether the offense ought to be dissolved, sidestepped, or embraced. In part II of this chapter, we shall observe how the idea of offense is thematized by Kierkegaard's Discourse, "Love Hides the Multiplicity of Sins." Following that, in part III, we shall locate the particular moments of offense in Kierkegaard's explication of 1 Peter 4:8. Part IV seeks to contextualize Kierkegaard's strategy as parabolic

---

[4] See above, chapter 2, pp. 61f. and n. 17. Cady is right to reject the solution to this dilemma proposed by certain reformist (as opposed to radical) feminists. That solution is the idea of a canon within a canon, the notion that there is a valid core to the Bible—a privileged selection of material—unsullied by the historical circumstances of its production and reception. The reformist move, the projection of a pristine text, underestimates the thoroughly historical nature of the documents (Cady, 135f.). I would take Cady a step farther and say that *theologically*, the reformist move naively dissolves the embarrassment of the Incarnation, the "scandal" that the invisible Word fully takes on visibly frail human flesh, but in such a way as to be visible as Word only to the faith the Word creates in its witnesses. If God has no objectively distinguishing signs, as Kierkegaard says, then the Bible has no texts immune from the traces of its humanity. It follows from this "scandal" that, as a humanly produced document, any and every part of the Bible is to be read, weighed, and assessed—i.e., critiqued—in light of its ultimate subject matter, which for Christians is the God of Love revealed in Christ. Our obligation to critique the text is sanctioned by the sovereign judgment which that subject matter—scripture's Transcendental Signified—exercises over its signifiers, its human witnesses.

Unfortunately, Cady's solution to the problem of a patriarchally infected scripture is no more adequate, for Christians, than the reformists' solution. As we noted of McFague and Schüssler Fiorenza in chapter 1, Cady simply dismisses (after misconstruing) the Bible's authoritative status. Christianity, for her, is a means to an end: justice for women and the creation of a non-patriarchal society. That is, she values it for its utility rather than any intrinsic truth. Methodologically, for Cady, social-scientific models are normative vis-à-vis theological discourse. Accordingly, she dissolves the scandal of the Incarnation with a materialist bias. For a fuller analysis of the place of social-scientific thought in some feminist theology, see Garrett Green, "The Gender of God and the Theology of Metaphor," *Speaking the Christian God: The Holy Trinity and the Challenge of Feminism*, Alvin F. Kimel, Jr. ed. (Grand Rapids: Eerdmans, 1992), 44-64.

discourse by comparing it with Nathaniel Hawthorne's short story, "Young Goodman Brown." Part V then asks how the application of a canon-contextual analysis to 1 Peter might re-focus the issue. Part VI draws conclusions from the preceding discussion.

II. The Offense

"Woe unto the man by whom offence comes; blessed is the lover who by refusing to give occasion hides the multiplicity of sins." (WL, 278)

Kierkegaard quotes Matthew 18:7 and pairs the scriptural woe-saying with a blessing to bring to a close his Discourse on 1 Peter 4:8, "Love Hides the Multiplicity of Sin." It is the second time in *WL* that he has cited the Matthean passage. The first came in Part One amid a sustained polemic against apologetic tendencies to make Christianity attractive by concealing the *skandalon* ("stumbling block," "offense") at its heart. The threat such tendencies pose evoked a bold prophetic rhetoric:

Since Holy Scripture says "Woe to the men by whom the temptation [*to skandalon*, "the offense"][5] comes, we confidently say: woe to him who first thought of preaching Christianity without the possibility of offence. Woe to the person who ingratiatingly, flirtatiously, commendingly, convincingly preached to mankind some effeminate something which was supposed to be Christianity! Woe to the person who could make the miracles reasonable, or at least sketch the prospects of its being done soon! Woe to the person who betrayed and broke the mystery of faith, distorted it into public wisdom, because he took away the possibility of offence! Woe to the person who could comprehend the mystery of atonement without detecting anything of the possibility of offence.... (*WL*, 192f.)

The emphasis on Christianity as a scandal runs throughout the Kierkgaardian corpus, and the terminology of offense punctuates *WL*.[6]

---

[5] The Hongs note that the Danish Bible has *Forargelsen* here, i.e. "the offence" (n. 122, p. 368). Why they follow the RSV's lead in using "temptation" in this context and not at the end of "Love Hides..." escapes me.

[6] Forms of the term "offense" occur no less than forty one times, in addition to the four instances in the passages quoted above. See 71f., 74, 145f., 191-94, 214, 264,

As we observed in chapter 1, the fact that Christian love should be *commanded* offends our natural sensibilities, as does the idea of Christian love as a triangle—that we love the neighbor by loving God (a "third party") in him or her.[7] Ultimately, what is offensive about Christian love is what is scandalous about a crucified Messiah. Love's having to die for humanity proves our insufficiency to save ourselves, rebukes our worldly conceptions of power, glory and honor, and calls believers to be followers in a cruciform, self-sacrificial service. Following Paul and Luther, Kierkegaard insists that this scandal, and the possiblity of taking offense at it, is constitutive of Christianity and, by extension, of Christian scripture. To disguise the occasion the gospel provides for taking offense is to cheapen the grace that the gospel offers.

What is curious about the Matthean quote at the end of "Love Hides..." is that it runs counter to the main thrust of the rest of *WL*. Whereas Kierkegaard typically condemns all efforts to conceal the gospel's offensiveness, eager as he is to guard the reader's freedom to respond as s/he will, here he praises love for providing no "occasion" for taking offense, no opportunity for sinning. This curiosity has overlapping Christological, moral, and exegetical dimensions. To bring these into sharper focus, let me situate the closing woe/blessing within the Discourse and the book as a whole.

The woe/blessing restates the last of four ways that love can hide sins. These four ways are: (1) by silence (268-71), (2) by a mitigating explanation (271-73), (3) by forgiveness (273-76), and (4) by "smothering sin at birth," i.e., by refusing to give sin "occasion" (276-78).

With respect to the last way, giving sin occasion means providing it an opportunity to express itself, which is not so strong as "causing" it but may nevertheless fall within the scope of one's volition and power. According to Kierkegaard, the loving person, alert to the smoldering anger, resentment, prurience, or other

---

268, and 271—the last four coming in our discourse, "Love Hides...." Though I haven't bothered with a word count, the terminology is doubtless even more frequent in *Practice in Christianity*, a book devoted to a full-scale exposition of "the offense." For an excellent analysis of the concept, especially as it relates to Kierkegaard's social and political thought, see Bruce H. Kirmmse, *Kierkegaard in Golden Age Denmark* (Bloomington and Indianapolis: Indiana University Press, 1990), his chapters on *The Sickness Unto Death* and *PC*, as well as his chapter on *WL* (318-23 in particular).

[7] See above, pp. 39-41. For the relevant passages in *WL*, see 40f. and 118, 70 and 280, respectively.

vulnerability in the neighbor, seeks not only to avoid igniting these passions, but to clear away the combustible behaviors that could fuel them. Thus love defuses the situation. The explosion that could have developed into multiple conflagrations is averted and a "multiplicity of sins" is hidden, covered, quenched.

In fact, this last way of hiding sins is less a separate way than an epitome of the first three, as the following paragraphs will demonstrate. The first three ways, in turn, are sub-sets of love's various forms of transitivity, which Kierkegaard develops in Part Two of *WL*. Having shown in Part One how neighbor-love relates to the imperative of the Law, in Part Two Kierkegaard turns to describe how such love works in practice and to describe the creative, transforming power it can have when motivated by grace.[8] This explains the interruption by our Petrine episode in chapter V of the Pauline-titled sequence of chapters I-IV and VI:[9]

I. Love Builds Up (I Cor 8:1)
II. Love Believes All Things...(I Cor 13:7)
III. Love Hopes All Things...(I Cor 13:7)
IV. Love Seeks Not Its Own (I Cor 13:5)
V. Love Hides the Multiplicity of Sins
VI. Love Abides (I Cor 13:13)

Love's hiding of sin is but another instance of the highly imaginative, active life of the *abidingly* eternal (chap. VI) Love that *believingly* (chap. II), *hopefully* (chap. III), and *unselfishly* (chap. IV) presupposes love in others and thereby edifies (creatively *builds up*, chap. I) both their true personhood and the lover's own. The abstract and difficult introductory portion of the text regarding love's "reduplication" (pp. 261-63) can be understood similarly. It serves to reiterate the "like-for-like" logic and the theme of love's reflexivity that run through these chapters and that help connect the Petrine and Pauline conceptions of love.[10]

---

[8] Kirmmse, 312.

[9] An especially scrupulous historical critic could be imagined to take offense at Kierkegaard's promiscuous mixing of Pauline and Petrine materials this way, which can only end up by producing an unhistorical synthesis of (slightly) divergent conceptions of love. Since the present chapter has greater exegetical offenses to cover, I am deferring this one to chapter 4, on James.

[10] The like-for-like logic serves as a key structuring element of the book as a whole. It is mentioned explicitly on 207 and 239 within the sequence of chapters under discussion, but also in the first and last chapters of the book (33, 345, and

III. Hiding Sin: Love's Injustice

1. Silence

"Silence" seems at first glance the most passive of the three methods by which the loving person hides sin. Giving sin no occasion in this sense means refraining from malicious gossip and scandalmongering. Further, silence's relation to the imagination appears merely negative, insofar as it is a refusal to indulge the "sick imagination" (277) that feeds on rumor. Nevertheless, to the extent that the act of refusal that silence performs suppresses rumor and retards the feeding frenzy that would otherwise "corrupt mind and soul," even "setting fire to a whole community" (271), silence can be said actually to decrease the number of sins potential in a situation. Moreover, by having just invoked the picture of Christ before the Sanhedrin and by twice reminding us that Christ "is the pattern" and "the highest example" (267f.), Kierkegaard implies that the would-be lover must actively engage the imagination in order to keep a Christ-like silence. Following an example is a highly imaginative activity.[11] Silence turns out to be neither so passive nor so unimaginative as we first might have thought.

But is this an example that *ought* to be followed? The feminist critique presses the ethical question. Silence in the face of wrongdoing can be complicity with evil, which those with more power are only too happy to advocate to those with less, and to advocate, if not impose, in the name of family, nation, and God. History and current socio-political analytic methods equip us to take offense at Kierkegaard's proposal. The fact that earlier in *WL* Kierkegaard insists that neighbor-love entails neither slavish compliance with the neighbor's desires (36f.) nor masochistic dependency on the beloved

---

348ff.). For a helpful discussion of both the like-for-like logic and Kierkegaard's emphasis on love's reflexivity, see Kirmmse, 308-16. Meanwhile, note their relevance to my broader hermeneutic proposal as formulated in chapter 2: one becomes loving by practicing love in one's living, which includes one's reading. We are conformed to what and how we read.

[11] On imagination as a quality of activity, a way of behaving, see David Gouwens, *Kierkegaard's Dialectic of the Imagination* (New York: Peter Lang, 1989), 158, 278f. On the use of the imagination in following an example, as in the imitation of Christ, see Gouwens, 253-61, especially his point that the imitation "requires improvisation" (254). Dialectically, on the effect of the example on the imagination, see Garrett Green, *Imagining God: Theology and the Religious Imagination* (San Francisco: Harper & Row, 1989), 80, 100-103.

(52f., 128) does not necessarily exonerate him. It may only be evidence that Christianity is incoherent and Kierkegaard naïve.

2. The mitigating explanation

It is in the nature of an explanation, says Kierkegaard, a speech-act hermeneutician ahead of his time, that it defines what is (271). Explanations legitimate "the world," giving things the objectivity of public being. To explain what in a person's behavior can be construed as ill-intended and criminal in a way that, instead, presupposes love as the ground of the behavior is to give that love the room to be. Thus, given the faith that love (i.e., God) really *is* the ground of the neighbor's existence, the loving explanation summons forth real love in him or her, much as "deep calleth unto deep" (or like unto like). Not only, then, does the lover's explanation give ill intention no occasion, smothering sin at birth; it positively occasions the birth of good intention.[12]

Kierkegaard's parable of the love sleuth (271-73) details the strenuous work imagination performs in this loving kind of explanation. The love sleuth tirelessly searches the terrain of the neighbor's deed, revisiting the circumstances for shards of evidence that might point toward an alternative hypothesis, a finding of love instead of malice. The imagery clearly attests the active quality of love's imaginative, interpretive work. More conspicuously than silence, the mitigating explanation shapes reality and reforms the world.

But the more actively love hides sin, the grosser the potential offensiveness. The loving interpretation looks like denial. As such it belongs to an ugly syndrome: the abused wife's mitigating explanation legitimates the husband's abuse and thus helps perpetuate it; she becomes his accomplice. In light of this all-too-common social reality, Kierkegaard's love sleuth looks like a dupe. By painting him/her so appealingly, Kierkegaard's Christian discourse may dupe us as well.

---

[12] This might be put more strongly: as a creative word, the loving explanation can actually "cause" the good intention—heretofore dormant, fetal—to come to birth. For more on the performative dimension of the creative word, particularly in the form of praise and blessing, see chapter 5.

3. Forgiveness

With forgiveness, Kierkegaard ups the ante of the sin-hiding game into the realm of pure miracle. The lover imagines that what is patently the case, not just dormant and waiting to be awakened or ambiguous and waiting to be defined, but incontrovertibly and factually there—namely, a neighbor's past sin—is annulled, canceled, "disappeared" by being forgiven. Giving sin no occasion in this instance means revoking its existence. Almost playfully, Kierkegaard analogizes love's power to forgive in terms of the seen and the unseen:

> The unseen is in this[:] that forgiveness takes away that which nevertheless is....The lover sees the sin which he forgives, but he believes that forgiveness takes it away. This, of course, cannot be seen, although the sin can be seen; and on the other hand, if the sin did not exist to be seen, neither could it be forgiven. Just as one by faith *believes the unseen* in the seen, so the lover by forgiveness *believes* the seen away. Both are faith. Blessed is the man of faith; he believes what he cannot see. Blessed is the lover; he believes away what he nevertheless can see!
> Who can believe this? (274; Kierkegaard's italics)

In posing the question "Who can believe this?" Kierkegaard clearly anticipates that he will provoke intellectual offense. What to the believer is pure miracle must seem pure fantasy to anyone else. Accordingly, the offense continues to escalate. In the case of silence and the mitigating explanation, hiding sin was a deflection of justice. With forgiveness, hiding sin becomes metaphysical as well as ethical, and cognitive insult is added to moral injury. For falsifying history and canceling consequences, which forgiveness attempts, are not simply deceptive; they are impossible. In other words, it is not just that, for justice's sake, love *shouldn't* forgive; for reality's sake, it *can't*. So the skeptic would insist.

However, the quotation also implies that love's hiding of sin by forgiveness belongs to the paradox of faith at the very core of Christianity. Kierkegaard reinforces that implication when he goes on to relate forgiveness (as a form of forgetting) to another basic Christian passion, hope. "...[T]o hope means to give being by thinking and to forget is by thinking to take being away from that which nevertheless is, to blot it out" (274f.). The issue is really a soterio-christological one; fundamentally, what is at stake in forgiveness is the "mystery of the atonement" (*WL*, 193; see above, p. 95).

But since faith and hope are also integral to both silence and the mitigating explanation, the question arises whether in those cases, too, the metaphysical/christological offense is not present. Indeed, might it not be the very *basis* of the moral offense? Perhaps we think love shouldn't hide sin *because* we think it can't. Subtly, indirectly, Kierkegaard asks the offended consciousness if the offense it takes might not in fact be unbelief?

IV. Offense in Parabolic Context

"Who can believe this?" The question has become one of writer strategy and reader response. It is important to remember that, while *WL* represents Kierkegaard's "Christian ethics," it works maieutically, not systematically. The purpose is not to present a formal set of mutually consistent rules and procedures for applying doctrine, but to induce in the reader a process of self-examination and a sense of "sacred discontent" vis-à-vis one's self and surroundings. Thus the Discourse keeps pressing the question of who its audience is, or just who they think they are, and it employs a rhetoric suited to that purpose—prophetic, poetic, parabolic—the rhetoric of "indirect communication." The implication is this: to take offense at inconsistencies within the book's "teachings" may be premature, a kind of category mistake or genre error that distracts one from the real rub. To read the book as a sort of parable, on the other hand, allows one to feel the friction where it belongs, namely at the specific, fleshy protuberances of egoism in one's own life and circumstances. A comparison with a parable contemporary with Kierkegaard's Discourse might be illuminating in this regard.

Nathaniel Hawthorne's short story "Young Goodman Brown" projects a kind of mirror image to that of "Love Hides...." Goodman Brown "covenants" with the devil in order to see beyond the pious exteriors of his Salem neighbors and into the (real or imagined?) snakepit of their hearts. To keep the appointment, he must depart from his young wife Faith, who, all innocence and "aptly named," nevertheless admits to being "afeared of herself sometimes," flirtatiously decked out as she is in "pink ribbons" (mentioned three times in the first six paragraphs). Despite her protests of fear—which he interprets, perhaps correctly, as doubts about him—Goodman Brown takes his leave of Faith, feeling "himself justified" (self-justified?) by his intention to quickly return. With an eye out for "a devilish Indian behind every tree," he sets out on his errand into the wilderness and is soon joined by an older figure "in grave and decent attire," whom Goodman Brown so resembles that "they might have been taken for father and son."

Indeed his companion turns out to be on intimate terms with Goodman Brown's ancestry and with three of his current spiritual mentors as well: Minister, Deacon, and the "very pious and exemplary dame who had taught him his catechism in his youth," Goody Cloyse, who now appears as a witch. All have the same destination, a witches' sabbath where the entire community has assembled to witness the initiation of two new members—Goodman Brown, of course, and, as he deduces in horror from a pink ribbon fallen on the path, his Faith.

It is in the initiation ceremony where parallels with Kierkegaard's view of the imaginative seeing or not seeing of sin are most striking. Imagine how Kierkegaard might have admired the satanic homily:

"Welcome, my children, ...to the communion of your race. Ye have found thus young your nature and your destiny. My children, look behind you!...There...are all whom ye have reverenced from youth....This night it shall be granted you to know their secret deeds....By the sympathy of your human hearts for sin ye shall scent out all the places...where crime has been committed, and shall exult to behold the whole earth one stain of guilt, one mighty blood spot. Far more than this. It shall be yours to penetrate, in every bosom, the deep mystery of sin, the fountain of all wicked arts, and which inexhaustibly supplies more evil impulses than human power—than my power at its utmost—can make manifest in deeds."
...Herein did the shape of evil dip his hand and prepare to lay the mark of baptism upon their foreheads, that they might be partakers of the mystery of sin, more conscious of the secret guilt of others, both in deed and thought, than they could now be of their own.

The phrase "sympathy of your human hearts for sin" strikes a chord resonant of our larger thesis about reader predispositions and the role they play in the hermeneutic circle inscribed by the Rule of faith. Reinforcing the motif of Goodman Brown's having pre-arranged

his rendezvous with Satan,[13] the phrase recalls Kierkegaard's parable
of the child in the den of thieves who hears and sees no evil:

> What, then, does the child lack? What is it which very often
> makes a child's narrative the most profound mockery of his
> elders? It is...that the child lacks an understanding of evil, that the
> child does not even desire to understand evil. In this the lover is
> like the child. But at the basis of all *understanding* lies first of all
> an *understanding* between him who is to understand and that
> which is to be understood. Therefore an understanding of
> evil...*involves* an *understanding with* evil. If there were no such
> understanding, the understander would not desire to understand it;
> he would flee from understanding it and would rather not
> understand it. If this understanding signifies nothing else, it is still
> a dangerous curiosity about evil, or it is cunning's way of spying
> out excuses for its own flaws by means of knowledge of the
> prevalence of evil, or it is falsity's scheme to peg up its own value
> by means of others' corruption. (*WL*, 266; Kierkegaard's italics)

The last sentence of the quotation explains the significance of
the pre-understanding as a potential strategy of evasion and
projection. That such a strategy can become a reading convention for
an interpretive community, e.g., witch-hunting American Puritanism,
suggests the ideological bite that Hawthorne's parable might have—
and the offense *it* might give.

Perhaps more allegory than parable, "Young Goodman Brown" is
a meditation on the "sick imagination," not just at the level of the
individual psyche but as a specific social and cultural phenomenon.
The naming of two characters after historic personages convicted in
the Salem witchcraft trials indicates an intent to engage the author's
and his American readers' relation to their common past. The story
deconstructs the religion of Puritan New England, a religion that
dooms rather than justifies its practitioners. The doctrine of total
human depravity has become the occasion for a neurotic fixation
on—and projection of—guilt. Hating sin transposes into an obsession
with exposing it, reverence for the elders into a devoted detailing of
their failures. A fragile faith, troubled by its repressed content, will act

---

[13] To be explicit, the pre-arrangement is an ingredient of their "covenant," by
which Brown indicates his predisposition to be sympathetic toward sin, or, in terms
of the Kierkegaard passage that I quote above, that his "understanding *of*
evil...involves an understanding *with* evil" (my emphasis).

out its ambivalence in titillation that portends pornography and will project its self-loathing in a racial paranoia that descends into genocide. The question of whether Goodman Brown has merely dreamt his journey reflects our confused efforts to clarify our own ambiguous experience of America with its surreal combination of wealth and squalor, valor and greed, idealism and violence. Ultimately, the question is moot: we share Goodman Brown's gloom at the end.

The point of my digression on Hawthorne has been to refocus the way Kierkegaard's parabolic discourse grates on us. Like Hawthorne, Kierkegaard would have us feel the offense at the level of ideology and culture critique. In Kierkegaard's case, the object of the critique would be the culture of unbelief that disguised itself as "Christendom" before fully coming into its own in the twentieth century. Let us inspect the way the Discourse articulates this critique.

Kierkegaard begins the critique subtly enough, singling out the word "multiplicity" from the title quotation (1 Peter 4:8) in what sounds like a lecture on linguistics:

> The concept *multiplicity* is itself ambiguous. Thus we speak of the multiplicity of creation; yet the same expression has considerably different meanings, depending on who uses it. (*WL*, 263)

The last clause recalls the linguistic principle he had invoked in the book's first chapter:[14]

> The same words in one person's mouth can be very significant and reliable, in another's mouth as the vague whisper of leaves.... —There is no word in human language, not a single one, not the most sacred word, of which we could say when a man uses this word, it is unconditionally proved thereby that there is love in him. Rather, it is true that a word from one person can convince us that there is love in him and the opposite word from another can convince that there is love in him also. It is true that one and the same word can convince us that love dwells in the person who uttered it and not in another who nevertheless uttered the same word.—There is no deed, not a single one, not even the best, of which we dare to say unconditionally: he who does this thereby

---

[14]The principle is cited and discussed above, pp. 7 n.9, and 36 n. 31. Its gist is that words don't refer, *people* do; and meaning is in use.

unconditionally demonstrates love. It depends on *how* the deed [word] is done [spoken]. (*WL*, 29f.)

Kierkegaard proceeds in our Discourse to illustrate the ambiguity principle with a contrast (263). He imagines the word "multiplicity" spoken in reference to creation by a nature-hating hermit, on the one hand, and by a naturalist on the other. From the first user to the second, the scope of "multiplicity" expands relative to their level of interest and observational acumen. Soon, however, Kierkegaard's subject has shifted to what we might call the *power of discovery*. By the end of the third paragraph, after the "discover"/"discovery" terminology has been used twenty-one times, we detect a satiric agenda. His target is what is valued in "the world" (ten times), which turns out to be...discovering gunpowder:

But to discover something is so admired in the world that we cannot forget this enviable good fortune: to have invented gunpowder. (*WL*, 264)

Kierkegaard's jump from linguistic to moral ambiguity is hardly casual. Just as the scope of multiplicity varies according to one's power of discovery, so the value of discovery varies according to who's doing the looking, what he or she's looking for, and why. The punchline hints that, for our culture, the marriage of science with capital—of the principle of discovery with "fortune"[15]—was a marriage made in hell, envy being the driving dynamic behind its interminable violence. The next paragraph develops the hint in terms of the "comparison relationship," which is presented in the book as a key feature of self-love.[16] Especially interesting is the sudden change

---

[15]To support the analogy I am suggesting between Kierkegaard's use of "fortune" in the sense of "fate" or "luck" and his use of "fortune" in the sense of "capital," see again the passage in *For Self-Examination* about the Danish bourgeoisie's self-interested misinterpretation of Luther's doctrine of justification by faith (41, quoted above, p. 32 n. 25). Relatedly, see the argument in *SUD* in which "good luck, bad luck, fate" are identified as categories of despair (Howard V. and Edna H. Hong, eds, and trans. [Princeton: Princeton University Press, 1980], 51). These categories reflect despair to the extent that one invests one's identity in them, equating the self's worth and meaningfulness with external circumstances. A classic instance of "external circumstances," of course, is: money, "fortune," "capital." (Cf. *Concluding Unscientific Postscript*, 388: "*Immediacy is fortune....* Fortune, misfortune, fate, immediate enthusiasm, despair—these are the categories at the disposal of an aesthetic view of life.")

[16] See *WL*, 43, 50, 177-81, 219, 228, and 336. See also above, pp. 41-43 and n. 42.

in tone effected by the first two sentences—from the jocular to the jugular, as it were—as Kierkegaard steers us back to the biblical text:

> Thus far it is easy to see that the lover, who discovers nothing, makes a very poor showing in the eyes of the world. For to make discoveries even in the realms of evil, sin, and the multiplicity of sin, and to be a shrewd, cunning, penetrating, and perhaps half-corrupt observer who makes accurate discoveries—this is highly regarded in the world. (*WL*, 264)

The abruptness of the shift from the discovery of gunpowder to the discovery of sin suggests that Kierkegaard finds a hook-up between the two processes deep in the fabric of his and his audience's lives. Kierkegaard's Denmark and Western Europe in general were newly outfitted with the ideology of bourgeois liberalism, which defined humans in terms of universal human rights, the least abstract of which was the right to own property and advance the self. Thus, with only property left to distinguish among individuals, it is quite logical that the essential dynamic in social relations would be competition and that the securing of one's individuality would come by comparing oneself (one's self-*qua*-property) to others. And since in the comparison game one seeks an advantage, the motivation is insuperable to spot the splinter in the neighbor's eye. As Kierkegaard says, one soon discovers that a "premium" is placed on one's knowledge of "how basically shabby every human being is...and what abominations reside in the purest people." One discovers how silly it is to remain "uninitiated into the inmost secrets of sin" (pp. 264f.).

Kierkegaard's rhetoric makes clear in what context he chooses to interpret 1 Peter's "love covers a multitude of sins." It is equally clear in what context he wants it read. It is not the abstract, ahistorical context of universal truth, but rather a specific historical context of powerful economic and social forces, which distinctively impinge upon one's concept of self and which structure personal relations. He has in view a pervasive spirit into which anyone living in that time and place can scarcely avoid being initiated. Accordingly, the gossip Kierkegaard targets in the section on silence is not a trivial matter of private morality, much less etiquette, but a condition of political life almost as pronounced in the mid-nineteenth century as it is in the late twentieth: that familiar condition in which the press's lust for libel is marketed as the public's right to know and what is newsworthy is assessed in terms of its entertainment value.[17] Parabolically interpreted, it is in the daily showdown with the insidious forces behind these symptoms, not in the matter of domestic abuse and flagrant criminality, that love properly hides the multiplicity of sins. It follows that Kierkegaard would have us take offense at his discourse at the points where our subjection to such forces is most convenient and our immersion in them most soothing. Of course, it may be that only as one takes God as love (262) and Christ as the pattern, the agent of atonement, that one might fully recognize how and why these forces are corrupting. But "who can believe this?"

Let us step back at this point and observe what my explication has accomplished. By reiterating Kierkegaard's question, I aimed to keep us cognizant of the Christian basis for his culture critique. To that extent his Discourse may retain some offensive power, but, to tell the truth, probably not much. For much of the current audience —largely academic, situated in "late capitalism," and steeped in the rhetoric of Marx and postmodern movements by the dozen—the critique has become commonplace. Many of Kierkegaard's readers, and mine, are no doubt active combatants against the dehumanizing forces systemic in our society. Already conscious of our own entanglement in the system's web, we find that Kierkegaard's attack, far from unsettling us, nicely reinforces our own convictions. We may even tolerate its Christian underpinnings, perhaps as harmless trappings, for the sake of the broader political content. Ironically, then, my move to contextualize Kierkegaard's offensiveness so as to sharpen its point, blunts it. I have redescribed his Discourse in terms that the current audience can readily accept. I have made it a discourse with which we are perfectly at home.[18]

I do not want to retract my explication; I think it still has descriptive merit. Perhaps, however, it would help to suspend it momentarily in order to approach the issue from a different angle. A major part of the agenda in this book is to see how well Kierkegaard's use of scripture stands up as "exegesis." Let us examine 1 Peter, therefore, with an eye for its relevance to Kierkegaard's purpose of prying his audience loose from their comforts. It may turn out that,

---

[17] For an equally savage treatment of the news media, contemporary with Kierkegaard's, see Anthony Trollope's novel, *The Warden* (Harmondsworth: Penguin Books Ltd., 1994).

[18] This rather disconcerting fact was brought to my attention, in a most gracious way, by Lee Barrett of Lancaster Theological Seminary.

in addition to the moral/metaphysical form of offense his exposition has produced, it yields exegetical offense as well. Scrutinizing that exegetical offense may allow us to resume the explication with enhanced precision...and bite.

V. The Canonical Context

At first glance the biblical text bears only the loosest connection to Kierkegaard's exposition—more pretext to his own agenda than text to be explicated. In *WL*, as we have seen, the chapter interrupts a sequence of four others all based on, and overtly explicative of, 1 Corinthians 13. The titles of those four chapters include the citation of biblical chapter and verse. But with "Love Hides," Kierkegaard does not identify the source, and, were it not for the two earlier Discourses on the same text (1843), one wouldn't guess he even knew the source. Curiously, however, the earlier Discourses reveal a profound sensitivity not just to the source (they both reflect extensively on the claim of apostolic authorship), but to many details of literary context. The second of the two earlier Discourses interprets "Love hides..." with reference both to the eschatological proclamation that precedes it ("the end of all things is at hand" [4:7]) and to the injunction to hospitality that follows, as well as with reference to various OT texts that lie behind it (Ps 32:1, Prov 10:12, 17:9). The first Discourse is perhaps the most densely intratextual writing in the Kierkegaard corpus with at least forty five direct and indirect references to scripture in the space of only thirteen pages. For Kierkegaard, apparently, the Petrine statement on love contains the rest of scripture in it, and to begin to open it up is to begin re-telling the whole biblical story. Both earlier Discourses culminate in stories of Jesus vindicating women scorned as sinners (Luke 7:36-50 and John 8:3-11). Thereby Kierkegaard points to Christ as the center of the gospel and affirms the christological basis of love's power to cover sin, a move reinforced by his invoking Christ as the pattern in our Discourse. The move is also fully consistent with 1 Peter. The specialist, therefore, need not take exegetical offense at the lack of citation. Kierkegaard knows who and what he's dealing with.

What all three Discourses show, however, is an application that appears to bear little or no relation to the Letter's actual address: "To the exiles of the Diaspora in Pontus, Galatia, Cappadocia, Asia, and Bithynia..." (v. 1b). Elsewhere Kierkegaard says that *his* discourses are addressed to "that single individual" who would bother with his reflections.[19] With his refusal to specify anything of the reader's social context, the effect is as universalizing as it is individualizing—in apparent contrast with 1 Peter.

The tendency in Kierkegaard's style of philosophical psychology to personify emotions only heightens the effect. Thus, while 1 Peter says "love hides sins," the poet Kierkegaard adds that "love strives," "love forgives," "cunning spies out," "evil desire watches," "sin becomes ill-natured," "embittered," "rages," "but cannot hold out against love" because "love gave it no occasion." The rhetorical use of disembodied attributes, nominalizing them into characters of a narrative, directs the reader's attention to an interior drama while implying that the same drama occurs in everyone, regardless of social context.[20] Thus, we detect a counter-current to the Discourse's historically specific thrust that I detailed in part IV above. The "single individual" is an Everyman.

As it happens, the question of the Letter's address and audience is a matter of current controversy within 1 Peter studies. Taking John Elliott and Brevard Childs as representatives of opposing positions in the debate, let us examine how the debate may bear upon Kierkegaard's handling of audience.

1. Elliott

Childs has written commendingly of Elliott's *Home for the Homeless* for the insight it generates into the socio-historical setting of the Letter and for the clarity of its profile of the community addressed.[21] Elliott focuses on the terms of the address in 1:1, "To the visiting strangers (*parepidēmoi*) of the *diaspora*," and on the related terminology in 1:17 and 2:11, "the time of your sojourning" (*paroíkia*) and "resident aliens" (*paroíkoi*). In the comparative literature and in 1 Peter itself, the language denotes an actual experience of displacement—geographical, political, social, and religious—with an attendant legal status of inferiority.[22] Elliott

---

[19] E.g., Kierkegaard, *Eighteen Upbuilding Discourses*, Howard and Edna Hong, trans. and eds. (Princeton: Princeton University Press, 1990), 5.

[20] I want to thank my friend and colleague, Nancy Holland, for helping me to define this operation.

[21] Brevard S. Childs, *The New Testament as Canon: An Introduction* (Philadelphia: Fortress, 1985), 453f., 457f.

[22] John Elliott, *A Home for the Homeless: A Social-Scientific Criticism of I Peter, its Situation and Strategy* (Minneapolis: Fortress, 1990, second edition and new Introduction; 1981 original), 24-49, 131.

sharply opposes any theological reductionism that seeks to construe the terminology as purely metaphorical (or, as he says at other times, "spiritual," "metaphysical," or "cosmological").[23] In particular, he insists that 1 Peter does *not* present a "pilgrim theology" universally addressed to Christians making their way through this earthly veil of tears to a heavenly home. Rather, it speaks to an audience who were estranged from their social environment *before* their conversion, who found that their newly Christian status only exacerbated the estrangement, and who were therefore the more strongly tempted to assimilate to the larger culture. "In 1 Peter," Elliott writes, "the actual social condition of the addressees as resident aliens and strangers is the stimulus for the encouragement that they *remain* so for religious and moral reasons."[24] Or again:

> 1 Peter does not state that the addressees *became paroikoi* by becoming Christians but that as Christians they should *remain paroikoi*....The context of the Christians' *paroikia* is said to be not the earth (in contrast to heaven), but the hostile pagan society of Asia Minor. The alternative to this predicament ... was not a future home in heaven but a place within the Christian fraternity here and now.[25]

As the last sentence indicates, what is at stake for Elliott is the Letter's profound ecclesiological emphasis. Getting clear on the socio-historical situation of 1 Peter's audience is, by his argument, crucial for appreciating the central role the Letter assigns to the church—particularly the church conceived as the "household of God" (*oikos tou theou*), the Christian "family" here on earth. This ecclesiological emphasis has two interesting implications.

First, the theme of the "household of God" establishes the context for correctly understanding the (to our ears, hopelessly patriarchal) "household code" of 2:18-3:7. Given the contrast the Letter sets up between church and society, the household instruction functions, not apologetically to legitimate a social status-quo and foster cultural conformity so as to avoid conflict and persecution (as David Balch has argued),[26] but to do precisely the opposite.[27] By

---

[23] Elliott, 29, 42.

[24] Elliott, 42.

[25] Elliott, 232f. The point is crucial for Elliott; cf. 44, 48f., 129, 130-32.

[26] David Balch, *Let Wives Be Submissive: The Domestic Code in I Peter*, SBLMS 26 (Missoula, MT: Scholars Press, 1981).

making "household servants" (*oiketai*) the paradigm of Christian humility for all believers[28] and by exhorting husbands to "*co-habit* with their wives as partners and not as masters (for in the Christian household of God wives are equal *co-heirs* of the grace of life [3:7]),"[29] the code presents an alternative vision of community life and social organization that works a startling inversion of values and entails a strong criticism of the dominant culture.[30] Whatever we want to say of Kierkegaard's Discourse, by Elliott's analysis 1 Peter is anything but propaganda for the status quo.

The second implication of the Petrine emphasis on the church is this: it is in the *church* that love will hide the multiplicity of sins. The injunctions to love are made to members of the household with respect to other members. For 1 Peter, love is significant as a distinguishing mark of that community's life over against the larger culture. Love is what defines the shape and identity of the church. From Elliott's perspective, to dilute the specificity of the Letter's address is to dilute the specific character of the love it commends. To do either would be bad exegesis and, at best, questionable homiletics. Kierkegaard does both.

2. Childs

Childs's canon-contextual approach to 1 Peter seems to produce the traditional exegetical picture of the sort Elliott attacks. Childs describes 1 Peter as a circular letter addressing "Christians at large" who live "in the light of perennial threats to the faith."[31] But Childs does not contest Elliott's conclusions that the Letter was *originally* addressed to a mostly rural, Asia-Minor readership who held resident-alien status prior to their conversion. Rather, he argues that in the Letter's *canonical* setting, once the literal socio-legal reference of the terms *paroikos/paroikia* recedes into "the background of the text," partly under the influence of 1:4, which serves as "the text's own explanation of the concept [*paroikia*]."[32]

Characteristically, Childs's statement of his difference with Elliott is succinct to the point of being cryptic. The reasoning behind

---

[27] Also Goppelt, cited by Elliott, 111.

[28] Elliott, 196, 205-207.

[29] Elliott, 136 (my parentheses). Cf. Elliott, 201.

[30] Ibid., 218f., 228-31.

[31] Childs, *New Testament as Canon*, 457.

[32] Ibid., 458.

his statement is this. Form critically, v. 4 belongs to the Letter's blessing (vv. 3-12). As illustrated in the thanksgiving/blessing sections of the Pauline epistles, one function of this part of the Letter is to elaborate the identity of the addressees by highlighting key facts and features of their situation that the body of the Letter then treats in detail. Thus the blessing further defines the addressee. To be specific, v. 4's eschatological reference to the "imperishable inheritance kept for you in heaven" is reinforced first by the parallel phrase "salvation ready to be revealed (*apokalupsthenai*) in the last time" in v. 5 and then by the corollary clause in v. 7, "when Jesus Christ is revealed (*apokalupsei*)." These reiterations cannot help but qualify "diaspora" in v. 1 as the contrasting dimension to "heaven"; conversely, they qualify "heaven" as the temporal-spatial locus that the exiles are in exile from. The apocalyptic tone and cosmic scope of the blessing, in other words, color the terms of the address.

To take Childs a step farther, the cosmic coloration actually begins in v. 2, which expands the address "To the visiting strangers" to include the notion of their election. They are strangers "who have been chosen according to the *foreknowledge* (*prognosis*) of God the Father..." and sanctified for obedience to Christ. As it happens, 1:20 applies the same concept of God's *prognosis* ("He was *destined before*") to Christ's work as was applied to the strangers' election. God destined them (v. 2) in destining Christ and *as* he destined Christ (v. 20). Their election and Christ's work are clearly part of the same divine plan. The readers can assume, then, that what is further said of God's foreknowing of Christ would pertain to his foreknowing of them: namely, that it was "before the foundations of the world," i.e., in time-before-time, in God's exclusive domain, in heaven. In other words, the addressees' status as exiles has been placed in the cosmological framework of a heaven-earth transaction, a transaction couched in imagery both temporal and spatial. In the terms that the letter itself specifies, the readers are exiles with respect to their election, not simply in virtue of their previous condition, although by ⁺ ˙s analysis they may be that as well.

An additional factor influencing a metaphorical construal of the phrase "the visiting strangers of the diaspora" in 1:1 is only alluded to by Childs. That is the reference in 5:13 to the "co-elect sister church *in Babylon*." On this factor, Elliott writes,

> The terms *diaspora* (1:1) and *Babylon* (5:13) indicate the similar condition of both Christian addressees and authors...[However,] the religious implications of the terms in

no way vitiate the social conditions of the strangers and aliens to whom they are applied. Nor do they suggest or, even less, require that *paroikoi, paroikia*, and *parepidemoi* be taken in an exclusively figurative or "spiritual" sense.[33]

Childs could easily agree, since his point is not to insist on an *exclusively* figurative sense, only to observe that the textual *inclusio* of 1:1 with 5:13 makes a figurative sense available to an audience who may not be literal exiles. If the authors claim to share in the situation of their readers by describing their own status as one of metaphorical exile (metaphorical in the sense that they do not necessarily occupy the legal status of resident aliens in Rome), then it follows that the status of the readers as exiles may be metaphorical as well. And with readers for whom a literal sense of exile would not apply, then the letter is telling them (*contra* Elliott) that their election has made them "exiles" with respect to their environment.

We need to be reminded at this point of two hermeneutic axioms at work in Childs's concept of "canon," one linguistic and one historical. The linguistic axiom is that an interpreter's purpose in interpreting a text, one's needs or wants as a reader, plays a decisive part in establishing textual "meaning." The historical axiom is that the process of forming scripture included the shaping of ancient texts so that they could address later generations of believers.[34] We may recall from chapter one that, for Kierkegaard, it is equally axiomatic that scripture functions as personal address to the contemporary reader; not to read it as directed to oneself is not to read it as scripture.[35] Thus, for purposes of theological interpretation, the Christian reader's expectation of being addressed informs the reading context. Any suggestion on Elliott's part that the Letter can be properly understood as addressing only literal exiles restricts its

---

[33] Elliott, 48.

[34] In *The New Testament as Canon*, Childs comments, "Central to the canonical process was the concern to render the occasional form in which the gospel was first received into a medium which allowed it faithfully and truthfully to render its witness for successive generations of believers who had not directly experienced Christ's incarnation and resurrection" (22). He goes on to emphasize repeatedly the kerygmatic force of the literature: e.g., the tradents and redactors seek to actualize the material "in such a way as to evoke faith in their hearers" (26). Or again, the literature renders Jesus as "not just a figure of past history but one who continued to *address* his readers..." (27). For this emphasis in his chapter on 1 Peter, see 457, 460-61.

[35] See above, pp. 32 and 37, citing *WL*, 31 and 62.

kerygmatic scope to the narrow limits of its historical setting and so blocks its contemporary appropriation. (We shall return later to ask what implications this point may have for my effort to historically contextualize Kierkegaard's Discourse.)

Childs's hermeneutic axioms notwithstanding, the route to contemporary appropriation is still bumpy. After all, the place names in the address—Pontus, Galatia, Cappadocia, Asia, and Bithynia— remain in all their particularity. Such is the case with most of the letters, Pauline and catholic alike, which fact only serves to underscore the basic conundrum of the epistolary part of the canon: highly occasional writings, most of them retaining clear marks of their occasionality, began to be collected, circulated, and read ensemble by a broader readership than originally addressed in the separate letters.[36] The collection itself then became a warrant for the continued practice of reading by the larger church. Beyond observing that broad warrant, Childs resists any single account of the way the particularity of the letters is transcended without being annulled. That remains a case-by-case business, often involving specific features in a letter's content and style of argumentation; sometimes it's a matter of intertextual references and sub-canonical groupings.

In our case, 1 Peter was grouped with the other "catholic" epistles. By that epithet the early church expressed its assessment that these letters had universal applicability.[37] The church's assessment thus establishes a reader-convention for the Christian "interpretive community": any group of Christians, of whatever time and place, can read 1 Peter as addressed to them. Relatedly, *Second* Peter's reference to itself as "the *second* letter I am writing to you" (3:1) assimilates 1 Peter's audience to its "you," who were defined in 1:1, in the most catholic of addresses, as "those who have received a faith as precious as ours."[38] By the intertextual reference, then, the readerships of the two Letters are identified as the same. Further, in terms of 1 Peter's specific content, the things said to the addressees about their faith—the notions of rebirth, of living hope, of suffering as a test, of salvation already tasted but yet to be fully enjoyed—all ring familiar by virtue of their currency in the rest of the NT. They

---

[36] Childs (*NT as Canon*, 251) cites two works: 1) Nils Dahl, "The Particularity of the Pauline Epistles as a Problem in the Ancient Church," *Neotestamentica et Patristica, Festschrift für O. Cullmann*, W. C. van Unnik, ed., Novum Testamentum Supplements 6, 1962; and 2) Harry Gamble, *The Textual History of the Letter to the Romans* (Grand Rapids: Eerdmans, 1977).

[37] Childs, *New Testament as Canon*, 495.

[38] Childs, 475.

thus constitute a terminology in which later readers are able to recognize themselves and by which they find themselves addressed. Finally, 1 Peter's claim in 1:10-12 that the prophetic witness of the Old Testament was "serving you" can scarcely be restricted to any local audience. Virtually definitive of all Christians' identity, this passage functions as one of several *meta*-comments in the NT about the power of scripture to speak into every reader's present to reveal Christ, disclose the self, and thus evoke an encounter with God.[39]

So where does this leave us? Recall that a primary thrust of Elliott's analysis was to recover a full sense of 1 Peter's ecclesiological emphasis. The question becomes: Does loosening the connection to the original historical situation *necessarily* dilute the ecclesiology? In my estimation, it does not. To put it in Elliot's terms, to say that the Christian's election *does* make one an exile—rather than that it just finds one thus and urges one to maintain that status on a Christian basis—does not commit the interpreter to a purely cosmological view of one's relation to the world. In 1 Peter, the election that calls Christians out of "the world" and orients them to the heavenly source of that call simultaneously calls them into the church, i.e., into the terrestrial wing of the household of God.

But is this any help in rehabilitating Kierkegaard's exegesis? In one respect, yes; in another, no. Yes, it helps in that the canonical shaping that extends 1 Peter's address beyond its original readership warrants, to some degree, Kierkegaard's universalizing mode of address and justifies his assumption that the ancient text wants to speak to his present readership. (I shall return to this point momentarily.) But no, it does not help in that 1 Peter's emphasis on the church as the place where love hides the multiplicity of sins, an emphasis equally clear from either the historical or canonical vantage points, is simply absent from Kierkegaard. Kierkegaard empties the passage entirely of its ecclesiological content. Faced with this striking exegetical offense, let me risk some concluding proposals.

VI. Offenses Revisited

Certainly, as my explication in Part IV already suggests, the absent ecclesiology is not a matter of any sociological naïveté on Kierkegaard's part; quite the opposite. We do better to seek the reason for it within the overall strategy behind the authorship. Kierkegaard conceived of his whole corpus as an attack upon

---

[39] Other such passages include 1 Cor 10:11, 2 Tim 3:16f., Heb 4:12, 2 Pet 3:15f.

Christendom from within. The hostile, unbelieving, pagan society against which 1 Peter urged Christians to maintain their stance of strangeness had become, well before Kierkegaard, "Christendom": the church *qua* culture. The very structure that the Letter proposed as the counter-cultural home for the alienated had become the alienating agent. As a primary instrument for legitimating the newly emergent industrial nation-state and the values of the recently ascendant middle class, the church had become the world. To restore it as a home for God's elect, Kierkegaard believed he first had to pry his readership loose from it and make them homeless once more.

In an important sense, then, Kierkegaard deliberately reads against the ecclesiological grain of the Letter, but he does so in order to revivify its transformative, edifying efficacy as scripture. Heard afresh, the Letter might then fulfill its purpose as God's Word of re-forming—building up, edifying—the church as Christ's Body. The hermeneutic point to make here, in keeping with the larger thesis, is that Kierkegaard's exegetical sin is covered by the liberty granted to the Christian interpreter by the Rule of faith. He uses scripture in pursuit of the ultimate good of the neighbor, his reader. His reading is, to use his phrase, a "practice in the art of interpretation in the service of love" (272).

Now let me return to the other issues of offense. Recall that two different currents were identified in Kierkegaard's Discourse. One is the current of historical particularity by which he forges the Discourse into a powerful critique of his culture. By immersing us in this current, however, I risked inadvertently diluting the gospel's potential for offense, which he meant to preserve. The other current, a kind of cross- or counter-current, is that universalizing mode of address by which he strips the readership of specific location in order to address them in whatever situation they find themselves. By finding warrant for Kierkegaard's universalizing mode of address in the canonical text's own drive for contemporaneity, we would, in effect, extend to Kierkegaard the same courtesy we extend to 1 Peter, that of allowing him to speak beyond his immediate historical situation.

Several possibilities now open up. One is that, if Kierkegaard's culture critique seemed too familiar to sting us, that may be because we failed to inspect our contemporary situation in sufficient detail for what I earlier called its "fleshy protuberances of egoism" (p. 101). For example, a primary aspect of the culture wars waged in academia and the larger society is the assortment of competing micro-political movements on both left and right.[40] Each often seems hampered from hearing the others by a perception of the others' failings and a passionate conviction of their own righteousness and ultimate importance. Thus, some pro-choice advocates may be deaf not only to their pro-life opponents on the right, but to people animated by other feminist concerns, not to mention gay rights, race relations, ecological issues, etc. At the same time, white feminists may be blind to their own racism, gay activists to their class prejudices, black civil-rights leaders to their sexism. The danger is that our critical versatility in detecting the holes in each others' positions may become an avoidance device, an excuse for not hearing the hard things others have to say to us.

Here is where Kierkegaard can help. In taking sin as seriously as he does, he recognizes that oppression and the unjust manipulation of power infiltrate, spoil, and compromise *every* effort to do the right thing. He therefore rejects, in a postmodernist vein, any simple totalizing scheme for eradicating our social ills. Instead, he tells me that when a privileged, white feminist speaks prophetically to me, I must strive *not* to discover her sins. I may do this through silence, with a mitigating explanation, or, when wounded, by non-condescending forgiveness. Put bluntly, he tells me to shut up and listen. If I try, perhaps my listening begins to interpret contemporaneously, not just the Kierkegaard text, but also Kierkegaard's biblical text, and precisely in the way that 1 Peter itself explicates the command to hide sin with love. The listening becomes the way to "practice hospitality ungrudgingly to [the] other" (4:9), a way of regarding her as a "steward of God's varied grace" (4:10), "who speaks as one who utters oracles of God" (4:11). Does this offend me? Very likely.

There is a second possibility that needs mentioning. To invite a hearing of Kierkegaard in our contemporary situation may be to allow him to speak into the context of domestic abuse after all. I had wanted to dodge that prospect; our canon-contextual considerations prevent me from doing so. I think Christians have to confess that fidelity to Christ does indeed ask the victim to love her abuser.[41] But

---

[40] For this point and its elaboration, I am indebted to Gerald T. Sheppard of the University of Toronto, in a personal correspondence.

[41] I am helped with the burden of this confession by a number of female students from my course in the Problem of Theodicy over the past several years. A frighteningly large percentage of each class have, in their journals, confided direct experience of domestic abuse, sometimes of the most horrific sort. They have been at various stages of coming to terms with the experience. What has been astonishing to

love is not witless, dealing in absolutes irrespective of situations. It is a spirit of wisdom and discernment and justice, the last especially if conceived not legalistically in terms of giving each what he deserves, but agapically in terms of giving the *neighbor* what he *needs*. Accordingly, the silence the victim exercises in order to cover sin need not mean failing to confront the abuser or to report the crime. Rather, it may mean refusing to speak inappropriately, glibly, of the incident, anywhere and everywhere. It may mean refusing to wear one's victimization as a badge of authority or a mark of reverse privilege. Or it may mean refusing to cash in on one's story in a way that fuels either public paranoia or prurience. Similarly, the mitigating explanation of the abuser's crime need not be ventured as an act of complicity perpetuating the crime, but rather as a form of understanding necessary for correcting the abuse and reforming the abuser, lest justice descend into mindless vengeance. Finally, even forgiveness may have its time and place in the process of recovery— the recovery of the full humanity of both the criminal and the victim.

As is so typical with Kierkegaard and with scripture, we are left in the tension of daily decision-making. We must decide whether to confront sin or hide it, in the text and in the neighbor, and we must decide how to do either, or in what proportion to do both, knowing that either can be a strategy for self-deception or a new occasion for the neighbor's sin. It is our endless task to try to discern the whether and the how, which is why working out one's own salvation is a matter of fear and trembling. Well might we be grateful that Love is a Subject who works out our salvation with, for, and through us. To speak of gratitude—and other forms of subjectivity correlative with Love—is the business of Part Two of this study, to which we now turn.

---

me is the eloquence with which many who have struggled their way through to the most advanced stages of recovery speak of their need to love their abuser, and not despite but *in* their anger. They tend not just to accept, but to insist on, the Christian confession that I here so timidly advance.

CHAPTER 4

"HEART ENOUGH TO BE CONFIDENT": DOUBT, RECEPTIVITY, AND THE EPISTLE OF JAMES[1]

The Apostle James must be dragged a little into prominence—not in behalf of works *against* faith; no, no, that was not the Apostle's meaning, but in behalf of faith.[2]

That which he emphasizes is that as God's all-powerful hand made everything good, so He, the Father of lights, still constant, makes everything good in every moment, everything into a good and perfect gift for everyone who has the heart to humble himself, heart enough to be confident.[3]

---

[1] An earlier version of this essay was published under the title, "'Heart Enough to be Confident': Kierkegaard on Reading James," in *The Grammar of the Heart: Thinking with Kierkegaard and Wittgenstein*, Richard Bell, ed. (San Francisco: Harper, 1988).

[2] Kierkegaard, "The Mirror of the Word," in *For Self-Examination*, 49. Emphasis Kierkegaard's, hereafter mine.

[3] Kierkegaard, "Every Good and Every Perfect Gift Is from Above," originally the second of the *Two Upbuilding Discourses* of 1843. This quotation and those in the rest of the chapter employ the Swensons' translation as it appears in *Edifying Discourses: A Selection*, Paul L. Holmer, ed. (New York: Harper & Row, 1958) 39. Subsequent page citations will be indicated in the body of the essay. Reference to the more recent translation by the Hongs (*Eighteen Upbuilding Discourses*, 32-48) will be given in the notes, e.g., for the present quotation, *EUD*, 40f.

How curious to suggest that a person might be both humble and confident at once! More curious still to suggest that the one is a precondition for the other. The world has never much favored humility, except in slaves and other subordinates. Nor does it easily imagine a confidence based on anything other than prowess, with all its potential for domination. The appearance of humility in persons wise to their own prowess, the world's reasoning goes, can only be an appearance. A tasteful restraint, perhaps; humility, never. The world of mass-produced individualism, full of self and empty of humanity, has like its mirror image, totalitarianism, no heart for humility. And its displays of confidence ring pathetically hollow. Often they are akin to terror, simultaneously suffered and imposed.

Like the virtues of humility and the confidence it sponsors, the Bible is ever more marginal to such a world. For the Bible speaks of God, the ultimate in marginalia, and of faith to people who have "gone further."[4] Even the church has marginalized the Bible. Indeed, the process of debiblicization has been scarcely less effective within mainstream Christianity than it has without. Kierkegaard's Christendom could feign familiarity with its canon; only the right wing can do that now, save occasional militants from the left and a few peripheral others. The choices appear limited to using the Bible in a privatistic pietism, or as a social bludgeon, or not at all. Many prefer not at all, their disregard ranging from obliviousness, through timid bewilderment and embarrassed incredulity, on to sheer contempt. And with the disregard comes drift: a loss of the language of faith that guides the practice of it, and the consequent formlessness of the practice. The tragedy is, to lose the stomach for scripture is to lose the heart for Christian living.

If the Bible has been marginalized, how much the worse for one of its already most marginal entries, the Epistle of James, to which the chapter title refers. Bad enough that the Epistle should speak commendingly of *works*, and so become automatically an item of

---

[4] Having "gone further" than faith is a satiric motif in *Fear and Trembling* (Howard and Edna Hong, trans. and eds. [Princeton: Princeton University Press, 1983), occurring six times in the Preface (5-7), once each in the Exordium and Eulogy (9 and 23), and at least eight times in the Preliminary Expectoration (32f., 36f, 50f.). Kierkegaard's point is that there is nothing further than faith, since faith is "the greatest and most difficult of all" (*FT*, 52).

orthodox offense.[5] Worse, in its endless moralizing it goes so far as to denounce *doubt*, that staple of critical inquiry, our culture's intellectual foundation.

But the Epistle creates further offense, saying that "every good gift and every perfect gift is from above, coming down from the Father of lights with whom there is no variation or shadow due to change" (1:17). Thereby it proves itself either perfectly banal ("If there is a God," common sense tells us, "of course it's the good things that come from Him") or horribly naïve ("What good things?" a more critical sense demands). In either case, it raises doubts of its worthiness, this letter which had as its purpose overcoming doubt.

Yet Kierkegaard champions James, deploying the Epistle of straw against a state-Lutheranism for which "justification by faith" had come to justify quietism and grease the skids of the free market. More specifically, he champions Jas 1:17, "every good and perfect gift..." in several of the Edifying Discourses of that title, suggesting in this one, the first, that the problem is less with the passage than with the way it is being read. Indeed, he suggests that the problem is with the doubter who reads it, that what it takes to read it is a humble and confident heart. He even goes so far as to say how one might get such a heart. That might be a lesson worth learning.

James and the Logic of the Heart

It is not only the misreading public that has been unkind to James. The scholarly discipline has done its part too, earning Kierkegaard's undying enmity in this as in so many of its ventures. With several notable exceptions,[6] the general impression gained from the literature, even of this century, is that while the Epistle poses some interesting historical problems, it is theologically quaint, if not boring. Relatively "superficial and undeveloped," we hear from one of the more balanced commentators regarding James's appropriation of Christianity.[7] Its ethics are, "from the point of view of conceptual

---

[5] If Luther is known in no other respect than this, generations of Protestants know at least to despise James's "Epistle of straw," although they do not know the Epistle.

[6] See especially the two works by Luke Timothy Johnson upon which the exegetical sketches in this chapter are based: "The Use of Leviticus 19 in the Letter of James," *Journal of Biblical Literature*, 101 (1982): 391-401; and "James 3:13-4:10 and the *Topos peri phthonou*," *Novum Testamentum*, 25 (1983): 327-47.

[7] Sophie Laws, *A Commentary on the Epistle of James* (San Francisco: Harper & Row, 1980), 3, 38.

pattern, the simplest in the New Testament," we hear from another.[8] It is that conceptual pattern, or lack of it, that seems to be the core of the problem: "the author moves from one subject to another with only a loose train of thought discernible." "Eclecticism" and "lack of continuity" are the key characteristics.[9] This view reaches its nadir in Dibelius's judgment that the Epistle's genre, *paraenesis*, is one so epigrammatic, so lacking in larger structure, that it is an exegetical mistake to try to interrelate its parts, i.e., to interpret in context![10] And if there is no larger structure, "there is no 'theology' of James,"[11] no depth grammar, nothing to think about except historical curiosities.

Now, *paraenesis* is essentially moral admonition, first-order language of the "heart." Part of Kierkegaard's appreciation of James, distancing them both from Dibelius, must have been James's appreciation for a certain pathos in *paraenesis*. James introduces the metaphor of the heart early in the Letter. In 1:22 we are told that hearing the word without doing it is self-beguilement, while 1:26 claims that thinking one is religious while operating with a loose tongue is deception of the heart. In both cases there is a hiatus between thought and action, a disconnection between the faith avowed and that practiced, a doubling of motive and objective that amounts to duplicity and proves the first terms, thought and faith, counterfeit. When it comes to "the word" and the knowledge of God that the word hopes to effect, any hearing that is hearing only and not a doing is a mis-hearing. As for "religion," unbridled speech (cf. 2:1-16, 3:10, 4:11-12, and 4:13-16) reveals the religion as "vain" pretense and "impure" (1:26f.). At stake are the God-relationship (one's standing "before God," 1:27) and the integrity of the human being (the salvation of the soul, 1:21), which of course are mysteriously, dialectically, related. The great weight, the pathos, of the "heart" metaphor is that it is used here, in relation to this foundational mystery of self- and God-relatedness and the wrenching human tendency to dissolve the mystery by delusively dissociating knowledge from action. For James, "heart" stands for the human self in its capacity either to become whole "in faith" (1:6) or to fragment

---

[8] J. L. Houlden, *Ethics of the New Testament* (Harmondsworth, Penguin, 1973), 66, as quoted by Laws, 28.

[9] Laws, 7.

[10] Martin Dibelius, *A Commentary on the Epistle of James*, 11th edn. by Heinrich Greeven, Michael Williams, trans. (Philadelphia: Fortress, 1975), 7-11, 69, 71, 77, 80, *et passim*.

[11] Dibelius-Greeven, 80.

itself in tragic self-deception. It is no accident that in this Discourse on James Kierkegaard, too, makes everything depend upon the heart.

To see the pathos of the heart in James is to see that there is a logic to it as well. Kierkegaard recognized that James's *paraenesis* was not a random prose scoring of the ancient vice-and-virtue lists, but a mapping of moral equivalencies and oppositions in which receptivity and doubt head the chart. To wit, 1:5-8 says that while God gives generously to all, the doubting (*diakrinómenos*), double-minded person (*dípsuxos*) who does not "ask in faith" will not receive. It is not that God does not give, but that the doubter is unreceptive. Faith is linked to receptivity as doublemindedness is linked to doubt. 1:21 then speaks of receiving the gospel with meekness. Receptivity, now virtually a synonym for faith, is humble. No other posture makes sense before the God who gives generously to all, the Giver of every good and perfect gift, of life and salvation both.

Faith's humility is identified in 3:13 with wisdom, which in turn is qualified as divine or true to the extent that it is not tainted by envy (i.e., "jealousy," vv. 14-16), but rather is "pure" (v. 17). Envy's close conjunction with pride and arrogance in 4:5-6 negatively mirrors wisdom's conjunction with meekness.[12] The dichotomy between the two pairs is emphasized by the wisdom saying that culminates the indictment of 3:13-4:6: "God opposes the proud but gives grace to the humble." The admonition that completes the call to conversion in 4:7-10, "Humble yourselves before the Lord and he will exalt you," underscores the infinite superiority of humility to pride.

Just as receptivity was seen in 1:6-8 to be opposed to doublemindedness (= doubt, uncertainty, *diakrinómenos*), so now the pure heart, one without envy, is also "without uncertainty" (*adiákritos*, 3:17b); and the purification of the heart, e.g., of envy, is clearly implied by 4:8 to be a matter of purging oneself of doublemindedness: "purify your hearts, ye doubleminded ones."

The equivalence of doublemindedness and doubt/uncertainty is central in James, though perhaps not as obvious as that between doublemindedness and hypocrisy. In fact, all three terms—doublemindedness, doubt, and hypocrisy—are closely related. The equivalence of doublemindedness and hypocrisy James illustrates in the critical observation that "From the same mouth come blessing

---

[12] The notorious crux of 4:5 has perhaps best been translated, "Or do you think that scripture speaks to no effect? Does the spirit which he made to dwell in us long enviously?" See Laws, 167, and Johnson, "James 3:13-4:10," 330f.

and curse" (3:10), and he finds hypocrisy rooted in a disposition to "show partiality" (2:1-13) toward the rich and against the poor. In that such partiality typically represents an effort to curry favor for oneself, it is clearly a doubleminded attitude that both violates the Royal Law of Leviticus 19:18 ("You shall love your neighbor as yourself," 2:8f.) and abandons "the faith of our Lord Jesus Christ, the Lord of glory" (2:1).[13] But to abandon the faith of Christ really means to have misconstrued the "Father of lights" (cf. "Lord of glory"), preferring one's own fractured and darkly unstable purposes (doublemindedness, 1:6-8) for the constancy—the singleness, the purity—of God, "with whom there is no variation or shadow due to change" (1:17). The human partiality that insults the integrity of God is therefore already rooted in a refusal to trust in, thus an uncertainty toward, the goodness of God. That is, it is rooted in doubt. Doublemindedness is by nature doubting, and doubt is doubleminded. Of course, neither is open to a purely cognitive repair, as if certainty would come with more information; for, remember, they are both a matter of the heart, which is to say, of the will. "Purify your hearts, ye doubleminded ones," says James. "Purity of heart is to will one thing," comments Kierkegaard, explicating James's understanding of purity as that which leads to wholeness. For both, the doublemindedness that is doubt means a lack of confidence.

Clearly, Kierkegaard saw in James an understanding of the human heart and the human dilemma that was far from superficial. He also saw that that dilemma bears directly on the way James gets misread. By calling for "heart enough to be confident" at the very centerpoint of the Discourse (see the title quotation), Kierkegaard must be seeking to correct a heartsick misunderstanding of James 1:17. Like James, he knows how meaning itself can be a function of the moral life, that it too is a matter of the heart. Significantly, immediately following the call to confidence comes an analysis of doubt, the confident heart's antithesis. Is it, however, also part of the corrective that, in his paraphrase of 1:17, Kierkegaard radically revises James's distributive syntax, "every good and perfect gift is from above," into the totalizing "He...makes *everything* good in every moment"? To see

---

[13] To spell out my logic here, the Royal Law establishes a single standard for assessing one's own good and that of one's neighbor, while the faith of Christ renders all people one's neighbors. Self-interested favoritism entails a double standard, one for the unfavored neighbor and one for the self. One therefore cannot subscribe to the Royal Law and engage in favoritism without being doubleminded.

why this is a faithful reading of James will be one aim of the close reading to which we now turn.

The Anatomy of Doubt

In his paraphrase of 1:17 it seems almost as if what Kierkegaard has in mind is the program his pseudonym, Climacus, set for himself in the *Postscript*, that is, to make matters more difficult.[14] At least, that is how he projects Doubt responding to his paraphrase, having Doubt say "that the words [of Jas 1:17] are difficult, almost mysterious" (40).[15] There follows Doubt's own way of reading the text, turning what Kierkegaard has just identified as a problem of the heart into a metaphysical question:

But how is this possible...either to determine what it is which comes from God, or what may rightly and in truth be called a good and perfect gift? Is then every human life a continuous chain of miracles? Or is it possible for a man's understanding to make its way through the interminable ranks of derived causes and effects, to penetrate all the intervening events, and thus find God? (40)[16]

Doubt wrenches the words of scripture out of their native habitat to place them in a foreign one (philosophy) in order to make a problem for itself, or so Wittgenstein might have described this operation.[17] Kierkegaard, following James, would call it sin.[18] In the meantime he continues to demonstrate how Doubt reads, and in the process doubt is anatomized, depicted in its demonic ("cunning and wily," "unobtrusive and crafty," [39f.][19]) enterprise of not just rendering the words useless (cf. "loose and idle," [29][20]), but worse, of

---

[14] *CUP*, 165f.

[15] *EUD*, 41. The dispositions Doubt, Carelessness, Defiance, and Gratitude are capitalized to reflect that personification in Kierkegaard's text. They are left in the lower case when my discussion is less paraphrastic or when Kierkegaard's usage is in less immediate proximity to mine.

[16] *EUD*, 41.

[17] Ludwig Wittgenstein, *Philosophical Investigations*, G.E.M. Anscombe, trans., 3rd edn. (New York: Macmillan, 1958), 48-51.

[18] The Journals (1847), as quoted in Walter Lowrie, *A Short Life of Kierkegaard* (Princeton: Princeton University Press, 1970, originally 1942), 122.

[19] *EUD*, 41.

[20] *EUD*, 32

putting them to "lip" service, to the work of self-deception and hypocrisy.

> [Doubt] had changed the apostolic exhortation into mere words...; it tore them out of the heart and left them on the lips. (40f.)[21]

Kierkegaard's phrase "idle words" at the opening of the Discourse aptly anticipates his subsequent dissection of doubt's workings, described in his next paragraph as "those anxious meditations in which thought exhausts itself but never makes any progress" (41).[22] The phrase and the subsequent description anticipate Wittgenstein again, who no doubt would have characterized those same workings as "an engine idling," "language...on a holiday."[23] Doubt of this speculative, endlessly cerebral sort *is* idleness. Hence the satanic imagery; doubt is basic equipment on the devil's playground. Wittgenstein would have agreed with Kierkegaard: the words have to "find a dwelling place in the heart of man" (41).[24]

Finding the words a "dwelling place in the heart" means more than merely adding feeling to thought, so as to have "heart-felt" thoughts, and it means something qualitatively different from sentimentally conjuring up feelings *about* the words, "so beautiful, so eloquent, so moving" though they may be (29, 49).[25] Finding a dwelling place in the heart refers to appropriation as a mode of reception. Whereas the careless reading forfeits appropriation by hastily abandoning the words, thereby proving its understanding defective (31),[26] Sophisticated Doubt worries them to death. Appropriation demands that the words be put to practice; the thought must involve itself in action. Reality being unremittingly situational, thoughts and words must get situated in real activities. They must get enacted for the reader to begin to apprehend the reality of which the words speak.[27] Otherwise, with the words "left on the lips," Doubt defeats understanding and the reader remains trapped in a realm of

---

[21] *EUD*, 41.
[22] *EUD*, 42.
[23] *Philosophical Investigations*, 19, 51.
[24] *EUD*, 42.
[25] *EUD*, 32, 48.
[26] *EUD*, 34.
[27] On apprehension as a fundamental component of knowledge, and the requirement of activity in its acquisition, see Charles M. Wood, "The Knowledge Born of Obedience," *Anglican Theological Review*, 61 (1979): 331-40.

abstraction. And needless to say, the subject matter, God and God's good gifts, never comes into view.

Invoking Wittgenstein these several times is useful to help clear the taint of romantic pietism and epistemological naïveté from the "heart" talk that epitomizes the Discourses. Otherwise it may appear that, in the Discourses, Kierkegaard himself had "gone on holiday," taking leave of his rigor. Then again, Wittgenstein would be the first to point out that Kierkegaard need not go begging for philosophical legitimation. Kierkegaard's language game is not one of generating new theories of knowledge but of explicating scripture, and clearly it is James's "epistemology," shared by all the biblical writers, that has shaped Kierkegaard's thinking and which he here mirrors with compelling credibility. And that biblical epistemology, never detachable from its ethics, is one in which knowing is always a function of doing, the knowledge of God always a matter of obeying God.

For ancient Israel it was axiomatic that one obeyed *in order* to know God, while disobedience was both the sign that God had been forgotten and the means of the forgetting.[28] The classic instance of the use of the heart metaphor to express the behavioral component of the knowledge of God is Jeremiah's New Covenant passage. The context is Israel's history of disobedience and consequent divine judgment. Then comes the promise of a miraculous reconstitution: "The Lord says, ...I will put my law within them, and I will write it upon their *hearts*...and they shall all *know* me, from the least of them to the greatest" (31:33f.; my emphasis). To take *Torah* to "heart," to have it "in" the heart, to do God's will, as it were, by second nature— that is knowing God at the most intimate. Clearly, the metaphor of the heart is as vital to the Bible's epistemological discourse as the metaphor of the mind is to Enlightenment discourse.

James, with his insistence that hearing God's word entails doing it, stands squarely within the biblical tradition. Faith, he argues, which is nothing if not the, at least incipient, religious mastery of the concept of God, is sterile so long as it remains at the level of mere intellectual assent: "So faith by itself, if it has no works, is dead. ...You see that faith was *active* along with [Abraham's] works, and faith was *completed by works*..." (Jas 2:17, 22; my emphasis). Once again, any thought that is presumably about God is not about God if it

---

[28] See, for example, the prophets Hosea and Jeremiah where "forgetting God" is thematic and disobedience is instrumental to it: e.g., Jer 5:25, "Your sins have put far the good from you." (Cf. Hos 5:4 and 7:2.)

remains at the level of thought. There is a discipline to knowledge, the biblical authors recognized, and the discipline constructs a certain form of life;[29] it etches a distinctive pattern into the "habits of the heart."[30]

Naturally, a recognition so reflexive is fraught with implications for the lives of the authors themselves. It is no surprise, then, that the question of authorship should arise again as the logical next step in Doubt's assault.

If a concept's mastery is revealed in its use, then a student's learning logically begins by observing the *teacher's* use of it. Hence, the lives of the tradition's paradigmatic teachers, the prophets and the apostles, were long acknowledged, in pre-critical tradition, as performing a modeling role. From the Bible's oral stages down through its canonization, the depiction of those lives underwent a shaping—Mosaic in the case of the prophets, cruciform for the apostles—to render them as trustworthy guides to the interpretation of their words. A canonical conception of apostolicity has its hermeneutic function in just this context, and Kierkegaard had already put the conception to use in his first paragraph in order to support confidence in the scripture:

> These words...are by an apostle of the Lord, and insofar as we ourselves have not felt their significance more deeply, we still dare have confidence that they are not loose and idle words, not a graceful expression for an airy thought, but that *they are faithful and unfailing, tested and proved, as was the life of the apostle who wrote them.* (29)[31]

But therein also lies the conception's vulnerability: Doubt, ever ready to subvert the word's hearing, can question its authenticity. Kierkegaard proceeds to show us how:

---

[29] Wood, "Obedience," 336.

[30] The phrase belongs to Tocqueville but has been borrowed by Robert Bellah and company as the title for their study on community and the concept of the self. They seek to adjust the American ideology of individualism by relocating the concept of the self in the matrix of the social as well as the private behaviors by which our identities are constituted. Their use of the metaphor of the heart is illuminating. See *Habits of the Heart: Individualism and Commitment in American Life* (New York: Harper & Row, 1985), 36-37, *et passim.*

[31] *EUD*, 32. My emphasis here and subsequently.

Was an apostle of the Lord perhaps *not* responsible for these words? ...Was it their intention to confuse men? (41)[32]

So *Doubt* entertains the possibility that the words were pseudonymously authored, or demonically inspired. Apparently, part of Doubt's cunning is to project its own "heartless" reception of the words onto their rendering—self-deceivingly, of course, as such projections typically work.

The hermeneutical issue here is the vexed question of how issues of authorship bear on the meaning of a text.[33] As one might expect of Kierkegaard, the relationship between the two, though deemed significant, is somewhat less than direct, and depends less on objective historical facts (who the author was and what he meant), or even on a rendering of the theological facts,[34] than on the disposition with which the supposed facts and interpretive rendering are received.

---

[32] *EUD*, 41f.

[33] The way this issue intersects with Kierkegaard's own authorship, pseudonymous and "direct," is intriguing to say the least, and sufficiently multi-layered not to touch here.

[34] As a language game with truth-telling aspirations, theology can be said to have "facts" just as legitimately as history and science can, though the different language games have different evidential criteria and verification procedures. Consider, for example, our constitutionally mandated practice of distinguishing between moral guilt and legal guilt. Morally speaking, a murderer is guilty from the moment he commits the act; legally, his guilt is not a "fact" until the judge and/or jury declare him "guilty." If the case is thrown out on a technicality despite otherwise overwhelming evidence against him, the defendant remains innocent. Again, even though a generation later historians establish his guilt as an historical fact, the legal fact remains the same: innocent. Facts are conventional constructs.

This issue is vital for understanding the strategy behind Kierkegaard's polemical literature. Kierkegaard continually confronts his nominally Christian readers with what were the generally acknowledged theological facts of Christianity to ask them how commensurate with those facts their intellectual speculation and practical behavior really were. His career can be viewed as a massive struggle against the category confusion that, since the Enlightenment, has been leading Christians to forfeit theological facts by privileging the historical and scientific paradigm of "fact."

Notice that my insistence on our right to speak of theological facts does not commit us to any particular fact claim, much less to an ahistorical, essentialist view of theological facts. Indeed, the notion of fact as social construct allows us to observe that while one century ago the assertion, "Christ died for our sins," was an undisputed fact among Christians, its status as fact has come into serious question today. Thus, facts may vary not just from one language game to another, but over time within the same language game. Of course, when enough of the facts begin to shift, one can question whether the game remains the same.

Further on "theological facts," see below, the discussion of canonical-theological exegesis vs. historical-critical exegesis, 148-52.

Moreover, that disposition has immensely creative and destructive(!) meaning-making potential, and not just for the text but for what counts as the facts behind the text as well. In Doubt's case, the facts prove no sure defense against suspicion.

Again, it is clear that for Kierkegaard the shape of the life that authored the words, and the disposition of the heart from which they sprang, are significant clues for how the words may be heard. The authorial heart does not, however, dictate how they must be heard, as if only one meaning, an "original" one, and that embedded "in" the text, were possible; it only suggests certain possibilities, likely construals, by modeling a set of purposes and practices that constitute a use. But Doubt suggests possibilities too ("Could it be this way, my hearer?"), by applying its hermeneutic of suspicion to the manner and motives of the text's composition.[35] Just how insidious we see it to be depends on how we construe Kierkegaard at this point, for his text is open to possibilities as well.

For instance, we could easily take the first question ("Was an apostle of the Lord perhaps not responsible for these words?") in a purely historical sense. In that case, the doubt at work would be the principled doubt of historical inquiry: If, as the evidence seems to indicate, the apostle James did not write the "letter" attributed to him (in fact, more a sermon than a real letter), then what Hellenistic Jewish-Christian of the late 1st Century did write it, the scholar asks, and what party interests was he promoting against which adversaries? Two centuries of historical criticism attest to how corrosive such methodological doubt can be to the ability to hear scripture as the Word of God.

The problem was not lost on Kierkegaard. In "The Mirror of the Word," the "newer science" takes its place among other forms of erudition as a means by which "I transform the word into an impersonal entity" (*FSE*, 61) so that, whatever else it has become (e.g., evidence for the history of Christianity), it is not God's Word that I am reading.[36] To begin to restore the ability to read it as such, the suspicion needs to be redirected against itself, that is, against the

---

[35] So as not to reify the concept excessively, we should remember that doubt is its own possibility; it is a manner of reception. It is *we* who doubt. Suspicious of authorship, we read doubtingly.

[36] The phrase "not reading God's Word" and its variants recur refrain-like on every page of *FSE* from 53-58. Kierkegaard calls on the serious reader to "make a distinction between reading and reading" (*FSE*, 52), for the different readings produce different texts. Obviously, for Kierkegaard the "Word of God" is not a static concept, not a property of the ink on the page.

doubt, which is to say, against *oneself*: "Seriousness consists precisely in having this honest suspicion of thyself, treating thyself as a suspicious character" (*FSE*, 68). For methodologically disinterested Doubt turns out not to be so disinterested after all:

> All this interpretation and interpretation and science and newer science which is introduced with the solemn and serious claim that this is the way to understand God's Word—look more closely and thou wilt perceive that this is with the intent of defending oneself against God's Word. (*FSE*, 59)

Even a principled doubt can be an instrument of evasion and self-deception. That is to say, Kierkegaard doubts its principles.

So taking the question ("Was an apostle perhaps not responsible for these words?") in a historical sense leads to a critique of historical criticism. Let us consider, then, another way of construing the question. Given the mythopoeic form of the questions that follow it—

> Were perhaps those spiritual hosts beneath heaven responsible for them? [Eph 6:12] Was there a curse which rested upon them, so that they should be homeless in the world, and find no dwelling place in the heart of man? Was it their intention to confuse men? (41)

—another sense seems likely, a supra-historical sense. Given the context, the question puts in doubt not so much the name of the author (the historical question) as the spiritual power and authority behind him, and the allusion to Ephesians clearly implies a demonic power and authority. From this perspective it matters little who the human writer(s) happened to be, whether the historical James or a later figure or community; Doubt suspects the quality of the inspiration. This is radical doubt, with which its historical-critical cousin (or guise) can seem almost trivial by comparison; for by its very nature, its target being spirit, there is no amount of historical information that can relieve it. It is fundamental doubt, challenging the ordinary Christian understanding of the concepts "apostle" and "Lord," implying that the confidence they are intended to inspire is bogus. Ultimately, of course, it is religious doubt, impugning the very goodness of God by suggesting that "God does tempt a man...by preaching a word whose only effect is to confuse his thought" (41).

What antidote can be found for so pernicious a poison? The words of scripture, instead of being instrumental to the love and knowledge of God, have through doubt become the occasion for making God the enemy. Scripture has again become, if not the criminal, at least an accomplice to theological crime. How does the exegete-expositor remedy such misuse? (And if misuse, is it not misinterpretation?[37])

We have reached a climactic moment in the Discourse. Kierkegaard has brought us to the very point at which three previously treated forms of misreading (carelessness, sorrow, and defiance) have culminated, namely, in "the error of thinking that God would tempt a man, [which is but a variant of] the error of believing that God would allow Himself to be tempted" (39).[38] And that is precisely the same error of which James warns: "Let no one say when he is tempted, 'I am tempted by God'; for God cannot be tempted with evil and he himself tempts no one" (1:13). In effect, doubt is itself the culmination of those other misreadings, or the diseased germ at their core. Occupying the center section of the Discourse, doubt represents a paradigm of all misunderstandings rooted in the heart. It is time now to turn back in the text to take stock of those other misreadings.

Carelessness

Admittedly, the "careless" readers to whom Kierkegaard refers (30f.)[39] were too unthinking to get so far as to tempt or be tempted. Their mode was "unconcern," their awareness nil ("without knowing"), and everything about them bespeaks a blithe mindlessness.

---

[37] The answer is clearly yes, assuming that the reader's purpose would be to put the words to *Christian* use, to interpret them "Christianly." Interpretation requires and implies a context of conventions, shared aims and purposes and practices—in a word, a use. The existential thinker Kierkegaard, like the canonical interpreter and the literary deconstructionist (e.g., B. S. Childs and Stanley Fish, respectively), recognizes that there are no a-contextual norms of "right" interpretation. Kierkegaard's context was consistently, if sometimes only implicitly, the Christian faith. Right interpretation in this context is interpretation that conforms to the Rule of faith. Or as Kierkegaard says in "Every Good and Perfect Gift," it is interpretation that works "to the honor of God" (43; *EUD*, 43).

[38] *EUD*, 40.

[39] *EUD*, 33. Comparing the Swensons' translation ("carelessly") with the Hongs' ("free from care") brings out the wordplay that captures exactly Kierkegaard's point. Carefree readers are likely to be careless, at least with texts whose subject matter is how to regard one's cares.

"For them life holds no riddle," Kierkegaard says. Elsewhere he might say that they are immersed in "immediacy."[40] Life having treated them well, they expect no trouble and are certainly not looking for any. Archetypic flower children, they happily take themselves and their "friendly fate" as what is only "natural." "Borne along on the wave of the present," they see no reason to give heed to apostolic warnings ("Do not err," Jas 1:16) "anymore than the wave gives heed as to whence it comes or whither it goes." Careless, heedless, and utterly immediate, they float upon the smiling surface of things—and read accordingly. In short, they are not deep enough for doubt.

Yet Kierkegaard's wave image rings familiar. It is James's image, of course, and Kierkegaard's double deployment of it suggests an association between his careless readers and James's doubters: "for he who doubts is like a wave of the sea that is driven and tossed by the wind" (1:6). If the careless are like the doubters in this one respect, their directionlessness, perhaps doubt is also more closely related to immediacy than first we thought. Further, if what underlies immediacy is really doubt, might there be method, and mind, to shallowness?

In point of fact, Kierkegaard credits the careless with all due deliberation insofar as they make "plans." And in his ironic commendation of their "wise and intelligent" deliberations, he intimates that they are actually proud and arrogant: "their plans, wise and intelligent, succeed since *they* are wise and intelligent" (my emphasis). Behind the commendation, it is clear, lie both James's rhetorical question, "Who is wise and intelligent among you?" (3:13), and his description two verses later of the "wisdom" that belongs to doublemindedness (in its form as envy): "This wisdom is not such as comes down from above, but is earthly, unspiritual [=Kierkegaard's "natural"], devilish." The spiritual predicament of the careless deepens commensurately.

James of course associates such wisdom with "the rich," whose status is as much a matter of mentality as material; one can belong to

---

[40] E.g. *CUP*, 218-21 *et passim*, where immediacy is identified with paganism: "The immediate relationship to God is paganism" (218). The same identification is suggested here by "friendly fate," which the careless readers equate with natural process, and by the sheer repetition of the terms "nature" and "natural" and their attendant imagery. Kierkegaard's "immediacy" is the equivalent of James's "friendship with the world," which is "enmity with God" (4:4). In *The Sickness Unto Death*, the deep connection between immediacy and doubt is laid out more explicitly in doubt's pure form as despair. As noted before (105 n. 15), there we also have stipulated immediacy's primary categories: "good luck, bad luck, fate" (*SUD*, 51).

their ranks purely on the strength of one's envy, i.e., double-mindedness.[41] And in James's accusation of the rich in 4:13-5:6 we find the same motifs that Kierkegaard applies to the careless: plans that are tantamount to arrogant boasts, transience (James's "mist" = Kierkegaard's "dream"), and the life of luxury and pleasure. Kierkegaard's careless are James's rich, and both are doubters.

What is lacking in Kierkegaard's depiction is James's explicit identification of the rich's arrogance as evil and hypocritical (doubleminded, 3:16f.), and of their actions as violent ("Behold, the wages of the laborers...which you have kept back by fraud cry out; ...you have killed the righteous [= poor] man; he does not resist you," 5:4f.). Yet when the James and Kierkegaard texts are juxtaposed (now James exegetes Kierkegaard), the careless people's complacent "giving...help to the needy in the way they believe is useful to him" turns suddenly sinister, and Kierkegaard's text becomes a commentary on exploitation and the contempt concealed in a patronizing sensibility. As for hypocrisy and James's theme of glib speech, the fact that "these words [every good and every perfect gift...] are again and again repeated in the world [the realm of the immediate], and yet many [the careless] go on as if they had never heard them," or say after a moment's consideration, "'Now we have understood them'"—that should be sufficient indictment.

In sum, carelessness is a symptom of doublemindedness, and even unconcern masks the deep malaise of doubt. "You have fattened your hearts," James accuses, recalling Isa 6:10 and the prophetic connection between callousness and self-aggrandizement. Similarly for Kierkegaard, the flight to immediacy is the neurotic avoidance of the painful consciousness of a lack of confidence in God, the means by which doubt is anesthetized. Mindlessness is repressed faithlessness, it turns out, a defect and a defection of the heart.

In the ensuing two misreadings, lack of confidence comes to consciousness. As Doubt surfaces, the heart engages its subject matter more actively than Carelessness cared to do, though no less defectively, with the result that the error of tempting God (Jas 1:13) becomes explicit.

---

[41] On "rich" and "poor" as spiritual categories in Hellenistic Judaism and Early Christianity, see Dibelius-Greeven, 39-45, and Laws, 7-9.

Sorrow and Defiance

What Kierkegaard depicts for us now are two closely related strategies of temptation. In the one (31-35),[42] sorrow is the primary disposition, issuing secondarily in defiance (33);[43] it begins piously but eventually reveals itself as impious manipulation. In the other (35-37),[44] defiance is primary, though always presupposing sorrow; but it discards sorrow's pious facade at the outset in order to use impiety as its means of manipulation. In both cases it is God they seek to manipulate ("tempt"), and in both the motive for manipulation is desire. Not surprisingly, we find the two ideas, desire and temptation, conjoined:

> With humble prayers and burning desires you sought, as it were, to tempt God...but the day you desired did not dawn. And still you made every effort, you prayed early and late, more and more fervently, more and more temptingly. (33)[45]

The connection between temptation and desire was made initially by James. Kierkegaard is only illustrating the relation between 1:13 and its compact elaboration in vv. 14f.:

> Let no one say when he is tempted, "I am tempted by God"; for God cannot be tempted with evil and he himself tempts no one; but each person is tempted when he is lured and enticed by his own desire. Then desire when it has conceived gives birth to sin; and sin when it is full-grown brings forth death.

The elaboration is pivotal for how Kierkegaard proceeds; his agenda remains exegetical. The depictions of Sorrow and Defiance are not free-form, but the function of a disciplined responsiveness to the biblical text.

As responsive exegete, however, Kierkegaard is also a hermeneutician, which leads him to see in sorrow a fierce dialectic, a conundrum in the very reading of scripture. Sorrow becomes both a capacity for understanding and a condition that incapacitates understanding. This bears spelling out.

---

[42] *EUD*, 34-37.
[43] *EUD*, 35.
[44] *EUD*, 37-39.
[45] *EUD*, 35f.

First, Kierkegaard recognizes sorrow as the condition that James's opening admonition addresses: "Count it all joy, my brethren, when you meet various *trials*" (1:2). It is sorrow, of course, not joy, that is the logical emotional accompaniment of trial, and James's assumption that his readers are encountering trials implies that they also know sorrow. This means that they will read the letter *through* their sorrow, and through their sorrow they will find its subject matter fitting. Certainly, without their sorrow they would hardly know what the letter is talking about. Thus the sorrow marks a capacity, the heart's qualification for a thoughtful and responsive reading (as opposed to a careless one).

And Kierkegaard recognizes how essential a capacity sorrow is for reading the words of Jas 1:17 appropriately, which is to say appropriat*ing*ly, by taking them to heart:

> These words are so soothing, so comforting, and yet how many were there who really understood how to suck the rich nourishment from them, how to *appropriate* them! Those concerned, those whom life did not permit to grow up and who died as babes, those whom it did not suckle on the milk of prosperity but who were early weaned from it; the *sorrowing*, whose thought attempted to penetrate through the changing to the permanent—those were conscious of the apostle's words and gave attention to them. (31)[46]

Moreover, Sorrow parents the humility and patience that James enjoins as necessary attributes of a faith receptive to God's good gifts (1:21, 4:10, 5:7-11). Ultimately, it is the requisite capacity for the repentance that makes available the exalted, transcendent comfort and joy that the good God gives:

> Be wretched and mourn and weep. Let your laughter be turned to mourning and your joy to dejection. Humble yourselves before the Lord, and he will exalt you. (4:9-10)

This is why James was able to say in the first place, "Count it all *joy* when you meet trials." As in the beatitude (Matt 5:4), the capacity for mourning is a measure of the capacity for comfort; so Sorrow aims at comfort and targets joy as its heart's desire. Sometimes desperately.

---

[46] *EUD*, 34.

And there is the problem. Sorrow is prone to despair, i.e., doubt. Often sorrow *is* doubt, as Kierkegaard warns us not only by resuming James's wave imagery ("your soul became restive, *tossed about* by the passionate wish...," cf. Jas 1:6), but by drawing out Sorrow's train of disillusioned thought, thought that focuses on the disparity between James's comforting words and the sorrower's felt reality, between heaven and earth:

> Or is there only a spirit who bears witness in heaven, but no spirit who bears witness on earth! *Heaven only* knows, and the spirit which flees from earth, that God is good; the earthly life knows nothing about it! Is there then no mutual harmony between what happens in heaven and what happens on the earth! Is there joy in heaven, only sorrow on earth, or is it only *said* that there is joy in heaven! Does God in heaven take the good gifts and *hide* them for us in heaven so that we may *some time receive them in the next world*! Perhaps you spoke in this way in your heart's bewilderment. (32f.)[47]

To exclaim that only God knows that God is good, that good gifts remain hidden, that joy is restricted to heaven, if it exists anywhere—that is Doubt talking, under the influence of Sorrow.

Hence sorrow is dialectical, necessary on the one hand, corrupt on the other, as Doubt distorts the sorrowing heart. Doubt works its distortion subtly, however, by transforming the heart's objects, the targets of its emotions. For instance, while James instructs, "Humble yourselves *before the Lord*" (4:10), Kierkegaard shows that Sorrow's humility is more likely to have as its object the *world*, life in its inscrutability, than God in his:

> So they sat in their quiet sorrow; they did not harden themselves against the consolation of the word; they were *humble* enough to acknowledge that *life* is a dark saying, ...so were they also slow to speak and slow to wrath. (32)[48]

The posture may be right, but surely the inwardness—what the self relates itself *to*—is misdirected. Similarly, the patience James commends, which establishes the heart on the ever-imminent coming

---

[47] *EUD*, 35.
[48] *EUD*, 35.

of the Lord, is not this patience that is willing to wait forever for the granting of *its own* "heart's desire" (5:7f.):

> Alas, it still did not come to pass! And you gave up, you would dispose your soul to *patience*, you would wait in quiet longing, if only your soul might be assured that eternity would bring you *your* wish, bring you that which was the delight of your eyes and your heart's desire. Alas, that certainty too was denied you. (33f.)[49]

The problem is verb-deep, for it is the very transitivity of the heart that is injured. The *way* Sorrow targets its objects, the manner of its desiring, has been disfigured by Doubt. Despair has turned the sorrower's desire into "his *own* desire," as James says, which "gives birth to sin" (1:13f.). All Sorrow's children will be tainted.

Even the comfort and joy that Sorrow seeks can be tainted.[50] The self-centered manner of the seeking makes them different from

---

[49] *EUD*, 36.

[50] Kierkegaard's idea of reading scripture with an expectation of comfort offers an interesting example of the larger thesis of this book, especially as worked out in chapter 2. Mentioned five times in Kierkegaard's first two paragraphs on sorrow (31f.; *EUD*, 34f.), the expectation of comfort is assumed as part of the equipment the faithful reader brings to the text. Like humility and patience, it is one of the dimensions of love (cf. 1 Cor 13:4-7), and thereby one of the components of the Rule of faith by which Christian sense-making of scripture is governed. Unlike the other two, however, the expectation of comfort is an extra-textual category not explicitly present in the text of James. In this regard it has more in common with certain other features of the Rule, e.g., the intent to interpret "to the honor of God" (43; *EUD*, 43). That is, while perhaps warranted by the biblical text when read from the perspective of faith, these categories are not inevitably imposed *by* the text on any and every reader as a requisite means for making sense of it, and in fact may not even *occur* to a reader of a different perspective intent on making a different sort of sense (or having utterly no idea of what sort of sense to make). In other words, a large-scale, Christian construal of scripture as a word of comfort or of judgment (i.e., as the Word of God) is not *arbitrarily* related to the text, the result of a capricious imposition by reader upon text, but neither does it arise automatically, univocally, and necessarily from the text to impose itself upon the reader. For the self-aware and self-consciously Christian interpreter like Kierkegaard, that construal represents a decision—an imaginative, canonical decision, no less—to take one's stand within an historical interpretive community of widely shared traditions (conventions, purposes, contexts of reading), among which is that of receiving scripture as a sure word of promise from a good God. The expectation of comfort from scripture is itself an act of faith. As such, it has no objective, independently ascertained grounding "in" the text. Theologically speaking, one ascribes it to the work of the Spirit. (Cf. Wood, *Formation*, 67.) See further, n. 51 below.

the sort of comfort and joy that God gives. As Kierkegaard suggests ("Alas, that certainty too was denied you"), the comfort desired is that of "certainty," a "sign or testimony" as clear evidence (that is to say, evidence that suits the sorrower's criteria) of a good gift from God. But the comfort of objective certainty can only be the fearful comfort of "bad faith"[51] and false confidence. It is bad faith in which the sorrower's expectation of comfort fails by not being radical enough, by being in fact doubleminded, wanting comfort from God but not God's comfort, wanting rather that of one's own passionate desiring. "You ask and do not receive, because you ask wrongly, to spend it on your passions—unfaithful creatures!" (Jas 4:3f.)

But for James and Kierkegaard the gospel renders comfort and the rest of sorrow's family in a different key:

As an example of suffering and patience, take the prophets who spoke in the name of the Lord [and were often martyred for their pains]. Behold, *we call those happy who were steadfast*" (Jas 5:10f.).

---

[51] The term "bad faith" figures in a powerful counter-construal to the Christian way of reading scripture, in particular the Sartrian-Barthesian (and Derridean) construal. The expectation of comfort is bad faith insofar as "comfort" signals a repressive eschatological fantasy and a self-delusive quest for certainty and closure. See Sartre, *Being and Nothingness*, Hazel Barnes, trans. (New York: Washington Square, 1966), Part One, chap. 2, "Bad Faith," 86-116; and Barthes, *Writing Degree Zero*, as described by Fish, 182f.

To be sure, this construal involves a faith decision, too, of sorts, one entailing conventional (i.e., shared) beliefs—say, in the *un*reliability or certainly the indeterminacy of the "Word of God," or in the irrelevance or sheer non-existence of the Transcendental Signified, or in the ethical reprehensibility of repression and the therapeutic virtue of play—beliefs which are no more independently grounded and justifiable than are those of the Christian construal. Deconstruction has its agendas, too, no doubt sometimes hidden from the practitioners but into which many of the practitioners genuinely invite their readers to inquire so as to expose. Sometimes the originally political program of the founders might deteriorate into the more private concerns of the followers, and one could speculate as to how much of the past three decades' deconstructing has been done in the service of self-advancement—if only one had more than one's own shaky legs to stand on. The point is that comfort can be banished out the front door only to sneak back in the rear, as every good deconstructionist knows that it will.

More to the point, Kierkegaard himself concurs in the critique of comfort to the extent that the comfort deconstruction critiques, i.e., the comfort of objective certainty, is of an entirely different quality from that which Kierkegaard expects. As we see below, his is a most discomforting comfort.

This is a grammatical remark defining the Christian concept of "happiness" and directing Christians to take comfort *in* their suffering, joy *in* the sorrow, and to receive God in all the minutiae of the mundane. As such, the remark represents an aspect of the Rule of faith, proposing how the Christian might best approach scripture. Again, however, Sorrow teaches the heart to doubt, and in doubt to absolutize the distance between heaven and earth, ideality and actuality, God's Word and human existence. And such a heart can only misinterpret the Word.

In this dialectic of sorrow, then, Kierkegaard demonstrates the conundrum of reading scripture, since it is in reading as in life. The heart's perfectly natural habit of meeting trial with sorrow, which is the very condition the text addresses so as to heal, obstructs the text's purpose, converting the text itself into a trial. James's words are then read sorrowfully, with confidence subverted at the outset in the habituated expectation that life will disappoint the comfort that the words seek to inspire. And the words themselves become the occasion for more sorrow, and doubt.

The precise form of Sorrow's misinterpretation is to read the words restrictively, though perhaps in the way a surface grammar and an arid scholarship would demand. The statement, "Every good and perfect gift is from above," says to sorrowers in doubt only that some things come from God and some things don't. The good things are from God, but if we cannot see them, the sorrowers reason, then the gifts must be like a "magnificent jewel": reserved for a "festal occasion" that has not yet come (32).[52]

But the deeper grammar of the text, its canonical logic, what it says when read by the Rule of faith, is entirely different. The humility of faith, which receives all things from God's hand in confidence that *whatever* God gives is good, reads accordingly: *everything* that comes is a good gift from God. But again, such single-minded and comprehensive receptivity is beyond the capacity of a heart beside itself with sorrow. Of course, when that heart turns defiant, it becomes utterly hardened. "God *does* tempt a man" (36),[53] concludes Defiance, in frustration at James's words, for the words seem only to mock its inability to receive from God what *it* desires as good. Thus Defiance hurls this Job-like accusation by which it tries to browbeat God into submission, tempting God to yield to its own hard-

---

[52] *EUD*, 34f.
[53] *EUD*, 38.

heartedness. But "God cannot be tempted with evil" (Jas 1:13), and "the anger of man does not work the righteousness of God" (1:20).

In either case, whether in sorrow or defiance, right reading seems impossible. Or an impossible leap is required. Kierkegaard thus depicts this hellbent human heart—"impatient and unstable," "hardened" and "barren" (34, 36)[54]—as undergoing what, by the logic of its own self-disintegrating constitution, is an impossible conversion:

> But when the busy thoughts had worked themselves weary, when the fruitless wishes had exhausted your soul, then perhaps your being became more quiet, then perhaps your heart, secretly and unnoticed, *had developed in itself the meekness which received the word* which was implanted within you, and which was able to save your soul, that every good and every perfect gift cometh from above. (34)[55]

> But, then, *when you humbled yourself under God's* powerful hand and, crushed in spirit, groaned: "My God, my God, great is my sin, greater than can be forgiven," then heaven again opened... (36)[56]

The wonder is how the faithless heart, having nothing to work with but diseased tools, is able to heal itself. The answer is that it doesn't. Rather, behind the conversion stands the Father of lights, still constant, with whom all things are possible, even creation *ex nihilo*:

> Then you acknowledged in all humility that *God had...created this faith in your heart*; when instead of the wish, which even if it could do everything, was at most able to give you the whole world, He gave you a faith through which you gained God and overcame the whole world. Then you recognized with humble gladness that God was still the almighty Creator of heaven and earth, who had not only created the world out of nothing, but had done the even more miraculous—*out of your impatient and unstable heart He had created the incorruptible essence of a quiet spirit.* (34)[57]

---

[54] *EUD*, 36, 37f.
[55] *EUD*, 36.
[56] *EUD*, 38.
[57] *EUD*, 36.

...then heaven again opened, then did God, as a prophet writes, look down upon you from the window of heaven and say: Yet a little while; yet a little while and I will renew the forms of the earth—and lo, your form was renewed, and *God's merciful grace had produced in your barren heart the meekness which receives the word.* (36)[58]

The development of the undeveloped heart is miraculous, as is the accompanying resolution of the conundrum of misreading. Neither happens naturally. The miracle is that the good gift given in every moment is God, if only one is willing to receive him, as well as receive the faith by which one does the receiving and goes on to read God's words aright. Now, if Doubt's deputies, Sorrow and Defiance, can be vanquished by grace, will it be any less so with Doubt itself? We return to Kierkegaard's answer to Doubt.

Gratitude and the Rule of Faith

Theological exegesis is like sin: sooner or later it must probe that deep layer of understanding where our decisions about what defines reason, what counts as fact, and where we stand are formed. And it is especially *when* it confronts sin that a theological exegesis must probe that layer.[59] For sin is its ultimate antagonist, the largest obstacle in its ground-clearing task of allowing the Word of God to be heard. But because sin is a spiritual condition, it remains highly resistant to exegetical argument and information. That is, Sin can take the argument, appropriate its reason, and marshal the information all to its own purpose and in its own spirit. In fact, in the face of Sin, exegesis itself is finally powerless; it cannot meet Sin's demand to guarantee the sense it makes. There is a critical point where all it can

---

[58] *EUD*, 38.

[59] It must do this probing, that is, if it intends to explicate what it is the words want to say and do, which is part of what it means to call it *theological* exegesis. It must to some extent enter into the words' subject matter and wrestle with the difficulties that such matter involves—again, if it is to be faithful to the intent of the words. Of course, the theological exegete's perception of the intent of the words is a function of the pre-understanding, the faith, s/he brings to the text. This is to say that theological exegesis, like *any* reading, necessarily entails a faith stance (even if that faith happens to be one of "Religiousness A" or outright non-belief). Theological exegesis, in other words, will be as much a constructive as a descriptive enterprise in which the traditional boundary between exegesis and exposition will blur.

do is to reaffirm *its* guiding spirit and re-invoke it. That is what Kierkegaard does.

In effect, Kierkegaard has defined sin as doubt. Having shown us Doubt's course from the supposedly naïve question, "How is it possible for the words to mean so?" to the direct assault, "God does tempt a man"—while diagramming Doubt's comprehensive, self-stultifying logic—he then simply re-invokes and reaffirms the counter-spirit. In the face of Doubt's subversion of apostolicity, Kierkegaard cites the apostle Paul. In the face of Doubt's impugning God's goodness and the meaningfulness of God's Word, he reasserts the fullest theological claim that the words can be construed as making:

> The apostle Paul says: "All of God's creation is good, if it is received with thankfulness." ...Would not the same hold true of every man's relation to God, that every gift is a good and perfect gift when it is received with thanksgiving? (41)[60]

What follows in his next two paragraphs can only be called a hermeneutic of thanksgiving. As always, the principle is that reading follows form of life. Reading James "Christianly" requires giving thanks in all circumstances. That is what it means to "obey" the statement made in 1:17 (i.e., to take it as applying normatively to oneself, to appropriate it), and that is what it takes to understand it. *And* that is what it takes to overcome doubt. Such continual gratitude will not be speculative and abstract, like doubt, because it will be confidently focused on the concrete specific, the gift itself, the character of which comes into focus by virtue of the gratitude with which one addresses its Giver:

> You did not anxiously ask what it is which comes from God. You said gladly and confidently: *this* for which I thank God. You did not concern your mind with reflections on what constitutes a good and a perfect gift; for you said confidently, I know it is that for which I thank God, and therefore I thank Him for it. (42)[61]

As in earlier chapters of this book, we should recognize the circularity here as intrinsically hermeneutic. Kierkegaard's statement

---

[60] *EUD*, 42.
[61] *EUD*, 42.

is another version of the circle inscribed by the Rule of faith, which finds in a problematic biblical text the love by which one reads it. To try to escape the circle would not only be a form of bad faith; it would be to forfeit the edification that gratitude performs. For gratitude shares in what I described in chapter two as the illocutionary force of the Rule. It has a reality- and self-constituting potency. In this case, gratitude is constitutive of the good. In a sense it is the gratitude that (re-)constitutes the gift (James's text) as good, whereas in doubt's hands the gift turns sour, even though God gave it as good.

Kierkegaard makes the hermeneutic point explicit when he adds to the statement quoted above the grammatical remark, "You interpreted the apostolic word." He is remarking on what constitutes both Christian interpretation and the apostolic word. He means that the life of gratitude effects an interpretation, a demonstration of the meaning of the words. And by interpreting the word with gratitude, one interprets it apostolically, in conformity with the apostolic intention and model; the word *becomes* apostolic (in contrast, say, to confusing or demonic)—it is actualized as the apostolic word—by having been read and interpreted through gratitude.[62]

Lastly, gratitude constitutes the self for the better, the self also being a good gift of God. Whereas carelessness, sorrow, and defiance diminish the heart, the practice of gratitude develops it, capacitating it for yet clearer purpose and stronger exertions—and for a still deeper grasp of scripture:

> You interpreted the apostolic word; *as your heart developed*, you did not ask to learn much from life; you wished only to learn one thing: always to thank God, and thereby learn to understand one thing: that all things serve for good to those that love God [Romans 8:28]. (42)[63]

Eventually, the heart's capacity is developed even to the point where it can sustain offense without taking offense, covering the sin, as it were, with the gratitude by which it receives it, transforming even sin into "a good and perfect gift":

---

[62] Recall the focus text in chapter 2, in particular the statements, "As we say, clothes make the man. Likewise one can truly say that the explanation makes the object of the explanation what it is." (*Works of Love*, 271). Kierkegaard's view anticipates the sociological definition of the objectivating, world-constructing force of language. See for example, Peter Berger, *The Sacred Canopy: Elements of a Sociological Theory of Religion* (Garden City, N.Y.: Doubleday, 1969), 8-14.

[63] *EUD*, 42.

And when men did you wrong and offended you, have you thanked God? ...[H]ave you referred the wrong and offense to God, and by your thanksgiving received it from Him as a good and perfect gift? (42f.)[64]

Obviously, the scandal addressed in the previous chapter is one Kierkegaard would locate very near the center of faith; here it is, four years prior to *Works of Love*. For emphasis the grammatical remark we heard before is repeated twice:

Then surely you have worthily interpreted the apostolic word to the honor of God, to your own salvation.... Then have you worthily interpreted that apostolic word, more gloriously than if all the angels had spoken in glowing tongues. (43, alluding to 1 Corinthians 13:1)[65]

The emphasis is significant. So is the allusion to Paul's paean to *agape*, which reinforces the earlier reference to Romans 8:28 ("all things serve for good to those that love God"). Again, Kierkegaard is connecting the hermeneutic of thanksgiving (so *self*-constituting is it that it works "to your own salvation") with the Rule of faith classically formulated in terms of the law of love. In Augustinian form the Rule has it that everything in scripture and the world is only properly read in light of the love of God, and points to the love of God when properly read. And again we are reminded of the focus text in *WL* which speaks of "the art of interpretation...in the service of love" (272). Now in "Every Good Gift" Kierkegaard is observing the obvious fact that gratitude and love are deeply wedded emotions, and that they are indispensably edifying (constructive) ones. With their application or atrophy, the world either waxes or wanes.

In all of this the hermeneutic circle remains unbroken, raising again the problem of how one breaks into it. The problem we saw with respect to sorrow and defiance is now raised with doubt itself. Whence this love and gratitude by which the undeveloped, indeed eviscerated, heart now begins to read? Kierkegaard asks the question himself, in the very next sentence: "Still, who had such courage and such faith, who loved God in this way?"

---

[64] *EUD*, 43.
[65] *EUD*, 43.

The Rule of faith seems to traffic in infinite regress. Certainly, courage would be required to receive everything as a good gift of God and thus to love God as the Good Giver, since such receiving means giving up all proprietary claims on our supposed possessions, our reality definitions, our very selves—things to which we cling as props in a doubt-cum-dread driven compulsion to secure our dubious existence. But then, whence this courage that Kierkegaard assures us we "will now and then gain to be thankful..., to understand that every good and every perfect gift is from above, [and] to explain it in love..." (44)?[66] To "gain" it must be to receive it "from above," "for it, too, is a good and a perfect gift." But then so also the *"faith* to accept this courage": even the spirit of receptivity must be received. Everything is received, including our recognition of the imperfection of the faith, courage, gratitude, and love by which we do our receiving. Yet even *this*, the imperfection (which, too, must be a gift, no less than the neighbor's/scripture's "sin"!) can point to the crucial and all-sufficient fact: the regress has a limit. In fact at every point it has a limit, though not a natural one. For at every point it is God who breaks through the circle of imperfection, who defines and constitutes the real reality, who does the giving, even the loving for and by which we thank him:

> Was it not this way, my hearer? You always wished to thank God, but even this thanks was so imperfect. Then you understood that God is the one who does everything for you, and then grants you the childish joy of having him regard your thanksgiving as a gift from you. This joy He grants you, if you did not fear the pain of remorse, nor the deep sorrow in which a man becomes joyful as a child in God; if you did not fear to understand that this is love, not that we love God, but that God loves us. (46, alluding to 1 John 4:10)[67]

For a third time Kierkegaard has climaxed a point with a biblical reference to love.[68] A deeper penetration of the mysterious dynamics of the Rule of faith would be hard to come by. Just as rare is his rigor in traversing the hermeneutic circle. That the Discourse does not in fact end with this cadenza but makes still another circuit through yet

---

[66] *EUD*, 44.

[67] *EUD*, 46.

[68] The previous two references are to Rom 8:28 (42 of the Discourse; *EUD*, 42) and to 1 Cor 13:1 (43; *EUD*, 43). See above, pp. 144f.

one more misreading (that of one "who in repentance will *only* suffer punishment") suggests that the circle is as hard to break out of as into. There is a misreading for every moment, for every stage along life's way; and the pattern—of misunderstanding, re-discovering our incapacity, being thrown back upon the love of God, renewing gratitude, and understanding anew that every good gift is from God—is a continuous process without systematic conclusion. It takes its shape from our imperfect lives, and only concludes when life does.

Canon and the Theological Exegete

Toward a conclusion, two aspects of that triple scriptural invocation of the law of love merit attention: first, its essential fidelity to James, second, its profoundly canonical character. As indicated, Kierkegaard uses the citations to underscore the identity of the law of love with the Rule of faith as a reading strategy. To make Christian sense of scripture one must live as well as read in the expectation of (a discomforting) comfort, in courage, and in gratitude—that is to say, in faith and love. James had worked the same hermeneutic. In his insistence that hearing the word entails doing it, "doing it" was summed up in 2:8 as "fulfil[ling] the royal law according to the scripture: 'You shall love your neighbor as yourself,'" a citation of Leviticus 19:18b. James follows the citation with five more verbal and thematic allusions to that verse's immediate context, the commands of Lev 19:12-18a, which he clearly regards as the appropriate biblical explication of the demands of love.[69] Taken with other statements relevant to the theme of love (e.g., 1:5, 2:13, 4:6, 5:11) and understood within christological perspective, the web of allusions to the law of love bears the burden of the Letter's argument. As Kierkegaard correctly saw, and induces us to see, the Letter of James rests entirely on the gospel of grace.[70]

---

[69] As listed by Johnson ("The Use of Leviticus 19," 399), the six passages with their allusions are Jas 2:9 (Lev 19:15), 4:11 (Lev 19:16), 5:4 (Lev 19:13), 5:9 (Lev 19:18a), 5:12 (Lev 19:12), and 5:20 (Lev 19:17b).

[70] Johnson ("The Use of Leviticus 19") is careful to point out how precisely these allusions are framed by explicit christological references. James's perspective on the Leviticus text, in Johnson's words, "is provided by the understanding of life and law given by the experience of Jesus Christ" (400f.). Thus, Kierkegaard's way of speaking about love as the love of God and the quintessentially good gift is not of a fundamentally different structure from James's emphasis on loving the neighbor. Christ is the middle term by which the two forms of love are mediated and by which the two perspectives are equated, however absent from Kierkegaard's Discourse

One does not have to show that Kierkegaard was aware of James's "halachic midrash" to argue that he rightly discerned the Letter's kerygmatic center of gravity. Nevertheless, it is striking how, like James, he sought an 'appropriate *biblical* explication' of the material he was presenting. As James went to Leviticus to explicate "the faith of our glorious Lord Jesus Christ" (2:1), Kierkegaard went to Romans, 1 Corinthians, and 1 John to interpret "every good gift...." Both worked intratextually, using scripture to interpret Christ-faith. The difference is that James's formulation of his gospel material itself became scripture, while Kierkegaard's remains exegetical only, as does all post-canonical commentary. What they shared was the conviction that scripture was deeply congruent with their subject matter because in every case (Old Testament or New, the life of the early church or 19th century Copenhagen) the subject matter was the work/Word of God. Accordingly, their intratextual practice of interpreting a given reality through scripture recalls another operation of the Rule of faith.[71] It is a singularly theological procedure and a thoroughly canonical one.

To what extent the theological character of this procedure of intratextual interpretation may account for the long scholarly neglect of Kierkegaard's exegetical work, one can only guess. Clearly, the procedure flouts historical-critical conventions, celebrating a harmony among diverse historical traditions where the modern critic would be compulsively precise. Indeed, Kierkegaard signals virtually no awareness of the diversity at all. To the "newer science," the theo-logic that he follows from James to Paul to John—it is not the diachronic logic of tradition history—would seem peculiar at best, more likely utterly naïve.

On the other hand, Kierkegaard's harmonization is hardly the sort favored by much of Protestant Orthodoxy, that of "correcting" James to Paul according to a "canon within the canon." To the contrary, Kierkegaard is adamant in seeing that James's distinctive

---

specific mention of Christ may be. It is as if, while nowhere visible, Christ is everywhere present.

This point about the implicit presence of Christ in the logic of the Discourse may bear on the relation between Religiousness A and Religiousness B, which are often thought to be modeled by the Edifying Discourses and the Christian Discourses respectively, the former reflecting a religion of immanence, the latter a religion of transcendence, i.e., Christianity. In the present case, however, the difference is less a matter of immanence vs. transcendence than of the implicit vs. explicit reference to Christ.

[71] See above, chapter 2, pp. 82-84.

voice is registered. For example, there is no compromising the charge
that hearing without doing is self-deception. Kierkegaard's is a
"canonical harmony" that seeks not to obliterate the different voices
in the ensemble, but to hear their full range while penetrating to a
grasp of the subject matter that allows them all to cohere.

Let me re-open the question from chapter 1: Is there an
alternative procedure, in particular, a non-theological, non-biblical
one? Again, I do not believe so, at least not for this particular subject
matter and the concomitant set of purposes and commitments; that
is, not for talking about restoring a person's life, not if the purpose
and hope are to go beyond talk toward actually cultivating a humble
and confident heart, and not if the procedure is to be Christian. A
form of life marked by the resiliency of courage, incessant gratitude,
and love such as James and Kierkegaard depict, specifically the
Christian life, does not happen naturally. Kierkegaard can write so as
to prompt a yearning for such resiliency, and surely it is a quality our
world is desperate for—but in desperation can never achieve. As
Kierkegaard has shown, the doubt that comes naturally to us can only
subvert it. And that is a fix unamenable to solutions afraid of
identifying and addressing God, since only thereby are we able to name
the poison and take the cure. As the canonical witness of faith, the
Bible remains the Christian paradigm for that naming and healing
process.

What Kierkegaard does time and again is to direct us back to the
Bible, where the lineaments of the confident heart are diagrammed
and where the heart's Creator and Sustainer is praised as its *sine qua
non*. For it will be in life as in reading. Without the text our life won't
know its lines. Of course, it is not just *that* we read and *what* we read,
but *how* we read that matters, with infinite suspicion of self and utter
confidence in God, and the faith to be not just a reader but a doer,
since it will be in reading as in life. I take it that it will be so even in
my life as a professional reader, a teacher who "shall be judged with
greater strictness" (Jas 3:1). Here, too, among a cloud of witnesses,
Kierkegaard is a guide, bold as he is to appeal to Paul and John in
order to interpret James, to hear the different voices of the canonical
ensemble but to hear the harmony among them as well. To prevent
doubt from invalidating the appeal, the miracle of faith will have to
be at work here too, and at every level, for ultimately the appeal is
only plausible in the context of a community of mysteriously
confident hearts.

In other communities, we should recall from chapter 2,
plausibility may be a problem. For instance, in the historical-critical

community the urge to doubt at this point would be especially strong. For if Kierkegaard's harmonization of traditions seems naïve, how much more his citation of "the apostle Paul" in the first place: "All of God's creation is good if it is received with thankfulness" (1 Timothy 4:4). What makes the move so dubious to critical eyes is that the passage is not "authentic" Paul by historical reckoning but *deutero*-Pauline. Kierkegaard not only blurs the sharp lines separating Pauline Christianity from the Jewish Christianity of "James" (not to mention the sectarian-inclined Johannine Christianity); he even mixes the former with its hierarchically stratified offshoot of more than a half-century later. We need to be clear about this: Kierkegaard's move is not one any form-, tradition-, or redaction-critic could make *per se*.[72] It is a move only a "pre-critical" or "post-critical" exegete would make, or a historical critic who forgets the rules of his game.[73]

But Kierkegaard's procedure is hardly less productive of understanding, depending on the kind of understanding one is after. Indeed, for a readership that shares his investment in James's words as sacred scripture and wishes to understand them as the Word of God, it may be that Kierkegaard's engagement with doubt and his recourse to "Paul" do more to move the mind over its obstacles than all the historical information the "newer science" can hope to muster. After

---

[72] For an opposing position, see Janet Forsythe Fishburn, "Soren Kierkegaard: Exegete," *Interpretation*, 39 (1985), 233. Fishburn claims that Kierkegaard's "approach to exegesis was similar to that of contemporary redaction criticism...." I believe there is a confusion here, the root of which may have to do with the fact that while redaction criticism *is* interested in theology, it is not interested in theology at a canonical level, as Kierkegaard is. The redaction critic's interest is rather in clarifying the theolog*ies* of the biblical authors and redactors *in their specific historical settings*. His/her work remains a branch of literary history in which the subordination of original settings violates the rules of the discipline. Characteristic of the canonical process, however, is that original historical settings often *were* subordinated to attributed, literary ones. As Charles Wood observes, "...the drawing of margins around these texts establishes new relationships among them, and between them and extracanonical tradition, past, contemporary, and future.... [Therefore,] they must be approached in a somewhat different way than is proper to their study as [historical] sources of Christian tradition." [*Formation*, 91.] This means that canonical exegesis and historical exegesis do not always operate by the same rules. Kierkegaard's exegesis may resemble redaction criticism in that it requires an imaginative and imitative involvement (Fishburn), as does all exegesis, but Kierkegaard's involvement occurs at a quite different level from the redaction critic's.

[73] The terms are Brevard Childs's in *Introduction to the Old Testament as Scripture* (Philadelphia: Fortress Press, 1979).

all, it was by his engagement with that subject matter, exegetically fitting since it was also James's subject matter (see again 1:6-8), that we discovered the essential obstacle to be, not lack of historical information about authors and settings, but doubt about the spirit working through them. Doubt had already relativized the historical issues of authorship. In the service of a Christian understanding, the exegete was forced to move to a different level, confront the threat itself, and articulate the *theological* facts at issue: the goodness of God and of God's creation, and the posture of gratitude from which the facts are recognized. From that perspective the appeal to Paul and John as interpreters of James is perfectly plausible since their solidarity had already been granted by doubt's assault on apostolic authority *per se*. As for the pseudonymous author of 1 Timothy, that Pauline disciple would stand under the same authority, whether impugned by doubt or confessed by Kierkegaard in the canonical appellation, "Paul."

What sort of community, then, would the community of confident hearts be? Perhaps it can be best described, again, in terms of the canonical harmony Kierkegaard hears among the biblical witnesses voicing the hermeneutic excellence of love. That harmony comes by virtue of the witnesses' shared experience and the shared interests, expectations, and purposes that such experience generated among them. More specifically, it comes by their having devoted themselves to what they attest to be one and the same subject matter: the God of Israel and of Israel's scripture and of Jesus of Nazareth and of the church. And it comes by their having already been so shaped by Israel's scripture and its Author as to warrant calling their experience a *shared* experience. Likewise, that Kierkegaard *finds* the harmony suggests that he too has tasted something of that experience and undergone a similar shaping by the church's canon. He belongs with those whose hearts have been developed by referring all things to God in gratitude. For our part, to be persuaded by Kierkegaard's reading so as to come to understand James's words similarly would be in some measure to enter into that same community. On the other hand, to fail to appropriate the words would mark an estrangement.

My concern in calling attention to the community of the heart must not be to draw invidious distinctions between insiders and outsiders, only to learn what it means to read and live seriously for those who call themselves Christians. In that vein, however, it merits asking if the undervaluation of Kierkegaard's exegesis, even more the long-standing scholarly impression of the banality of James's Christianity and its lack of conceptual coherence, but most of all the church's neglect of scripture are not an indictment, a cultural witness to a collective heart failure. For if we fail to see or care how the emotion concepts cohere—concepts like confidence, humility, gratitude, receptivity, courage, and love—it may be because in life and in reading they have fallen out of use with us. If we remain unimpressed with Kierkegaard's understanding of James, perhaps it is because we have lost the tools to see what impedes our own.

Not that being impressed proves we have mastered the words. All talk of mastery is out of place. For life darkens, the words become hard again, the interpretation even more so. We wonder if the man who in 1843 could write that everything is a good gift from God is quite sane, or just hopelessly naïve. Perhaps then we should remember that in the same year that same man published *Fear and Trembling*—and an Edifying Discourse on Job!

Chapter 5

THE PRAISE OF JOB: EDIFYING DISCOURSE AGAINST THEODICY

Mouth and meat by grace amazed,
God upon my lips is praised.[1]

In the previous chapter, I elaborated the Rule of faith in terms of the subjective elements of humility, confidence, and gratitude that it takes to read the Epistle of James as scripture. In this chapter I want to elaborate the Rule in terms of praise and test it against a crisis situation, the Book of Job. The Book of Job is the Bible's quintessential exercise in theodicy, a paradigm of religious crises. Terence Tilley concluded a recent essay with a list of reasons why readers might rightly fear speaking of Job.[2] I want to concur with his assessment and extend his point to the subject of theodicy in general.

The problem of theodicy is, as Gustavo Gutierrez said of the Book of Job, the problem of how one speaks of God in a crisis, particularly in the face of evil.[3] My thesis will be that, for Christians, doxology is as preferable to theodicy as blessing the name of God is to cursing it, and that what is true of our speaking holds for our reading of scripture as well. Reading doxologically makes better sense than reading metaphysically, or sociologically, or cynically.

---

[1] Archibald MacLeish, *J.B.* (Boston: Houghton Mifflin, 1986; originally, 1956), 26.

[2] Terence Tilley, "The Silencing of Job," *Modern Theology* 5 (1989): 257-70.

[3] Gustavo Gutierrez, *On Job: God-Talk and the Suffering of the Innocent*, Matthew J. O'Connell, trans. (Maryknoll: Orbis, 1987), xi-xix.

Kierkegaard again serves as a proto "post-critical" model and guide, this time in the short novel, *Repetition*, and in the Edifying Discourse titled after Job's infamous proverb, "The Lord Gave, the Lord Took Away; Blessed Be the Name of the Lord."[4] Prefatory to Kierkegaard, I shall offer two contrasting examples to Kierkegaard's doxological reading, counter-types of reading Job, which I shall be calling the metaphysical and the sociological readings. But here the interest will be not simply to present a critique, but also to ask how my own speech in presenting the critique may be self-incriminating. So permit me, at the outset, this obligatory postmodern gesture of confessing the double-binds in speaking of theodicy and Job.

I. Double Binds

Readers of the Bible do not fear theodicy for nought. Theodicy is not an innocent venture. Believing readers might well be warned that the intellectual "problem of theodicy" has a way of transforming itself into an existential problem *with* theodicy. The poignancy of the problem grows in relation to one's concern for the Bible's normative status, its character as canonical scripture. Theodicy often involves a drastic distancing from the biblical idiom and an even more drastic redirection of scripture's performative force. The danger is that theodicy itself may thereby effect disbelief—even more than the evil does that it seeks to explain. Whether defined etymologically as the justification of God in the face of evil, or more broadly as any response to anomy in terms of the given nomos, in practice theodicy usually involves stepping outside the relationship with God that Christians call faith. Such disrelationship with God Kierkegaard called despair. Despair he called disbelief, or sin.[5]

1. The Metaphysical Reading

Of the two counter-types of reading we shall consider, the first is so distant from the biblical idiom, it scarcely refers to the Bible at all. It is theodicy done in the way Kierkegaard no doubt knew it best, as a

---

[4] "The Lord Gave...," *Edifying Discourses*, vol. 2, David and Lillian Swenson, trans. (Minneapolis: Augsburg, 1944), 7-26. (Hereafter *ED.*) Page numbers will be given in the body of the text. Corresponding pages in the Hong edition (*Eighteen Upbuilding Discourses* [*EUD*], 109-24) will be given in the footnotes.
[5] *The Sickness Unto Death*, Part Two. Cf. *Works of Love*, 54f.. Subsequent citations to these texts will be given parenthetically in the body of the text.

topic in metaphysics. Illustrative is the collection of essays-in-dialogue, *Encountering Evil: Live Options in Theodicy*.[6] Tailoring their text for classroom use, the authors perhaps had little room for niceties of nuance, much less for exegesis. But that is symptomatic of a more basic difficulty. Much academic work proceeds in an entirely different context—and spirit—from that which forged the biblical materials thought to be normative for the theological task.[7] Divorced from that context, in particular from the activities of praise central to that context, theological scholarship easily slips into a logic foreign to that which makes Bible into scripture.

Nowhere is this more evident than when Stephen Davis, the book's editor and most orthodox participant, frames theodicy in terms of "threats to *theism*" (2-4, my emphasis). Immediately, God has been made to occupy a function within a particular metaphysics. Nowhere is it asked whether in fact biblical faith in God entails or depends upon "theory"—ideology, systems of theoretical propositions—in quite the way "theism" implies.[8] The presumption that it does is precisely the target at which Kierkegaard would aim the a-theistic barb that, objectively, God does not exist.[9] His point of course was not to question *whether* God exists but in what *manner*. One's concept of God should reflect, he believed, the manner of God's existing as attested by the primary witnesses of faith. That manner has more in common with the activity of praising—and other such elements of subjectivity—than with the task of anchoring ideology.

---

[6] Stephen T. Davis, ed., *Encountering Evil: Live Options in Theodicy* (Atlanta: John Knox, 1981). Page citations will hereafter be given parenthetically in the body of the text.

[7] I am thinking of theology here as a historically distinctive Christian activity. Often the term "theology" is extended to cover second-order reflection on and within any religion, however misleadingly (since not all religions are theistic). Clearly, Christian scripture is not normative for the enterprise of reflecting on and within non-Christian religions.

[8] I would agree with Paul Holmer that it does not. See the chapter, "Theology, Theism, and Atheism," in Holmer's *The Grammar of Faith* (San Francisco: Harper & Row, 1978), 159-78.

[9] The formula is my own midrashic conflation of two statements Climacus makes in *Concluding Unscientific Postscript*: "Passion is subjectivity, and does not exist objectively" (117); and "To bring God to light objectively...is in all eternity impossible, because God is a subject, and therefore exists only for subjectivity in inwardness" (178). The equivalence between what is said of passion *qua* subjectivity and what can be said of God *qua* subject is possible only if we are speaking, not of the fact, but of the *how* of God's existence. (See the earlier discussion of "God as subject" in chapter 2, n. 4)

So when transferred out of the language game of worship via biblical story, poem, and moral suasion, into that of system building, the concept of God becomes a different concept, one egregiously inadequate to its supposed referent.[10]

At least two of *Encountering Evil*'s other contributors, John Hick and David Griffin, conceive of theodicy similarly to Davis. Theodicy is, in Hick's words, "an exercise in metaphysical construction consist[ing] in the formation of large-scale hypotheses concerning the nature and process of the universe" (39). Again, the assumption is that religious beliefs are justified primarily by having a place in a theoretical scheme. Or as Griffin has it, there are "common notions" about the world, universally valid "facts" (typically the ones disclosed by western science), which the hypotheses attest and to which one's concept of God must conform in order to be "plausible" (40f., 114-19). In both cases the criterion of plausibility is invoked as if it were simply a given—a non-perspectival, self-authenticating datum as neutral as the "facts" themselves and formed in no particular context.[11] It is arguable, of course, that this criterion is really quite specific to that of the science that disclosed (produced?) the facts, and that the modern worldview is not necessarily the non-prejudicial bar of reason before which all beliefs must ultimately be judged.

What Kierkegaard would insist is that it is precisely our sense of what is plausible that needs reforming by the God of scripture, the God for whom "all things are possible." But that would take more than the essentially propositionalist view of scripture, doctrine, and even of possibility,[12] that our metaphysicians employ, liberal and conservative alike.

---

[10] Daniel Hardy and David Ford put it well in their book, *Praising and Knowing God* (Philadelphia: Westminster, 1985), 109:

In the case of knowledge of God, as with any other claimed object of knowledge, the question is whether the criteria and the way they are applied are appropriate to the object. If, for example, the only way to know God is to interact with him in particular ways, then criteria which demand a neutral, non-involved knowing will be inappropriate.

[11] One's "comprehensive view of the world," Griffin says, needs to be "*intrinsically convincing*" (118, his emphasis). The word "intrinsically" begs the question of exactly what criteria of plausibility are adequate to the subject matter and in what context they are formed.

[12] For Kierkegaard it is not just scripture and doctrine whose truth belongs to the realm of subjectivity, and which are thus to be conceived in more than propositional ("aesthetic," objective) terms. Possibility, too, can work as an existential, personal category. In ethico-religious terms, possibility is a reality in relation to which one must learn to live and understand oneself as a human subject. Indeed, God is himself

Griffin, the process theodicist, dismisses the Bible on the grounds of its failure to be clear, precise, or accurate enough in the doctrines of *creatio ex nihilo* and divine omnipotence, doctrines for which scripture once served as an "external guarantee" (before historical criticism debunked it). In place of the Bible, a more logically and scientifically consistent account needs to be given of why God's power is persuasive power (104f., 118f.). Left out of account is this prospect: that by reading the creation story as a narrative hymn to be sung through one's living, one might actually refashion the objectionable doctrines into virtual paradigms of the persuasive power with which Griffin believes them to be incompatible.

For the evangelical Davis, the Bible's function seems indeed to be one of external guarantee.[13] One of the things the Bible is supposed to guarantee is the doctrine of "divine foreknowledge," which to Davis logically implies, and apparently requires asserting, double-predestination (80-82). But here the force of systemic entailment has overcome that of appropriate context. The whole discussion proceeds mindless of the fact that in the New Testament the actual root, "foreknow" (*proginosko*), is used only for purposes of comfort, always to assure readers of God's determination to *save*, not damn.[14] Even with the infamous "vessels of wrath made for destruction" (Rom 9:22), Paul's main point is to insist that "all Israel will be saved" (Rom 11:26). For Paul, whatever sense the concepts "foreknowledge" and "election" make, they make only as they effect confidence in God's plan of salvation, that is to say, only as they "perform" the gospel. Apart from that use, they are invalid.

"Foreknowledge" is only one of the biblical concepts to suffer distortion.[15] The point is that flattening doctrines becomes easier the

---

the very power of possibility, known through hope (i.e., in subjectivity). See *WL*, 233-43; cf. *CUP*, 286-89.

Thus, God's reforming our sense of what is plausible would require that we submit our lives to the scrutiny of scripture, to a transformative reading of it, by which, Kierkegaard would say, we would appropriate what we read. The contrasting style involves submitting scripture to the scrutiny of the modern worldview, presuming scripture's primary content to be truth claims about the "nature and process of the universe."

[13] Thus, Griffin's antipathetic view of biblical authority is not entirely unprovoked.

[14] Romans 8:29, 11:2; 1 Peter 1:2, 20; Acts 2:23.

[15] Others include "love," "freedom," "hope," "the fear of God," "God" itself (as we saw above), even "good" and "evil." Two of these, hope and fear of God, will figure later in my reading of Job. Suffice it to note here that in the essay of John Roth, a fourth contributor to the volume, "hope" is virtually equated with "optimism"

more remote one gets from the biblical context. But it is not as if the remoteness is remedied simply by getting more "biblical," or even more "exegetical," since there are vastly different uses of the Bible and a different way of doing exegesis for each of them. As we saw in the Introduction, much turns on the "imaginative construal" (David Kelsey), or "imaginative paradigm" (Garrett Green), under which one approaches the text in the first place.[16]

My insistence throughout these chapters is that the appropriate construal for Christian theological purposes requires approaching the Bible in *canonical* context, that is, as scripture. This means more than just addressing the "final form of the text." It means considering the text in relation to the communities that formed and shaped it, and that continue to read it, as scripture. It means taking into account the rules that normatively guide their reading—summarized under the Rule of faith—as well as the web of beliefs, commitments, practices and purposes that surrounded and informed the shaping.[17] Praise is a

---

(15), a pale substitute. Optimism is to hope roughly what adolescence is to adulthood.

I should add that only Frederick Sontag, the fifth contributor, consistently asks how these concepts *should* be defined, and only he structures his essay maieutically, that is, in a manner that captures some of the performative force of scripture as challenge and address.

[16] David Kelsey, *The Uses of Scripture in Recent Theology* (Philadelphia: Fortress, 1975); Green, *Imagining God: Theology and the Religious Imagination* (San Francisco: Harper, 1989).

[17] I continue to use "canonical" in the broad sense Brevard Childs employs it in order to refer to a historical process of composing, redacting, transmitting, and preserving the biblical literature with religious uses in mind, and to the interpretive stance of realizing the literature in relation to those uses. It should be emphasized that while a concern with the final form of the text figures strongly in this notion of canon, it hardly exhausts it, as numerous scholars mistakenly assume. See, for example, Tilley, "The Silencing of Job," 259, 268.

In light of Tilley's particular misreading, a distinction should be noted between biblical "text" in the sense of a particular collection and arrangement of writings and the more technical term "text-type," which refers to manuscript tradition. The trick is, in the canonical process there could be relative stability of the former while there remained great diversity of the latter. With the Hebrew Bible, for instance, the number, order, and shape of the books was reasonably well established long before the Masoretic text-type (MT) won out in the synagogue over its rivals. Indeed, the MT did not itself achieve its present degree of stability until the tenth century of the Common Era. For the church, of course, differences over the OT canon persist because Roman Catholicism sought to honor the importance of the Septuagint (a Greek text-type) for early Christianity, while the Reformers believed that the decision of Jews vis-á-vis Jewish scripture should be normative for Christians as well, since "to them

continuous thread in that web and a staple of the Rule. Too often theodicy à la metaphysics obscures the canonical context and fails to hear the praise. But it is not alone in doing so.

2. The Sociological Reading

Our second counter-type of reading does not set out to "do" theodicy so much as study it. Sociologically understood, theodicy itself becomes the paradigm under which the Bible is to be read, such that the Bible as a whole is construed as a giant project in theodicy. The virtue of the sociological approach is that the scholar employing it does at least read the Bible. Not surprisingly, he/she gives Job pride of place. Moreover, as an invaluable tool of ideology-critique, sociological analysis attends to a performative dimension of the Bible qua scripture. Sociologically viewed, scripture serves to legitimate a religious community's world order (*nomos*), especially in situations of crisis. Reading Job effects, to paraphrase Peter Berger, a pact with anomy and helps keep one's social world—and its institutional arrangements—intact. Of course, this performative force would be differently described under the Rule of faith. I want to mark that difference. Later, a question to be asked is whether the sociologist's reading might not perform a theodicy for the sociologist, too.

Berger's *The Sacred Canopy* offers a classic illustration of the sociological approach.[18] Berger develops a typology of theodicies on a rational-irrational (theoretical to non-theoretical) spectrum.

---

belong the covenants, the giving of the law, the worship, and the promises" (Rom 9:4; cf. 3:2).

The upshot is twofold: first, "canon" does not imply "rigid fixity." Second, there can be (and are) notable areas of ambiguity within the canon and disagreement among faith communities about its peripheries without the reality and value of "canon" as a critical category being utterly vitiated.

Further, it bears keeping in mind that arguments over text-critical issues (e.g., text-type), as over translation, are of a quite different order from arguments about whether, say, the J stratum of the Pentateuch, which exists only as a hypothetical construct of historical criticism, has a claim to authority equal to that of the "final form of the text." By canonical logic, it is the Pentateuch in its final form (LXX *or* MT)—i.e., as a text that actually exists—that is authoritative for synagogue and church. As applied to Job, an analogous question would be whether the poetic dialogues should be abstracted from and read against the prose framework, or should be read in "canonical context." On this question, see below, p. 162 and part II of this chapter.

[18] Peter Berger, *The Sacred Canopy: Elements of a Sociological Theory of Religion* (Garden City, NY: Anchor, 1969). Page citations will be indicated parentheticaly in the body of the text.

Though compelling, the typology requires highly abstract distillations of the religions under comparison. In the inevitable oversimplification, biblical religion is defined rationalistically (i.e., in terms of its propositional content) as "radical ethical monotheism," for which the task of theodicy is said to be at its most difficult. At hand to the believer, however, is a useful antidote, Berger argues, a fundamental religious attitude prevalent at the irrational end of the spectrum but oddly fitting, if not tailor-made, for the biblical situation. It is the "masochistic" attitude of "submission to the totally other"; it is a posture of self-abasement before the radically transcendentalized, omnipotent, wholly righteous and unchallengeable deity, "who by his very nature is sovereignly above any human ethic and generally nomic standards" (74).

The gist of the masochism is this: given the reality of evil, if God cannot be at fault, humanity must be. The Book of Job is then read in light of that theoretical necessity. In Job, Berger writes, "the implicit accusation against God [for permitting evil] is turned around to become an explicit accusation against man....The question of human sin replaces the question of divine justice," and the problem of theodicy resolves into one of "anthropodicy." Thus Job is said to present us with "the pure form of religious masochism *vis-à-vis* the biblical God." Job is "the masochistic solution *par excellence*" (74f.). In sum, the biblical religion having been defined as if it were little more than a theory about God's nature, according to which God is known primarily by such abstract predicates as "cannot be at fault," the Book of Job is read as if it were defending the theory, and to do so it has to denounce humanity.

Berger maintains that the sociologist uses "masochism" in a purely technical, non-pejorative way. Still, one cannot help but suspect that the term is motivated by a sense of offense at the "negation of man" it describes (75), and that the offense has been projected onto, read into, the biblical text.[19] To wit, Job's confession

---

[19] The suspicion is reinforced by the hyperbole that attributes Yahweh with *absolute* otherness. In fact, the Hebrew Bible's emphasis on God's otherness (transcendence) is matched by its insistence on his immanence. This is reflected in the theomorphic depiction of human beings, male and female having been created in God's own image, and in the constant adverting to the divine pathos. Indeed, as Psalm 113:5-9 attests, God's transcendence is conceived as his power to be near to the lowly of the world. It is the power by which God's pathos is effective. The New Testament gives heightened expression of the interrelationship of transcendence and immanence via the Incarnation. Further on the significance of the divine pathos, see

in 42:5-6 is taken as a confession of *sin*, his submission and self-abasement as self-*condemnation*. Yet nowhere in the text does either Job or God concede that Job has offended. Indeed, the whole force of the prose prologue and epilogue to the story is that Job has *not* sinned—there has been no offense—a fact three times affirmed by Yahweh himself (1:8, 2:3, 42:7) and three times underscored by the narrator (1:1, 22, and 2:10). The logic governing Job's confession, therefore, and driving the book as a whole, must be something other than repentance for sin.

Various commentators have made the point about Job's sinlessness. Where Berger sees a "cosmicizing" motive in Job's masochism (the sacrality of the nomos is maintained by Job's submission), Matitiahu Tsevat sees the book's effect as *de*-cosmicizing. The Yahweh speeches in particular (chaps. 38-41) work to demythologize the physical world, showing that the moral principle of retribution is not necessarily built into the cosmos, as Job's three "comforters" assume it must be. On the contrary, there is no necessary connection between sin and suffering whatsoever, Job's or anyone else's.[20] In a variation on Tsevat's thesis, Edwin Good persuasively argues that it is not only the friends who buy into the doctrine of retribution but Job himself. The world *should* follow the law of just desserts, Job assumes, but somehow the law has misfired: the wicked prosper and the good suffer, he especially.[21]

Tsevat and Good allow us to distinguish, as Job himself must, between Job's being a sinner and his simply being wrong, i.e., mistaken, about how God and the world operate. Accordingly, Job's confession need not be, and makes no sense as, a confession of sin. Further on, I'll be making the case that it is a function of praise. Meanwhile, it is enough to say that with theodicy as his paradigm,

---

Abraham Heschel, "The Theology of Pathos," *The Prophets*, vol. 1 (New York: Harper & Row, 1962), 1-11.

[20] Matitiahu Tsevat, "The Meaning of the Book of Job," in *Studies in Ancient Israelite Wisdom*, James L Crenshaw, ed. (New York: KTAV, 1976), 341-74 (originally, *Hebrew Union College Annual*, 37 [1966]: 73-106). Comprehensive and exegetically acute, Tsevat's article is one of the most influential pieces of scholarship on Job in recent decades.

[21] Edwin Good, "Job and the Literary Task: A Response," *Soundings* 56 (1973): 446-85. Good's essay has been less widely influential than Tsevat's, but it will later be apparent that I am deeply in Good's debt.

Berger has had to ignore crucial particulars in the text in order to find there a moralistic masochism.[22]

Berger has also had to ignore the canonical shape of the story. He tacitly follows the modern scholar's tendency of privileging the poetic dialogues (3:2-42:6) over the older prose framework (chaps 1-2, 42:7ff.) and pitting the poet's "Protesting Job" against the "Patient Job" of the folktale.[23] The tendency is understandable. The folktale is generally felt to be pietistic to the point of fantasy; some would call it a "fairytale."[24] The outraged protests of the dialogues and the depths of suffering they reveal ring truer to late twentieth-century sensibilities. Nevertheless, it is in the prose that the protester is vindicated, while in the poetry, read in isolation from the framework, God's speeches are perhaps too easily heard as "...the voice of [a] terrible God...so overwhelming as to drown out the cry of protest of tormented man" (74). The canonical shape of the text, however, holds the protest and the piety together in a dynamic far subtler than that of simple opposition, and it suggests an altogether different tone of voice for God.

Ideology critique, important as it is, does not come without costs, and a high price is paid for the sociologist's approach. Maybe costliest is the irony that Berger ends up reading the Book of Job the way the comforters read Job's character. They find Job guilty in order

---

[22] Berger may also be operating with a loose conception of sin uninformed by canonical context. As we shall see below, Kierkegaard reads the Book of Job as a test, or "ordeal," which addresses a different religious problem, a different set of existential issues, from that associated with the NT (Pauline) conception of sin-consciousness. In other words, reading Job by the (Christian) Rule of faith does not require reading into it, or reading it as about, the Christian doctrine of human sinfulness.

Incidentally, while Kierkegaard describes suffering as an essential expression of the religious life, he explicitly denies that this constitutes masochism. See *CUP*, 387 and 414, and the discussion of this issue in C. Stephen Evans, *Kierkegaard's* Fragments *and* Postscript: *The Religious Philosophy of Johannes Climacus* (Atlantic Highlands, NJ: Humanities Press International, 1983), 172.

[23] See, for example, H. L. Ginsberg, "Job the Patient and Job the Impatient," *Vetus Testamentum Supplements* 17 (1969): 88-111. Christopher Seitz describes this model for reading the material as the "developmental" or "correction theory," whereby the author of the poetry is viewed as having sought to replace or "correct" the purportedly mechanistic view of God and suffering presented in the naïve folktale. Seitz's critique of the model is succinct and, in my opinion, devastating. See his "Job: Full-Structure, Movement, and Interpretation," *Interpretation* 43 (1989): 5-17 (esp. 8f.).

[24] E.g., David Robertson, "The Book of Job: A Literary Study," *Soundings* 56 (1973), 468.

to defend their theory about God (that he rewards his friends and punishes his enemies). Berger misconstrues Job as confessing sin in order to keep a tidy typology. But he doesn't go so far as some.

James Crenshaw shows just how far one can go. Crenshaw has elaborated on Berger's analysis in many venues. None better reflects the intellectual parentage than his essay, "The Shift from Theodicy to Anthropodicy."[25] The purpose, to count the costs of defending God, assumes with Berger that God's defense is what the biblical writers are really up to.[26] More plainly than Berger, Crenshaw finds the costs in human dignity excessive, and more palpable than in Berger is the tone of an offended consciousness, of a felt need for self-defense. The essay's title thus becomes a self-description: Crenshaw's cost analysis becomes anthropodicy in action.

Were Crenshaw to use Berger's term "masochism," there would be no doubt as to its pejorative force. Job's submission is again taken as a confession of sin, but now it is further cast as "abject groveling" (6). Such submission is the "fatal flaw" of theodicy, because it involves a "sacrifice of human integrity," of "human dignity," of "self-esteem," resulting in the "loss of self" (6-9). Meanwhile, the God the self is sacrificed to is "this blustering deity" (9), whose pathos and concomitant capacity for change amount to a "divine inconstancy" (10).[27]

It is curious that the fatal flaw is located in what happens to the self rather than in, say, our prior construal of God as cosmic bully, which we guilty theodicists then try to deny by jumping to God's

---

[25] See *Theodicy in the Old Testament*, James L. Crenshaw, ed. (Philadelphia: Fortress, 1983), 1-16. (Page citations will be given in the body of the text.) No essay better displays Crenshaw's exegetical acumen than the one on Job, "Murder Without Cause," in *A Whirlpool of Torment: Israelite Traditions of God as an Oppressive Presence* (Philadelphia: Fortress, 1984), 57-75. The latter no doubt presents a rounder, fairer picture of Crenshaw's interpretive stance. On the deliberately provocative design of the "Anthropodicy" essay, see below, pp. 164-66.

[26] While there may be considerable agreement within biblical studies that theodicy is ideological—and that all biblical writings have an ideological dimension—a quick survey of the widely conflicting opinions about exactly what ideology any particular writing is pushing, about precisely what its propagandistic *tendenz* actually is, shows how speculative and conjectural our knowledge is regarding the agendas and motives of the biblical writers. Indeed, we rarely agree about their identities and dates, much less their politics.

[27] This contrasts with Heschel, who understands God's pathos not as opposed to his constancy but as a function of it. It is because of God's passionate commitment to human beings, because of a faithful will to save which is eternal and *un*changing, that God suffers change.

defense. The flaw is made to reside more in the act of *confessing* sin than in any actual sinning. And finally, it is the text and its writers that Crenshaw holds responsible—though, as we have seen, incorrectly—for depicting the necessity of such confession.

Once again, the tendency to fix the issue on sin is characteristic of the dialogue section in Job, for which the sociological approach, like the modern sensibility, seems to have a borne affinity. As with Berger's, Crenshaw's argument really repeats that of the dialogue, certainly its anthropocentric focus. The "Protesting Job" is engaged, not in defending God (the writers are said to do that), but in defending himself, as Crenshaw would. The good God who in the prologue presents himself as Job's advocate, whom Job had known previously as his friend and who only the reader knows remains constant, blurs for Job under the ordeal of suffering. Like the offended Job, the critic Crenshaw represents God as hostile.

The existential limits that the narrative levies on Job's knowledge—he cannot see what transpires in heaven between God and the satan—thus correspond with the epistemological (and ontological?) limits of the sociologist's methodology. Self-restricted to the horizon of what the eye can see unaided by revelation, the critic gradually adopts the posture of defending the seer so restricted. "Human integrity" gets confused with the questionable integrity of humans in their alienated state. "Self-sacrifice" and "submission," which for believers mean the yielding over of alienated selves in the hopes of being made whole, appear as violations of our dignity instead of steps toward its restoration. Subtly, the study of theodicy has become like that which it studies, an enterprise in human self-legitimation. Sociology has become anthropodicy.

Our two counter-type readings, the metaphysical and the sociological, are meant to illustrate what can follow from the project of theodicy theoretically formulated, and from construing Job as an instance of that project. These readings assume a language game in the material's production quite different from the first-order language of faith itself, and they tend to repeat that game in their own discourse.

Or so it seems at first blush. Crenshaw's piece turns out finally to resist this arduous dismissal. On the last page he says his intent was "to be provocative" (13), and elsewhere he acknowledges having purposefully adopted the restricted perspective of the sufferer.[28] What seemed a straightforward mis-reading now appears to have been

---

[28] *Whirlpool of Torment*, 117.

a deliberate one, which qualifies the work as something on the order of Kierkegaard's "indirect communication," maybe even "edifying discourse." And we are reminded of Kierkegaard's claim that in Christendom, or in its wake, truth takes a polemical form.[29]

The reasons for polemical indirection are well known. They are grounded in issues of class and culture. My every instinct, particularly as part of a reader-elite, is to get to the other side of Job's protests as quickly as possible, to shield myself from the discomforting fact that, for the greater part of humanity for much the greater part of history, life has been a relentless ordeal of disease, deprivation, and grief, an ordeal aggravated by false comfort from privileged counsellors.[30] In the face of that, Crenshaw's repetition of Job's perception of "God as an Oppressive Presence" is a rhetorical strategy for arresting my vagrant attention in order to force a hearing of what Job has to say.

This, after all, is only to follow the lead of God in the narrative. God *allows* Job that mis-perception of him. Job is permitted to experience God, as Barth says, in alien form.[31] For that is part of the test, part of this ordeal that injects the dimension of *life*-time, lived time, into the epithet "the Patient" and into the ascription "Blessed be the name," and thus converts clichés back into troubling profundities. So, in a sense, it is the narrative's God that clears a space for the poetic dialogue, and honors it with God's own hearing (thus the speeches from the whirlwind), and declares Job's part of it "right speaking" (42:8). And just as the rhetoric of Job's protest turns increasingly general —"Has not man hard service on the earth?"

---

[29] *WL*, 336.

[30] See Job 6:14-21, 12:1-6, and 13:4-12. Job's analysis of the friends' advice is stunning. First, he points out, their advice simply adds to his anguish. Part of the situation he laments is that he has become "a laughingstock to my friends," a fact that illustrates his precipitous fall and confronts him as a matter of radical cognitive dissonance: "I, a just and blameless man, am a laughingstock!" (12:4). Second, the advice adds to his anguish because it is so condescending. Having mistaken the vicissitudes of fortune as an index of worth, the friends are secretly contemptuous: "In the thought of one who is at ease there is contempt for misfortune; it is ready for those whose feet slip" (12:5). And finally, the contempt is shown really to be a displacement of fear, a self-distancing denial of the possibility that the horror that has overtaken Job could just as easily befall them: "you see my calamity, and are afraid!" (6:21)

Job's analysis anticipates Terrence Des Pres's account of the responses typically given to the testimony of Holocaust survivors, including responses of the psychoanalytic community. See *The Survivor: An Anatomy of Life in the Death Camps* (New York: Oxford, 1976), 38-45.

[31] Karl Barth, *Church Dogmatics*, G. W. Bromiley, trans. (Edinburgh: T. & T. Clark, 1961), IV/3/i, 402-405. Hereafter *CD*.

$(7:1)^{32}$—and we come to see Job and his experience as representative, so the exegetical focus on that section, along with its rhetoric and experience, serves to re-present the poetry's wide human content and the common voice of human anguish it divinely behooves us to hear.

If this is the case, then Crenshaw's language game has shifted more subtly than first thought. Previously I described the shift as one from the study of theodicy to active anthropodicy. Second-order discourse was doing the work we often associate with the first-order language of personal involvement, self-legitimation in this case, although practice in suspicion has accustomed us to that particular linguistic maneuver. Now, however, we see the same formal disguise, first-order business garbed in second-order language, but find we can construe it differently. The ostensibly objective, analytic discourse of the sociological and biblical-critical disciplines, with all their rationalistic biases and blindspots, has been put to the work of *faith*. What looked like a too familiar style of academic exegesis was, it now appears, *witness* incognito. Crenshaw writes as a faithful witness to suffering humanity.

This raises the question of who the offended consciousness really belongs to. It does seem incongruous that my advocacy of praise should begin with a critique that verges on the *ad hominem*. How odd that to propose doxology as a speech form preferable to theodicy, I find myself defending God's praise-worthiness at someone else's expense! In a word, I end up doing theodicy. One safely objective conclusion to draw from this embarrassment is that any given language game can be played in strange and diverse uniforms; wearing the proper speech does not guarantee that one is playing the proper game. Another conclusion is that our games are never proper (just as our intratextuality is never clean[33]). A third is that my thesis has a quirk.

The thesis has been that for Christians to read Job in good faith, they must read by the Rule of faith; that is, read it as pointing to the love of God, read it to the honor of God, to the greater glory of God, i.e., doxologically. The Rule indicates the requisite intentionality and dispositional equipment for receiving and perceiving scripture as the Word of God—to the degree that humans can of themselves do *anything* to receive and perceive it so. Obviously, however, this

---

[32] See also 3:20, 7:17-18, 9:2, chaps. 14, 21, and 24.

[33] See Terence Tilley's proposal of a "dirty intratextuality" in his critique of the Lindbeck-Frei thesis, "Incommensurability, Intratextuality, and Fideism," *Modern Theology* 5 (1989): 87-111.

entails the reader's already believing in God. It entails at the outset a hoping-believing *knowledge* of God as praiseworthy and good: a knowledge informed by the revelation of God paradigmatically in Christ but also typologically in the covenants with Noah, Abraham, and Moses, in the Exodus from Egypt, indeed, in all God's wondrous works with Israel and the world, not least with Job. In short, to read Job as scripture and in the hope of meeting God, is to read it already in God's favor. Thus the normative reading of scripture becomes, *qua* witness to the mysterious and oft-hidden goodness of God, a legitimation: an implicit theodicy. To praise God is to justify God, despite myself...and my objections to theodicy.

This quirk, that doxology turns out to be theodicy after all, is compounded by a further embarrassment: the fact that the Rule of faith proposes a *dogmatic* starting point. In chapters two and four I treated the embarrassment by insisting, first, that the Rule simply marks one more instance of the well-known hermeneutic circle: readers make the sense they are looking for and are equipped by the Rule to look for; and second, that the Rule simply defines the interpretive community the readers belong to as Christians, in analogy with the reader conventions and competences that define any interpretive community. The Rule, in other words, is no more irrational or less circular a starting point than the underlying principles and assumptions for any other reading enterprise.

The Book of Job magnifies the embarrassment nonetheless. It does so because to recommend the Rule, to advise a doxological reading, is to find *oneself*, like Berger and countless others, repeating what Job's friends say. Thus Eliphaz in 5:8-9: "As for me, I would seek God, and to God I would submit my cause; who does great things and unsearchable, marvelous things without number...." He goes on to number the marvelous things, doxologically of course. So when it comes to commending doxology, I am only following the lead of the pious windbag, Eliphaz.

Barth touches the nerve of the issue in this analysis of the stance of the friends:

Their representations rest on the assumption that, on the basis of the tradition in which they stand..., they have information about God to which they have only to refer back to be able to speak appropriately concerning Him, i.e., information about His nature, that He is always wise and righteous, and about the degrees to which He is always faithful to this nature of His in His action and rule, and is thus to be feared and loved as

God....To them in their belief that they are thinking and speaking for and with God, [Job's] is an attitude which they can only resist and attack in the hope of breaking it....As Job himself said clearly enough, somewhere behind the laborious mildness which controls their instructions there is already prepared an *auto-da-fe* to be celebrated *ad maiorem Dei gloriam*. This is what disqualifies their speeches in advance, however full of content they may be.[34]

The question is painfully clear: how does reading by the Rule of faith, doxologically in the light of Christ, differ formally from the procedure Barth sees at work in the friends, "disqualifying their speeches in advance"? Indeed, how does Barth's own way of reading differ? Does he not, like they and I, rely on a knowledge of God mediated by tradition and the past, i.e., by dogma? Kierkegaard might say that resorting to a dogmatic beginning point is a "temptation," a temptation to retreat from "the religious," that sphere of naked exposure to the living God in an open text, to the security of "the ethical," the sphere of conventional definitions that enclose the text before it is read.

---

[34] *CD*, 456-57. David Clines cites K. Fullerton to the same effect ("Double Entendre in the First Speech of Eliphaz," *Journal of Biblical Literature*, 49 [1930]: 336f.). Clines comments:

However true [Eliphaz's words] may be in theory—and we are not meant by the author to doubt that these are divinely inspired words—they are plainly inappropriate to Job's case....Eliphaz, says Fullerton, is "a certain kind of dogmatic theologian whose presuppostions are supposed to be divine revelation...and whose eyes are therefore blind to all that does not fit into the preconceived pattern. Now the difficulty with such persons is that they are *unintentionally* cruel....They may have sympathy, but it is an abstract sympathy....They are unable to feel their way into ideas or experiences alien to their own. Dogma has a terrible power to dull the imagination, and without imagination sympathy is unable to help." The author does not mock the dogma of Eliphaz; he mocks the presumed efficacy of dogma to alleviate suffering. (*Job 1-20*, vol. 17, Word Biblical Commentary (Dallas: Word Books, 1989), 132f.

What Clines, Fullerton, and Barth all seem to be saying is that without imagination *dogma* is unable to help. But the positive implication is worth noting, and lends itself well to Kierkegaardian formulation: Dogma (teaching) can be true, vital, indeed essential to the degree that it is inwardly—and that means imaginatively—appropriated by the learner; and that requires that it be indirectly—i.e., imaginatively—communicated by the would-be teacher. If there is a way out of the dilemma posed in this part of the chapter, it is in the direction of this business of imaginative communication and appropriation. But that also makes it a matter of the heart, as we have seen throughout this book.

Is it the case, then, that the effort to read Job in good faith inevitably ends up as an exercise in bad faith?[35] At the very least, the effort becomes what Kierkegaard might call an "ordeal." But if an ordeal, then perhaps a "repetition" is possible, indeed necessary (for reading in good faith): a repetition of the book itself, of Job's confession, praise, and faith.

II. Kierkegaard and the Ordeal of Praise

1. Repetition

Whether a repetition is possible is the question driving Kierkegaard's short novel, *Repetition*. Though speculatively posed by the pseudonymous author-aesthete, Constantin Constantius, the question takes shape as an existential ordeal for the anonymous "young man" who is the story's protagonist. It is the young man's fascination with Job, prompted by his own situation of lost love, that sharpens the two key categories, "repetition" and "ordeal," and gives them their pathos. No doubt their pathos is what impels Kierkegaard to embed them in so ironic a narrative that the reader cannot quite tell how the question has been answered and so must re-ask it for herself.

What "repetition" means is hard enough to say, let alone whether it is possible. Kierkegaard's use of it is characteristically equivocal, the sense shifting according to the form of life, or stage of existence—aesthetic, ethical, or religious—of the person attempting it. Repetition begins with our capacity for imaginative self-consciousness. Aware of ourselves in our concreteness and finitude, we are also able to project possibilities for ourselves, possibilities that are ideal by virtue of being imaginatively projected but authentic because consciously grounded in the actual selves we happen to be. Accordingly, we *repeat* the ideal to the degree that we enact it in actuality, realize it in the medium of existence, do it in our day-to-day living. As David Gouwens succinctly puts it, "In repetition a person raises reality to ideality, and then repeats that possibility in actuality."[36]

The emphasis on actual existence points to the ethical as the normative sphere for repetition. Repetition is a (if not *the*) *self*

---

[35] On the concept "bad faith," see pp. 139 and 143.

[36] David Gouwens, *Kierkegaard's Dialectic of the Imagination* (New York: Peter Lang, 1988), 206.

building operation; that is, it is the process through which we construct and become selves, full human subjects. And it is in the ethical sphere, as Kierkegaard defines it, that a person recognizes the achievement of self and subjectivity as one's proper life-work and sets about doing it. Now, the fact that in the second literature Kierkegaard refers to this construction process with the *religiously* laden term, "edification" (or "up-building"), hints at a paradoxical quality within the idea of repetition, a kind of transgression of spheres or confusion of categories.[37]

However, the term's etymology points back to the primacy of the ethical sphere. C. Stephen Evans observes that "repetition" in Danish "literally means 'again-taking.'" "The self is not merely taken or assumed as already real; it must be 're-taken.'"[38] Again, the recognition that one does not simply "have" a self but must become one, and the consequent striving to become a self-in-fact, are marks of the ethical life. For persons in the aesthetic stage of life such recognition and striving are a problem. Some are so immersed in their immediate environment that they merely take themselves for granted. Others, aesthetes proper, relate to their possibilities only hypothetically; they balk at undertaking a commitment to any one of them. They cannot bring themselves to "set about doing it." Either way, there can be no repetition. Repetition is simply not possible within the limits of aesthetic existence. Repetition belongs to ethics virtually by definition, so only there can the question of its possibility be realistically raised.

The tragic irony is, once the question is raised in the ethical sphere, its normative province, it becomes urgent and anguished in the extreme. And it *is* raised, for even the great ethical virtuosos seem never to forge themselves without suffering some breach of consciousness in the process. The self one wins always turns out to be a broken self, never the ideal. (We hear Kierkegaard the Lutheran here: there is no doubt that it is a Christian psychology he gives us.)

Yet precisely at this point another irony may emerge, even greater than the tragic one. For it sometimes happens that in—and despite—crushing failure, in the collapse of the ethical striver's world, the self is found and "re-taken" *outside* one's striving, i.e., outside and in violation of the ethical principle of repetition that it be one's *own*

---

[37] See especially the chapter "Love Builds Up" in *WL*, 199-213. See also Johannes Climacus's discussion of edification and the Edifying Discourses in *CUP*, 229-44.

[38] *Kierkegaard's* Postscript, 154.

actualizing of one's possibilities that forms the self. This is a paradox, a transgression of spheres, as mentioned above: Repetition's fulfilment is an exception to its own ethical logic.

This fulfilment of repetition is part of the paradox—the exceptionality and the higher irony—that for Kierkegaard marks the religious stage of existence. Outwardly, and ironically, the person who actually experiences repetition resembles the person still caught in aesthetic immediacy who takes herself as given. Inwardly, however, she is different for having gone through the struggle of the ethical and been educated by it. Having learned and acknowledged that she cannot establish her self by herself, she receives herself not from nature as a product (aesthetically) but from God as a gift (religiously). Thus the religious fulfilment of an ethical category suspends the ethical and so looks like the aesthetic; nevertheless, the ethical is indispensable to it.

Where is Job in this abstract scenario? Louis Mackey boils it down to basics where the Joban flavor is unmistakable: "Repetition," book and concept, are really about "the possibility of restoring a personality to integrity after it has been broken by grief and guilt."[39] For the young man, and Kierkegaard, Job is a paradigm of such restoration.

At the same time, Kierkegaard's interest in Job's repetition has a polemical edge and needs to be set in the context of his campaign against Christendom and speculative idealism. In his view, recall, these two villains form an unholy alliance in which vital ethico-religious categories are assimilated into the larger cultural agenda of capitalism and the nation-state. The resulting distortions threaten human community at the core. In the face of modernity's vast depersonalizing and demoralizing force,[40] repetition stands for the task each individual has of appropriating for his or her own life the faith of old Father Abraham, the wisdom of Job, and the grace of Jesus Christ, each won *in extremis*. "Going beyond"[41] these simple gifts to

---

[39] *Kierkegaard: A Kind of Poet* (Philadelphia: University of Pennsylvania Press, 1972), 322, n. 20. Mackey's mention of guilt points to an interesting psychological fact: Job *feels* guilty even though he isn't—indeed, even though he *knows* he isn't.

[40] It is important to note that for Kierkegaard "de-moralization," a term used frequently in *CUP* (120, 129, 135, 179), means more than "discouragement." It refers to large cultural processes and individual forms of self-deception whereby people fail to develop their capacities for ethical thought and action and thus forfeit their nature as moral beings. (See also above, p. 43 n. 43.)

[41] Mentioned above in chapter 4, this expression is a satiric leitmotif in *Fear and Trembling*, 7, 9, 32, 36, 37, 50, and 51. The novel *Repetition* was published in

something more sophisticated (like Hegel's wanting to go beyond the primitive images of story to universal concepts systematically displayed in Theory) is the grand illusion of Kierkegaard's and our age. In place of our addiction to novelty, our compulsion for progress, and our infatuation with theory, Kierkegaard thought it enough that we should strive for a repetition.

The novel *Repetition* is styled and structured to promote that very goal, as is the Kierkegaardian corpus as a whole. As Mark Lloyd Taylor has shown,[42] the novel's appearance in tandem with *Fear and Trembling* was scarcely accidental. Thematically, the one repeats the other. Both are aimed at introducing the concept of repetition. Both are "the story of an ordeal that ends with a repetition by virtue of the absurd, which, in some fashion, illustrates religious faith."[43] Of course, for illustrating faith, Job more closely repeats Abraham than does the young man himself, and what Abraham and Job illustrate faith to be is, essentially—and in keeping with what we found in chapter 4—receptivity. The restoration of health and household to Job, like the restoring of Isaac to Abraham, represents a re-taking, a "taking again," a receiving, of life in its finite immediacy. But the repetition is also a receiving life in a new way, not naively as at first but in a "second immediacy," "whereby," Taylor says, "the finite is received from the hand of God."[44]

The absurdity of Job's fairy-tale restoration was of course a natural magnet for Kierkegaard's interest, since the restoration so clearly violated both his age's skepticism, grounded in its essentially aesthetic-objectivist worldview, and its ethical sensibilities. "Who would have imagined this ending?" marvels the aesthete Constantin, who can imagine (but not enact) an ethical repetition (*R*, 212). Job's *religious* repetition goes quite beyond his ken.

In this Constantin mirrors Johannes de Silentio, pseudonymous author of *Fear and Trembling*, whose inability to fathom Abraham generates his four depictions of what Abraham might have done

---

tandem with *FT* and appears in the same Hong edition as above. Page citations for both will hereafter be given in the body of the text.

[42] Mark Lloyd Taylor, "Ordeal and Repetition in Kierkegaard's Treatment of Abraham and Job," *Foundations of Kierkegaard's Vision of Community: Religion, Ethics, and Politics in Kierkegaard*, George B. Connell and C. Stephen Evans, eds. (Atlantic Highlands, NJ: Humanities Press International, 1991): 33-53.

[43] Taylor, p. 39.

[44] Taylor, 8. On "second [also "new" or "later"] immediacy," see among other places, *FT*, 82 and *CUP*, 235. See also the "knight of hidden inwardness" in *CUP*, 417ff.

differently had he "doubted"; i.e., had Abraham been unreceptive, an ethical hero of self-constituting precocity rather than a "knight of faith," one disciplined in receptivity.[45] Marvelous, verging on offensive, was Abraham's ability to receive Isaac back again with joy, once having resigned, if not steeled, himself to the catastrophic loss (*FT*, 35, 45, 48-50). Analogous is Job's apparent willingness to *accept* the restoration—which of course includes a new set of children (42:13-16), the first set having been killed (1:18-19). Offense is given not just by the intellectual absurdity that arises from an appraisal of "what is plausible," but by Job's overcoming an ethical repugnance at one's life not belonging to oneself—the children's to the children, his to himself, much less theirs to him—but rather all to God, who gives and takes (1:21) and gives again, inscrutably.

Like Silentio, Constantin is constructed to represent (repeat) a dominant perspective among Kierkegaard's readership. Accordingly, his wonderment serves to articulate a common reader response to the bizarre ending of Job and to prod that response to deeper levels. Like Silentio vis-à-vis Abraham, Constantin's discourse fills with *our* questions the space of Job's silence after his restoration, questions more disturbing for the fact that the divine restoration includes no divine guarantees that catastrophe won't strike crazily again.

A slow clarification may come by having our questions thus mirrored for us. The difficulty of again-taking may come to be seen as the difficulty of surrendering to God all proprietary claims to life and goods—and still have soul enough to care, love, and rejoice in that which we are given.[46] We ask with personal urgency how such repetition is indeed possible. To the degree we do, edification may already be under way.

Kierkegaard works his repetitions at another level as well. Constantin mirrors not just reader reaction to Job's story but narrative action within it. As dubious advisor to the young man, he is related to the young man as Job's hapless comforters are related to Job. Thus we find ourselves as readers of the story, to the degree we see it through Constantin the counsellor, closest in kind to the least sympathetic characters *in* the story. Whether or not we go on to recognize ourselves in shame—which I shall argue is the substance of

---

[45] The Exordium I-IV, 9-14. See also Silentio's remark in the "Eulogy": "If Abraham had doubted, he would have done something else..." (20).

[46] See Edward F. Mooney, "Understanding Abraham: Care, Faith, and the Absurd," in *Kierkegaard's "Fear and Trembling": Critical Appraisals*, Robert L. Perkins, ed. (University, AL: University of Alabama Press, 1981), 100-114.

Job's "confession" in 42:5-6 and an implication of the friends' response to Yahweh's chiding in 42:9—Kierkegaard has given us occasion for such self-recognition. No human being can do another's repetition for her, Kierkegaard believed; only God can do that. But if one is suitably indirect, he may, edifyingly, help to induce it.

Constantin is not our only window on Job in the novel; we also get to view him through the young man's eyes. Naturally, if Constantin typifies the friends, we expect to encounter the young man as a type of Job. To an extent, our expectations are supported. Beginning to view his own life in light of Job's, the young man presents himself as Job does to his friends. "No doubt wisdom will die with you; but I have understanding as well as you" (12:2-3), Job sarcastically insists. Similarly, the young man can quote wisdom with the best of the pedants: "If anyone asks me anything, I have a ready answer...quite a few poems, pithy sayings, proverbs, and brief maxims from the immortal Greek and Roman writers..." (*R*, 203). Through his Joban self-interpretation, the young man interprets Job for us as a master of wisdom's standard speech forms, but as a master with a sense that such mastery can be empty. We are also shown the prospect that one might, like the young man, find oneself impelled to repeat Job's passion to fill the forms with substance.

Ancient Israel's concern with wisdom as right-speaking is sharpened in the Book of Job into this concern with the *substance* of speech, and this in turn is framed in terms of human integrity (1:11, 22; 2:3, 9-10). At bottom the issue of integrity is related to the question of how humans might properly fear God, or whether they *can*, which of course is the satan's question that generates Job's ordeal (1:9). The young man re-introduces us to this constellation of themes by again mirroring the role of Job. As Job rejects the self-falsification urged upon him by his friends (11:6, 13-15; 22:5, 21), and clings to his integrity (13:16; 19:7, 23ff.; 23:7), so the young man clings to his, by refusing the charade proposed by Constantin as a way out of his dilemma: "I demand my rights—that is, my honor" (*R*, 202).

It is significant that the young man conceives of his integrity, his "honor," in terms of "rights," for so does Job. Job's enumeration of duties done (see especially the innocence oath of chap. 31) constitutes the basis of his claim upon God for what Job sees to be his rightful due. This is integrity defined ethically, Kierkegaard would say: a wholeness of self won by the self through the embracing of duty. With Job it is won through the fulfilment of covenantal obligations. The question of religious repetition is precisely the question of whether *another* form of integrity, rooted in an enhanced relationship

with God, is possible. That Job's integrity does shift in quality with
the divine revelation, and that his fear of God deepens, seems a
reasonable conclusion to draw from his "confession."

This conclusion is not indisputable, however. It turns out that
Kierkegaard's young man has led us into a hermeneutical thicket, that
of deciding how to construe the quality of Job's integrity in light of
the book's ending. For instance, Job's restoration can also be read
deconstructively as the reinstatement of the doctrine of retribution
that the divine speeches appeared to shatter; or in Kierkegaardian
terms, as the reabsorption of the religious by the ethical, the
domestication of the transcendent by the social.[47] In other words,
when Job repents, he finally does what the doctrine of retribution
requires and the friends advise: confesses the sin of which his suffering
was a symptom, according to the doctrine (as read—backwards—by
the friends).[48] And he is rewarded by God, winning back from the
appeased Yahweh the goods his good deed (the confession) deserves.

Of course, which reading one chooses may turn on whether one
will entertain the notion that a repetition is really possible. For it
only takes a dialectical twist to render the deconstructionist reading
less toxic. Yes, the doctrine of retribution does seem to have been
reinstated, but, if one can believe it, it has been reinstated only in the
manner of a repetition; that is, only after being filtered through the
dialectic of experience, de-ossified and revivified, no longer to be
taken in naïve immediacy, but taken again by a heart transformed by
its testing.

Similarly, the restoration need not be construed as the religious
being reabsorbed by the ethical; rather, the ethical has been taken up
into the religious and acknowledged as dialectically essential to it. Yes,
the doctrine affirms the pleasure God takes in the good done by the
creature, for doing good relates creature and Creator in good
proportion and so good grows. And the doctrine affirms the divine

---

[47] See, for example, David J. A. Clines, "Deconstructing the Book of Job," *The
Bible as Rhetoric: Studies in Biblical Persuasion and Credibility*, Martin Weaver,
ed. (London: Routledge, 1990), 65-80. The point of the essay is neatly summarized in
Clines's commentary, *Job 1-20*, xlvii. See also Tilley, "God and the Silencing of
Job," 267.

[48] The doctrine of retribution has it that good deeds result in happy
consequences, evil deeds in unhappy consequences, such as suffering and death. To
read the doctrine "backwards" is to reason that any happiness people experience is
the result of goodness on their part, any suffering the result of their sin. As I shall
argue two paragraphs below, the backwards reading does not follow logically from
the doctrine itself.

displeasure at evil, which yields disproportion and disrelationship and so more evil; so it is essential to seek the good and shun the evil. But no, a syllogistic doctrine of retribution is inadequate to the pluriform complexity of human experience, let alone of the universe, or indeed of the divine mind. Yes, sin creates suffering, but no, every instance of suffering, Job's in particular, is not the direct effect of the sufferer's sins.

Or again: yes, dutifully striving to embody divine will in human works—as one would do if one took the doctrine as instruction for one's own practice, rather than as a weapon for judging others— forms the self. But no, ethical striving does not complete it. Yes, God restores and completes Job after Job's confession, conferring upon him the integrity Job sought. But no, chronology need not imply causality. The fact that the restoration is subsequent to Job's confession does not mean that it must be—and the text does not say that it is—a *consequence* of the confession. The restoration may simply be the free gift of God's good pleasure. And we should remember, the wonder may be less whether God freely gave it than where Job got the heart, the integrity, to gladly receive it, if not from God as a free gift.

The way the restoration bears on the status of the doctrine of retribution has raised an important point, one related to the purposes governing our reading in the first place. Of the last two questions (did God give the gift freely and where did Job get the heart to receive it?), Kierkegaard would see the first as the stuff of idle speculation and as a standard means of evading the second. The second is serious because so potentially edifying. By asking how Job got the heart to receive new children gladly, one may be opening the door to do some receiving oneself. In fact, that opening of the door would itself be an increase in receptivity and so a building up of the self.

Still, whether the text actually answers either question is less important to Kierkegaard than that it communicate a passion to ask the second one. Indeed, the passion of reader involvement may be in proportion to the text's opaqueness on certain crucial questions. In any event, something in the way the Book of Job is styled, something Kierkegaard sought to repeat in *Repetition*, clearly signalled to him an edifying intent. We see from that repetitive styling where his hermeneutic investment lies: in inducing a religious passion in the reader.

That is why the young man is a type of Job only to an extent. Not fully identifiable with Job, he, like Constantin, is a reader with possibilities we are likely to share. Standing too close to Job for his own comfort, too close to us for ours, he articulates what might be called Kierkegaard's epidemiological model of scripture: the text carries a contagion; if we read it, we might catch it.

> And yet anxiety comes over me, as if I still did not understand what someday I would come to understand, as if the horror I was reading about was waiting for me, as by reading about it I brought it upon myself, just as one becomes ill with the sickness one reads about. (*R*, 206)

Apparently, for the person willing to entertain it, the possibility of repetition is not without dread.

The horror that the young man refers to, the dreadful prospect he sees looming before him, is what I have already referred to as Job's "ordeal." It is interesting that it is through the young man as anxious observer, i.e., as a type of the passionate reader, that Kierkegaard introduces us to this most decisive category in his description of Job. It is the ordeal that the young man/reader must repeat, if repetition is possible.

It is noteworthy that the ordeal is understood to include the "powerful cries" of "Job's tormented soul." In other words, the ordeal includes the dialogue section of the book, both with its complaints and with Job's announced intent to "take God to court as a child of man does his fellow" (*R*, 206). In a religiously serious reading (i.e., in a canonical one), Kierkegaard makes clear that Job's protests are not to be silenced but must be allowed to reverberate with utmost significance, not unlike the cry of abandonment from the cross.

That makes it more interesting still that Job's ordeal becomes the focus for the dithyrambic praises that so markedly distinguish the young man's voice from Constantin's. At the same time, the voice the young man's paeans most closely resemble is that of Kierkegaard's own authorial persona in the Edifying Discourses, most especially in the Discourse on Job, "The Lord gave, the Lord hath taken away; blessed be the name of the Lord" (from Job 1:21). The similarity in voice can only suggest yet another step in the maieutic intratextuality we saw between *Fear and Trembling* and *Repetition*. We can therefore expect to see the Edifying Discourse work to induce a repetition, just as we have seen *Repetition* serve as edifying discourse. Both texts give us a Job bathed in praise, and a Job praised precisely for the complex form of praise with which he confronts his ordeal. We turn now to inspect the ordeal and the praise more closely, under the continued guidance of Kierkegaard's doxological discourse.

2. Edification, Proverbial Wisdom, and the Fear of God

"It is true of all edification that it must first and foremost produce the *necessary adequate fear*, for otherwise the edification is reduced to an illusion," says Johannes Climacus in describing the relation of edification to religious ordeal.[49] The point is directly relevant to Kierkegaard's Edifying Discourse and the proverb after which it is titled. Whether Kierkegaard chose Job's proverb because it is so selfless a response to loss that we are repulsed by the frightening claim it makes upon us, or because it has been stripped of its fear through mindless parroting, Kierkegaard saw fit to attempt the *tour-de-force* of reading all of Job through it.

It is clear from the young man's astonished question that he was aware of the proverb's potential for being reduced to a cliché.

> Job! Job! O Job! Is that really all you said, those beautiful words: The Lord gave, and the Lord took away; blessed be the name of the Lord?—no more, no less, just as they say "God bless you" when one sneezes! No, you who in your prime were the sword of the oppressed, the stave of the old, and the staff of the brokenhearted, you did not disappoint men when everything went to pieces—then you became the voice of the suffering, the cry of the grief-stricken, the shriek of the terrified, and a relief to all who bore their torment in silence, a faithful witness to all the affliction and laceration there can be in a heart, an unfailing spokesman who dared to lament "in bitterness of soul" and to strive with God. (*R*, 197)

The answer, a categorical "No," points in the direction of another possibility for the proverb. The young man's allusions to Job's protestations in the dialogues shows he knows that more was said indeed, and thus that what was said in the proverb could not have been said in the same vein that "they say 'God bless you' when one sneezes!" It was not a cliché because the life situation out of which it was spoken was not a cliché. In *Job's* mouth the proverb means more. It means more because of who Job is, because of what happens to make him what he is and to show him as he is, or better, because of

---

[49] *CUP*, 231 and 235. "Ordeal" is translated as "trial" in the *Postscript*.

what he *does* with the proverb.[50] This is Kierkegaard's claim at the very outset of the Discourse:

> ...the expression itself is not the guidance, and Job's significance lies not in the fact that he said it, but in the fact that he acted in accordance with it. The expression itself is truly beautiful and worthy of consideration, but if another had used it, or if Job had been different, or if he had uttered it under different circumstances, then the word itself would have become something different—significant, if, as uttered, it would otherwise have been so, but not significant from the fact that he acted in asserting it, so that the expression itself was the action. (*ED*, 7-8)[51]

Job's speaking not only asserts God's blessedness, it performs the blessing. Job not only tells what God has done, the telling relates him to God, identifying God as the one by whom he is confronted and with whom he has to deal in both good and bad. Given the "circumstances," Job's insistence that it is with God that he has to do in the evil he suffers makes for fearsome edification indeed.

What Kierkegaard proceeds to do with the proverb in the Edifying Discourse, and what we heard the young man do in his quotation above (31), is exactly what the Book of Job does with the proverb: namely, narrativize it, fill it out with the story of a life that practices the wisdom it asserts. The book depicts the "circumstances" in light of which we begin to discern this wisdom's dreadful implications. This of course is the canonical intent of Israel's proverbial wisdom, that the proverbs be tried and tested in the lives of the community. Artful distillations of wisdom, they can only serve to make one wise as they are taken by the reader out of the realm of the purely aesthetic and carried into the storm of experience. Proverbs are only validated in that theater of action known as the fear of the Lord.[52] The hermeneutical upshot for the Book of Job is that it be

---

[50]This point corresponds with the Wittgensteinian principle that has been invoked throughout this book and that Kierkegaard enunciated so clearly in the early pages of *Works of Love*—namely, that meaning is in use and that to understand any particular use one needs to see the speech act against the "life situation," what Wittgenstein called the "form of life," of the person performing it. See *WL*, 29f., and chapter 1 above, pp. 7 and 132 n. 37.

[51] *EUD*, 109f.

[52] On the foundational status of the "fear of God" in traditional wisdom, see the prefatory poem in the Book of Proverbs, 1:1-7 (cf. Pss 111:10 and 112:1; Prov 9:10),

read canonically, too, as an experiment in wisdom, the prose in context with the poetry, the proverb in context with the full ordeal.

To narrativize the proverb is to problematize it. No sooner has Job blessed God than we hear him, if not cursing God to his face—as the satan stipulated (1:11, 2:5)—at least cursing God's work, namely, the day of Job's birth, which of course is part of God's creation (3:1-26). Surely, if anyone could make a persuasive case for equating the two, cursing God to his face and cursing his work, it would be the satan, though the matter would no doubt remain problematic. The ensuing dialogues make it nonetheless clear that even in the self-loathing in which Job would annihilate himself, Job knows that it is truly *God* with whom he is dealing. It is "the Almighty's arrows," not the slings of fortune, that pierce him. The "terrors of God" himself are arrayed against him (6:4). It is God who is destroying Job, despite his innocence (9:15, 22). Job insists that God has made him an enemy (13:24 and 19:11)—tearing him, gnashing at him, seizing, dashing, slashing him open to pour his gall upon the ground:

> He breaks me with breach upon breach;
>   he runs upon me like a warrior. (16:9-14)

God has put Job in the wrong (19:6), and therefore it is this accuser God, not some obscure satan or perverse fate, whom Job insists on facing—and who, remarkably, appears.

As Kierkegaard sees it, Job's theocentric obsession in the dialogues is explicit in the proverb's "the *Lord* hath taken away," at least when the proverb is spoken by Job. Thus, part of the proverb's problematization is that it now embraces the dialogues. Or we could say that the dialogues, read canonically, explicate the proverb. At the same time, Kierkegaard observes, in Job's mouth the proverb articulates the fear of God (and is validated as wisdom thereby):

> Was it not a wind-storm from out of the desert which overturned the house and buried his children in the ruins? Did the messenger mention some other perpetrator, or did he name someone who sent the wind? Yet Job said, "The Lord took"; in the very moment of receiving the message, he realized that it was the Lord who had taken everything. Who

---

plus Job 28:28. As evidence that the term refers not just to an emotion state but rather to the manner in which daily life is conducted—that is, to faith-in-action, to obediential striving—see Exod 20:20, Deut 6:2 *et passim*, and Prov 8:13.

told Job this? Or was it not a sign of his fear of God that he thus shifted everything over to the Lord, and justified him in doing it: and are we more devout, we who sometimes hesitate a long time to speak thus? (*ED*, 19-20.)[53]

Kierkegaard's assessment is supported by the narrator in 1:22, and, more impressively, by God in 2:3. Here, in the second audience with the satan, God repeats the question that triggered the whole plot: "Have you considered my servant Job, a blameless and upright man *who fears God* and shuns evil?" (emphasis mine). Now if the proverb implies the dialogues and articulates the fear of God, what of the dialogues and even the curse of chap. 3? Then they, too, with all their protests and laments, must express the fear of God, not least, as we have already seen, because they demonstrate that in all things Job knows that it is God with whom he has to do.

It would appear that in problematizing one cliché (Job's proverb), another cliché, the "fear of God," has been cracked open. Clearly, this is how Kierkegaard's young man reads the matter when he contrasts the paltry fear and sanctimonious smarminess that "does not dare to complain to God" with the brave and awful fear of

unforgettable Job...you powerful spokesman who, fearless as a young lion, appears before the tribunal of the Most High! Your speech is pithy, and in your heart is the fear of God even when you bring complaints.... (*R*, 197f.)

Such fear of God is at the heart of Kierkegaard's description of Job's plight as an ordeal. In general, an ordeal is a situation of such apparent God-forsakenness and in which God's rule seems so unlikely that the God-fearer's response of clinging to God, madly clinging to the God-relationship and insisting on God's sovereign relevance, looks like Godlessness. By conventional standards of piety, it looks like blasphemy. But God takes it as praise. To say any more about the ordeal, we need to look into the dynamics of praise.

3. "Blessed be the Name of the Lord": Praise and the Character of God

Certainly, part of the significance of Job's proverb as an articulation of the fear of God is that it makes praise explicit. Praise

---

[53] *EUD*, 119

is significant because it is an ingredient in the fear of God. Praise makes clear a crucial element of asymmetry in the God-human relationship: the fact that the relationship is initiated by God, draws its strength from God, and is judged, vindicated, and consummated by God. Peculiar as the grammar of fear already appears, apart from this fact of God's priority, it might make no sense at all to speak of fear. But praise gives God God's due, and so is God-fearing.

Further, praise gives God his due gladly, gratefully. Without the element of joyful gratitude, God-fear would not be the fear of *God*, who is the source of value, the initiator of our good, who *is* our good, indeed is Good itself. If the latter is the case, as scripture depicts and believers try to believe, then praise would appear to correspond to something in God's own nature.[54] As an activity of attending to others, affirming their excellence as other, and communicating that excellence so as to raise the objects of attention to their true status and thus "arouse in others the emulation of this,"[55] praise works as God does—performatively, creatively.

Like God, praise creates space for others freely to be themselves, to grow up into themselves, as it were, enlarging their capacities, their sphere of relevance and relationships, and thus their very selves. So, like God, praise is creative. It is also performative, for praising establishes relationship with the one praised. It not only comments on the relationship, the very act adds something new to it. Thus the praise itself becomes part of the relationship. As it does, as praise becomes an item of increased mutual delight and appreciation, it creates space for yet further praise. So praise is itself ever expansive and self-generative in character, again like God. One might even say that as God is love, so God is praise, praise being the linguistic form of love *par excellence*.

The specific form of praise that Job's proverb takes happens to be that of blessing. "Blessing" in the biblical world, far from being a verbal reflex to a sneeze, is one of those power-laden, sometimes quasi-magical, always super-intentional speech acts by which reality itself was believed to be materially influenced. Nearly synonymous with the Hebrew for "praise," *hll*, and often parallel with it, the term "to bless," *brk,* means to influence things for the good.

---

[54] This is the core of Hardy and Ford's thesis in *Praising and Knowing God* (cited above, n. 10). My paragraph summarizing the thesis draws especially from pp. 6-10, 153-163 of their book.

[55] Hardy and Ford, 158.

Therefore, blessing may well be the quintessentially performative doxological speech act, particularly when performed by God. The paradigmatic case would be the blessing God speaks over creation three times in the opening chapters of Genesis (1:22, 28, and 2:3). Blessing is the speech act through which God affirms the world in such a way as to enliven it, bestowing it with potency and freedom. The blessing therefore goes hand-in-hand with God's declaring the world "good." Neither the blessing nor the declaration is a mere afterthought to the creative activity; rather, each is intrinsic to divine creation while integral to the three aspects of creative praise: attending ("God looked/saw"), affirming ("It is good"), and communicating ("be fruitful and multiply," the blessing formula itself). So as part of praise, blessing is the very form of God's creating.

When humans bless, then, it should properly be regarded as a response to God's creative blessing. Indeed, it is the appropriate response to our being created in God's image. As a form of naming (Gen. 2:19f.) and a work of language, our blessing is a sharing in the creative activity of the God who spoke reality into being ("'Let there be...'") with his blessing. In blessing others, we not only "let them be" themselves, but we invite God to be God with them and to grow in them, while creating (as Praise itself), the space that is the widened relationship constituted by the creative speech act. Our blessing thus invokes God's growth into ever new spheres of creation, while registering our participation in "the spiral of mutual appreciation and delight which is the fulfilment of creation."[56]

Now, that humans can bless even *God*, the source and substance of all true blessing, is no oddity. It follows from the superfluity of praise, from the virtuous circularity of the praise that is God's very nature. And bless God is precisely what Job does. He blesses God in response to all that God has given. What is remarkable of course is that he blesses God even in response to God's taking away, as if even that, the taking away, were a function of praise by God (of God's being God).

My argument, like Kierkegaard's, depends on being able to read the taking-away doxologically, as a function of praise. To read it so, recall, would be to read it by the church's Rule of faith, which asks us to read all of scripture by the love of God and as pointing to the love of God. Is it inconsequential, then, that when God steps onto the scene in the Book of Job, and later speaks out of the whirlwind, it is as

---

[56] Hardy and Ford, 82.

one who obviously loves Job? His first words are words of praise, praise for Job's uniqueness and integrity: "Have you considered [lit. "set your heart on"] my servant Job, that there is none like him on the earth, an upright man of integrity, who fears God and shuns evil?"

The interrogative form encourages the satan to attend to Job by fixing his heart upon him in the same way that God has fixed God's heart upon him, with the consequence that surely Job's integrity would be made manifest thereby, and creation's joy enlarged.

4. The Satan and the Curse

It is a suspicious age, or perhaps just a worn-out one, that will read God's question only as the braggadocio of a buffoon or a despot's taunt.[57] The text itself does not demand that construal. That reading comes from what one brings *to* the text, not from what one finds *in* it. It is the projection of a predisposition, the product of a paradigm, of a prior imaginative construal. Of course, the doxological reading is a product too, though it also happens to be one consistent with the broad canonical depiction of God as Creator. The point, however, is this: hermeneutically, we seem to have a choice.[58]

Certainly, our choice, too, can be seen as a function of the freedom with which we have been empowered by God's respectful praise. As readers of the text, the readers implied by the textual world, we are free to respond with suspicion no less than praise. Obviously, as a character within that storied world, Job is also free. According to the grammar sketched thus far, God's praise would effect new possibilities for Job, opportunity either for enhancement and growth in freedom, or for the self-constriction and disintegration that comes from rejecting the praise, from answering blessing with curse. Now, the plot device for the playing out of this freedom, both Job's and ours as readers, is the satan, who is also free to be suspicious.

The role of the satan is easily trivialized. For instance, when the book is viewed as an exercise in theodicy, the invention of the satan is liable to be passed off, as it is by Crenshaw, as just "another means of protecting God's honor"—a bad means, however, since it requires

---

[57] Crenshaw, "The Shift from Theodicy to Anthropodicy," 9f. (cited above, p. 163). Before Crenshaw, the interpretation of God as bully-buffoon was presented by Robertson, "The Book of Job: A Literary Study," (cited above, p. 162 n. 24.)

[58] Recall from chapter 2 our hermeneutic focus text in *WL*, where Kierkegaard says, "Variation in explanation is possible—a choice" (271). The argument of chapter 2 was that reading by the Rule of faith is an exercise in the hermeneutic freedom that all interpretation entails.

"compromising ethical monotheism." Even so the device fails, by this line of thought, since "God is still at fault," the satan being just one of the subalterns in the employ of the divine court.[59] However, if the issue is not defending God but describing him, if it is not assigning blame for evil but learning how to praise in spite of it, the satan's role seems much more interesting, much less contrived. For the satan instantiates the fact that the negative possibilities inherent in our freedom are real, and that at least some of these real possibilities have been actualized, suspicion not the least, cursing one of the worst.

The connection between the satan and cursing is crucial. When the satan responds to God's appeal for praise—first, of course, answering the question with another question[60]—he proposes that Job will curse God if subjected to affliction. Moreover, the very form of his proposal is a curse.[61] The standard translations obscure the point, no doubt because in Hebrew the expression is elliptical. First in the satan's statement, as in the genre generally, is the stipulation of the relevant circumstances: "Only stretch forth thy hand and touch all that he has" (1:11), or, "...his bone and his flesh" (2:5). The point is the revocation of all God's blessings—excepting life itself. Next comes the standard protasis, the negative formulation of which is the generic marker for oaths and curses: "If he does *not* curse thee to thy face..." (identical in 1:11 and 2:5). Whether because too horrible for words or just too obvious, or both, the apodosis is omitted, leaving the protasis dangling. But everyone knows what is implied: "then let the curse be on me," or, in current idiom, "then I'll be damned!"

In terms of its form and logic, then, the satan's proposal is no mere *bet*, which Yahweh takes up on a lark. It is a curse, the most directly, potently antithetical challenge imaginable to the character of God as praise, and of God's creation as praiseworthy. It is in fact, as a speech act, the exact antithesis to blessing. All the features of blessing—its attending to the other, its determination of value, its communication of love, and its person-making and self-expanding nature—are negatively mirrored in the curse. Just as praise is the

---

[59] Crenshaw, "Shift from Theodicy to Anthropodicy," 11.

[60] The Hebrew term שָׂטָן may not exactly mean "attorney," as some have suggested. (See Clines's discussion in *Job*, 19-21). Nevertheless, the satan certainly thinks like one.

[61] This is a feature typically neglected by the commentators. Clines recognizes the form of the oath in the satan's speech, of which the curse is a sub-genre, but makes little of it (*Job*, 26-30). To my knowledge, only Edwin Good has fully explored the implications ("Job: A Response," 475-82).

paradigmatic linguistic form of love, so cursing is the paradigmatic
linguistic form of hatred:

> At the heart of hatred is the phenomenon of the curse....The
> curse is the meaning of hatred come to its point of greatest
> intensity....In its intensity it concentrates the identity of both
> curser and accursed; for in the act of cursing there is a whole-
> hearted other-directedness which commits the very self of the
> curser in the relationship of hatred.[62]

The self-committal mentioned here is reflected in the (elided)
apodosis of the curse formula ("then I'll be damned!"). Certainly, part
of the significance of the character of the satan, especially as later
developed in apocalyptic literature, is this personal, subjective,
agentic quality of evil, which though imperial and cosmic in
dimension is nevertheless *not* God and is characterologically distinct
from God. Relatedly, as a *supra*-personal, cosmic entity, the heavenly
figure of the satan represents the objective, oppositional status of evil
over against God. He is the narrative attestation that evil as a real
possibility of creation has in fact been historically actualized and now
exists as a ubiquitous environment threatening to suffocate blessing at
every turn, and which blessing must overcome even to be spoken.[63]

Exactly how that historical actualization of the possibility of
opposing praise ever occurs in the first place is a mystery.[64] That is
the relevance of reading Job in canonical relation to Genesis 2-3,
which shows not *how* evil is possible but rather *that it is* and what it's
like as an experienced actuality. (The presence of the serpent, being
one of God's creatures, does not explain the mystery; he is part of it.)
The Garden story witnesses to the fact that human life is, tragically,
lived under a curse, a curse that once actualized becomes potent and

---

[62] Hardy and Ford, 100.

[63] Accordingly, we may not be so free to praise as earlier I suggested (see above,
p. 184). We may well be trapped in suspicion—or at least profoundly disposed to
it—by the environment of the curse. (I owe this observation to my friend and
colleague, Garvin Davenport.) Whether and how we *can* praise, and of course
whether and how we can even *read* doxologically, can thus become an existential
question for us.

[64] Johannes Climacus says that every becoming, every instance of possibility's
becoming actuality, is a mystery. See *Philosophical Fragments*, Edna and Howard
Hong, trans. and eds. (Princeton: Princeton University Press, 1985), 72-86; and
CUP, 86-113.

self-actualizing. The satan of Job's story narratively confirms that witness.

In terms of the logic of our story, then, and as the opposite number to blessing, the satan's curse is a powerful, self-actualizing, reality-shaping word-event. That means, it will generate plot. The satan is capable of naming his game and stipulating the rules, and Yahweh, the sponsor of blessing, will continue to play. But the authority of cursing is not itself ultimate, since it owes its own possibility to praise. Thus the satan cannot stipulate *all* the rules, and we see in 1:12 and 2:6 God setting limits on the chaos the curse can work. But to be true to God's own character as non-coercive praise, God cuts the satan his slack and lets the game run. To do otherwise would be to grant cursing (and determinacy) the victory over blessing (and freedom). So a contest, a struggle, is set in motion, and the relevant question is: Is there a blessing that can meet cursing without being itself transformed into a curse?[65]

5. Ordeal and the Paradigmatic Exception

We are at last in a position to see the pertinence of Kierkegaard's category of the ordeal. At one level it seems obvious, for an ordeal is precisely what the working out of the plot will mean for Job. Job is the battleground between curse and blessing, the place where the integrity of praise is to be tested. God's praise, spoken into a condition in which cursing is an active reality comprehensively structuring the affairs of men and women, makes trouble for Job. We begin to get a fuller sense of Kierkegaard's understanding of "ordeal" when we note that Job's situation foreshadows a later ordeal in the Gospel of Mark when the divine confirmation of the apocalyptic hero (1:11) occasions all hell to break loose against him, beginning with "Satan" in 1:13, followed by a procession of demonic and human opponents, all leading to the crucifixion.

Recall that Kierkegaard situates the ordeal in the sphere of uniquely religious experience. A struggle is an "ordeal" precisely when it takes one beyond the ethical. As the young man says,

> This category...is not esthetic, ethical, or dogmatic....[It] is absolutely transcendent and places a person in a purely personal relationship of opposition to God, in a relationship

---

[65] Hardy and Ford, 101.

such that he cannot allow himself to be satisfied with any explanation at second hand. (*R*, 210)

"Dogmatic" here would refer to religious doctrines. Included of course would be the doctrine of retribution, that conviction of Job, his friends, and the rest of ancient Israel's sages that sin leads to suffering and righteousness to life, or should. But even doctrines are really part of Kierkegaard's ethical sphere insofar as the "ethical" includes all socially objectivated knowledge of existential import, anything that can claim "universal" or "eternal" validity and require personal commitment (even when the claim and requirement are recognized only within a specific interpretive community).[66]

Accordingly, much of what conventionally passes as religious belief and behavior, though genuinely *part* of the religion, is not *uniquely* religious. There is always the possibility that one may be encountered by the Absolute, God, in such a way as to put one at odds with the "universals" that norm our understanding of God but are not identical with God. The encounter would put one in conflict with the conventions that aim to invoke God but cannot contain him. The person, the "one" so encountered, would be an exception, a peerless enigma to his "peers," perhaps even to himself, to whom now even God appears alien. His paradoxically exceptional situation is the ordeal.

Canonically, the appropriateness of the category "ordeal" is illustrated by Kierkegaard's having applied it also to the Abraham-Isaac episode. In doing so he was following the biblical writers who used the concept in verbal form in the story's superscription: "And God tested (*nissah*) Abraham" (Gen 22:1). At stake in the ordeal/test is Abraham's ethical integrity as a member of his community (his household and descendants, the people Israel), for whom killing one's child is murder, and killing *Isaac* is betraying God's Promise. The Promise is a dogmatic category and the focal point of Abraham's covenantal relationship with God. Hence Silentio speculates that had Abraham performed the sacrifice, he may have had relationship with God, but he would have had difficulty talking with Sarah—to say nothing of losing sweet communion with Moses, David, Isaiah, etc.

Although the author of Job does not use "ordeal" explicitly, the concept is nevertheless implicit, embedded parabolically in the narrative structure that counterposes heavenly scenes to earthly ones. Specifically, it is implicit in the satan's curse, which, unknown to Job,

---

[66] On "universal," see Evans, 59-61 and 73-75.

generates the earthly action. The curse is thus analogous to the superscription that sets up the dramatic irony for Abraham. In other words, the satanic oath is a fictive expression for the "ordeal." Clearly, its logic is as transcendent as its setting. From the human point of view, the curse is not only unheard but inexplicable, having virtually magical efficacy. One incants the formula and it goes into effect, God knows how or why. Once again, Job's ordeal is a function of the curse, which is a response to God's praise.

The category of the ordeal is also apt in highlighting the theme of the "exception" and a curious pattern of substitution[67] that grows out of it. As the characters in *Repetition* and Kierkegaard in his *Edifying Discourse* all repeat, Job is exceptional.[68] The ordeal singles him out. It makes him an exception to the conventional wisdom that one suffers because of sin, and his exceptionality singles him out for ridicule, which isolates him further. He is exceptional as a *mortal* whose judicial oath (chap. 31) can summon even God to take the stand. He is exceptional in holding to his integrity so faithfully that when God answers him, he can confess God to be in the right, honestly—that is, without becoming demonic, without gulling God.[69] Kierkegaard holds, with the young man, that Job is exceptional as one who is in the right by virtue of God's putting him in the wrong. The ordeal turns out to be the stuff of paradox.

> The secret in Job, the vital force, the nerve, the idea, is that Job, despite everything is in the right. On the basis of this position, he qualifies as an exception....The explanation is this: the whole thing is an *ordeal*. (*R*, 207, 209)

So says the young man, and for Kierkegaard, too, everything turns on the fact that Job is innocent. As we have seen, prologue and epilogue confirm him in this. The whole ordeal presupposes Job's innocence; otherwise it would not be called an ordeal.

Moreover, the category is appropriate in that it allows the reader to distinguish between a generalized human guilt, which our text and Job himself acknowledge (4:17, 9:2, 14:4, 25:4), and the sin-

---

[67] On this pattern of substitution, see below, pp. 194-198.

[68] *R*, 207-10, 226-28; *ED*, 25 (*EUD*, 123).

[69] The interpretation of Job's confession as rebellion-in-disguise, an ironic jest, was offered first by David Robertson (see above, n. 24), then by Elie Wiesel in *Messengers of God*, Marion Wiesel, trans. (New York: Random House, 1976), 235. For Kierkegaard's discussion of the demonic, see *R*, 207, and *SUD*, 72-74.

consciousness that Christians tend so readily to project upon both book and Job. But the latter, sin-consciousness, is a category peculiar to the Christ-event, Kierkegaard believed, and thus pertains to a subsequent stage in the divine-human relationship—or the history of salvation, if you will—than that which the OT Book of Job addresses.

The difference between guilt and sin-consciousness corresponds to the difference between Kierkegaard's "Religion A" and "Religion B."[70] In the former a person knows guilt to the degree he recognizes the "infinite difference" between himself and the goodness of God. He recognizes that he has fallen short and that it may be a long, long stretch before he even begins to achieve the total reliance on God that constitutes human righteousness, our right-relatedness to God. But for him the question is how long the stretch is, not whether one can eventually make it—that is, until one reaches the upper limits of the stretching. Then doubts begin to emerge as to whether God-relatedness is an immanent capacity, whether the infinite difference might not be an "infinite *qualitative*" one. However, it is only in the encounter with the God-Incarnate, in Religion B, that one recognizes this to be the case in fact. Here one realizes the extent of the damage sin has done, how utterly incapacitating it has been. In Christ it is revealed that one has to rely on God even to be able to rely on God, and, in Christ, God accomplishes for us that act of self-emptying God-reliance. For the Christian, then, guilt is magnified into a sin-consciousness that only God in Christ can resolve.

The story of Job is not *un*related to the story of sin-consciousness and its resolution, but it is not the *same* as that story. It may prepare one for that story, by showing that the God-relationship goes beyond ethical categories and dogmatic definitions, but it does so by positing Job's innocence. It may foreshadow and prefigure the other story (e.g., see above, p. 187), but it does so by positing Job as the righteous sufferer of life under the curse. It is *not* a story about Job coming to a recognition of sin. Thus, through the category of the ordeal, Kierkegaard helps us to read the OT with Christian interests but without crudely Christianizing it or assimilating its terms to those of the NT.

But if the book is not about Job's coming to recognize himself as sinner, what is it of which he "repents" in 42:5-6? As we saw earlier

---

[70] The discussion here owes much to Gouwens, *Kierkegaard's Dialectic*, 232. For Kierkegaard's (Climacus's) formulation of the relation between Religions A and B, see *CUP*, 493-98.

in this chapter, this is a classic crux in the interpretation of the Book of Job. How is Job's "confession" to be understood?

Job's words are not a confession of sin, I have argued. Rather, as Charles Muenchow contends, they are a confession of shame. In the agonistic societies of the Mediterranean, to "repent upon dust and dirt" was a stereotypic gesture for expressing shame before the greater honor of another whose integrity one had contested.[71] The case holds even more obviously for Job's self-silencing in 40:4-5.[72] Job had imagined the world to operate by an order whereby his suffering implied the enmity of God and a hostile assault upon Job's own integrity. Job thought he was being dishonored, shamed, by God. His misconstrual pits order against order, honor against honor, his against God's.

"Who is this that darkens counsel by words without knowledge?" Yahweh asks (38:2). Job's initial curse had sought to roll creation back into primeval "darkness" (3:3-10), to rouse the chaos monster, "Leviathan" (3:8), and so obscure God's historical intention in Creation, i.e., God's "counsel."[73] Misreading the doctrine of retribution as he did, Job felt wronged, and in his hurt he wanted to relocate blame (chaps. 21, 24), correcting injustice, he believed, but in fact only threatening more disorder. Thus Yahweh questions, "Would you really annul my order ["justice," $mišpat$]? Must you make me out to be wicked for yourself to be righteous?" (40:8).

Muenchow is right, God's whirlwind tour of Creation serves to rebuke and thus shame Job,[74] but it does so by revealing to Job something of Creation's truer order, the grander scope of it, than Job from his mortal perspective and through the lens of curse-inflicted grief can perceive. The strategy is not just one of intimidation. God's rhetorical questions serve to re-focus Job's mind, not unlike the effect on Dickens's Scrooge of the spectre's pointing finger. The questions call Job to attention, and they focus his attention away from the self,

---

[71] On the word-pair ʿapār waʾēper per Muenchow cites Gen. 18:27, Job 30:19, and Sirach 40:3, in all of which the expression connotes humble or diminished status relative to another. Apart from Job 42:6, these are the only attestations. See "Dust and Dirt in Job 42:6," *Journal of Biblical Literature,* 108 (1989), 608f.

[72] The general connection between shame and praise will be made below. On silence as a specific and primary mode of praise, see Hardy and Ford, 21.

[73] On this reading and the rest of this paragraph, see Good, 479-81.

[74] Muenchow, 607.

which already works a kind of liberation,[75] onto the riot of nature—consider the ostrich, of all things! (39:13-18), not to mention the mountain goat, wild ass, war horse and hawk—and onto a radically de-anthropomorphized world where "rain falls on the desert where no one lives, to satisfy wasteland and make the ground put forth grass" (38:26-27). And with all the detail of imagery and its value-laden language ("satisfy"), the questions cannot help but communicate the good that God sets upon this kaleidoscopic scene which extends so far beyond the human vista. It is the encyclopedic praising of the Psalms Job hears,[76] rather pointedly addressed at him. Finally, in the climactic peroration, God's praise is lavished even on Leviathan (chap. 41), the Chaos that Job (and the satan) would have unleashed with cursing but could not and cannot because God has been restraining it from the beginning even until now.

The order of Creation turns out to *be* praise, when seen from the divine perspective. The abundance of its riotous inexplicability, its very riotousness, belongs to God's *mišpat* as a quality of *non*-order that is essential to praise.[77] There is in this non-order a principle of laughter, a spontaneous overflow of play and enjoyment, that reflects something of the divine purpose, a purpose obscure to the lately-arrived Job but attested at the world's foundation "when the morning stars sang together and all the sons of God shouted for joy" (38:7). To quote G. K. Chesterton, "One cannot help feeling...that they [the stars] must have had something to shout about."[78]

But Job would have replaced the greater *mišpat* of God's non-order with a usurpative over-ordering of his own. Consequently, God's praise shames him. As is generally the case, so here: God's praise works to recreate proper order, raising reality to its true status and clarifying the lines of relationship within it. God rectifies Job, and,

---

[75] See Hardy and Ford, 84: "Praise takes one out of oneself into enjoyment of God, and into appreciating and sharing his desires for the world. The focus is on God, his will, and other people, and there is a liberation from concern for self."

[76] Patrick Miller recalls Gerhard von Rad's having related Job 38f. with the doxological hymn Ps. 148. Both texts reflect the propensity in wisdom literature for cataloguing the elements of creation. See Miller's "Enthroned on the Praises of Israel: The Praise of God in the Old Testament," *Interpretation*, 39 (1985), 14.

[77] See Hardy and Ford, 7, 96-99, where they distinguish "non-order" from "disorder."

[78] G. K. Chesterton, "Man Is Most Comforted by Paradoxes," in *Job: A Study and Selected Readings*, Nahum N. Glatzer, ed. (New York: Schocken Books, 1969), 235 (abridged version of Chesterton's original introduction to *The Book of Job* [London, 1916]).

anthropologically speaking, shame is the characteristic response to such rectification. "The phenomenon of shame," Muenchow argues, "is broader than just the feeling of being acutely embarrassed. It is a recognition of the legitimacy of the relative distribution of power and privilege in a given society."[79] Theologically, too, Job's shame behavior is a recognition of who is who in the relationship and what is what. Hence the appropriateness of the vision metaphor in 42:5: "I had heard of thee by the hearing of the ear, but now my eyes see thee...." Again, Muenchow:

> In "seeing" Yahweh, Job also knows undeniably that he himself has been seen for what he is and must now admit to being—a mere creature of lowly status in the eyes of his lord.... And yet as a final note, one must return to the fact that Yahweh has bothered with Job enough to shame him.[80]

That final point—that Yahweh has bothered with Job enough to shame him—is part of the paradox of which the young man spoke in *Repetition*: God honors Job in rectifying him, justifies him even while putting him in the wrong. In the contest of honor, it was not a judicial verdict Job was after so much as it was some response by God to his complaints. "Response itself is recognition, and recognition is the *sine qua non* of honor."[81] God's response, even in the form of an indictment, would be for Job a badge of honor, as he says in his climactic oath:

> Oh, that I had one to hear me!
> Here is my signature! Let the Almighty answer me!
> Oh, that I had the indictment written by my adversary!
> Surely, I would carry it on my shoulder,
> bind it on me as a crown.
> I would give him an account of all my steps;
> like a prince I would approach him. (31:35-36)

God's speeches, then, are the effective recognition of Job's honor, to which of course Yahweh was committed from the first.

So Job's shaming is a kind of backhanded praise from God. But, typical of praise, there is a reciprocity by which the praise is

---

[79] Muenchow, 610, n. 57.
[80] Muenchow, 611.
[81] On this point and the following verses (31:35f.), see Muenchow, 606.

expanded. Job's shame behavior, his silence and self-prostration, are the returning of the praise to God. Job has been overwhelmed by God's praise, and he responds with the most primal gestures of worship.

But we need to return to the exceptionality of Job's laudatory innocence, part of which is its "repetition." Recall, it is Job's innocence that occasions the ordeal in the first place. And Job was praised as *uniquely* innocent: "There is none like him," insists Yahweh, *twice*. Thus Job not only suffers undeservedly; he suffers because he is the best. At the conclusion, Job's integrity is repeated by virtue of being re-established by God's praise, wonderfully reconstituted by God's direct revelation, and thus received anew by Job. Clearly, in all of this Job is exceptional. But as the exception he is also, paradoxically, a paradigm. Johannes Climacus best states the peculiarity of the situation as it applies to the ordeal in general:

> ...the religious paradigm is an irregularity and yet is supposed to be the paradigm (which is like God's omnipresence being evidenced by His invisibility, and a revelation being through a mystery). The religious paradigm expresses not the universal but the particular (the irregular, the exceptional...), and yet it is assumed to be paradigmatical. But to be a paradigm is precisely to be for all, and one can surely be a pattern for all only by being that which all are or ought to be, i.e., the universal; and yet the *religious paradigm* is precisely the opposite (the irregular and the exceptional).... (*CUP*, 231)

So the religious paradigm is a "set" of one who is taken as a representative for all who are unlike him. Certainly, the young man discerned Job's paradigmatically representative status when he praised him as "a *faithful* witness to all the affliction and laceration there can be in a heart" (*R*, 197f., my emphasis). That is, he praises Job as one whose heart, by complaining to God for brothers and sisters who suffer in silence, bears the fear of God. And we have already seen how Job himself generalized his plight, seeing in his case the human case: "Indeed there is hope for a tree....But man dies and is laid low...and rises not again....So thou destroyest the hope of man" (14:7-19).[82] Similarly in the Discourse, Kierkegaard observes that for the readership passionate enough to see him so, for all struggling and striving individuals, "Job is again present, takes his place, which is the

---

[82] See above, p. ??? ("And just as the rhetoric..." [re: Crenshaw]).

outpost of humanity" (*ED*, 7). Taking his stand thus, Job as it were stands *in* for humanity, as a kind of substitute.

Again, Job's role as representative, i.e., as a substitute, is textually reinforced by reading the epilogue in canonical relation to the dialogues. The silence of shame is not in fact the last word we hear from Job, for God assigns him that peculiarly substitutionary task of interceding for his friends: "Now therefore take seven bulls and seven rams," God instructs the counsellors,

> for you have not spoken rightly of me, as my servant Job has, ...and go to my servant Job, and offer up for yourselves a burnt offering; and my servant Job shall pray for you, for I will accept his prayer not to deal with you according to your folly; for you have not spoken rightly of me, as my servant Job has." ...[A]nd the Lord accepted Job's prayer. And the Lord restored the fortunes of Job, when he had prayed for his friends. And the Lord gave Job double what he had before. (42:7-10)

Four times in short order Yahweh refers to Job as "my servant," doubling the number of times he uses the epithet in the prologue. Apparently, intercession is part of Job's service to God. Job's prayer will, mysteriously, i.e., by God's good pleasure ("grace" in NT parlance), render the sacrificial service of the foolish friends acceptable. In fact, Job's intercessory service stands in for them as proper praise, as paradigmatic perfecter of their praise.[83]

Further, as the paradigm of human righteousness, Job serves to represent even God. Indeed, God puts him forward to the satan as the paradigm of God's fear. There is, it would seem, a theodicy to be performed after all. And Job will perform it, not of course by defending God's honor and reputation, as if God were constituted by passive attributes to be seized and argued in the abstract, but by actively representing God's passion for human well-being and God's passionate interest in the relation that humans bear to God (a relation which is part of God's self, by Kierkegaardian definition). Job will perform a theodicy as he manifests the reality of God's presence, which is what the biblical writers from Isaiah and Ezekiel, through the Priestly school of the Pentateuch, down to John the Evangelist and the Apostle Paul, called "glorifying" God. Job's will be a theodicy of praise.

---

[83] On intercession as praise, see Hardy and Ford, 16.

As might be guessed, this is a theodicy that also accomplishes an anthropodicy. Perhaps the climactic way in which Job represents God's passionate interest in humankind is in letting God be God-for-us, precisely by asking God to vindicate him. Job justifies God by letting God justify him, which, as we have noted before, is the only way a human *can* be justified. Moreover, God does it. God accepts Job and all Job's speaking as right-speaking of God. Even though *objectively* it smacked of blasphemy, scandalized the sages, mistook the order of the world, and even took the form of a curse, God took it as praise. But of course, *objectively*, God does not exist.[84]

6. *Euphemism, Hope, and Canonical Witness*

Lest the substitutionary logic that I see running rampant through the Book of Job appear, as it were, too subjective, two small textual notes should be considered. In 1:5 a euphemism is introduced reflecting a piece of conventional Israelite piety. To explain why Job would regularly perform intercession for his children, the narrator cites Job's words, "It may be that my sons have sinned and cursed God in their hearts." Or that is the gist.

In fact, in place of the word "curse" (*qll*) stands "blessed" (*brk*). Wisdom had it that the fear of the Lord requires right–speaking of God, and to speak rightly of God is to *bless* the Name. So antithetical to God's nature was the idea of cursing that the very word is not to be used in proximity to the Holy One, blessed be His Name. Accordingly, the biblical authors/redactors "build a hedge around the law," as the rabbis say, and substitute the God-fearing "bless" for its dangerous opposite. As proof that this is not merely the author's way of expressing Job's particular scrupulosity, or of suggesting that he was pharisaically *over*-scrupulous (a too familiar Christian reading), the euphemism occurs even in the satan's speech—"and if he does not *bless* thee to thy face..."— "bless" for "curse," twice of course (1:11 and 2:5).

Thus, in a book whose plot is whether humans can bless God in their hearts and whose theme is precisely what counts as genuine blessing, the text plots and thematizes itself in the most concrete yet vertiginous way imaginable. It substitutes "bless" for "curse" in the interest of keeping faith, of disciplining the self in the fear of God, but the substitution yields a situation in which blessing stands in for cursing and literally *is* cursing (in the most literal sense of "literally").

---

[84] See above, p. 155 and n. 9.

The text unleashes the question—and the friends provide evidence for an answer in the affirmative—whether what conventionally passes for blessing might not be cursing in disguise.[85] But if so, might not there be the opposite prospect, that what looks the part of cursing may be a hidden form of blessing? It is a cursed situation indeed in which none of the conventional answers suffice for making a clean discrimination. Whatever it is that Job offers, however, the text shows God cutting through the confusion to declare it his praise, as if by final clarifying substitution.

But that is Job's story, the story of God's response to Job, which can become a conventional answer itself. The problem of self-referentiality brought on by the euphemism means that the text cannot confine its own question. The question having been unleashed, it spills out beyond the textual borders, calling the text's own answer into question. Readers can only hope that the Yahweh who answers Job might be their God, too, who substitutes his blessing for and against the curse. The prospect of hope brings us to the second textual note.

It comes in 13:15, another interpretive crux. Job is declaring his intention to "take my flesh in my teeth" (v. 14) and take God to court, so as to "defend my ways to his face" (15b). This he will do, the context implies, despite overwhelming odds, despite the fact that the deck is stacked entirely against him and that all the power is on the side of the prosecution. Now, in v. 15a the Hebrew consonantal text reads, and the RSV translates, according to what we would expect from the context: "Behold he will slay me; I have no hope." To be precise, the consonantal text has לֹא, which indicates the negative particle *lō'*, "not" or "no." The Masoretes, however, who vocalized the text to create what for Rabbinic Judaism became the *textus receptus*, recommend reading the particle as the preposition *lĕ* plus the third masculine singular objective suffix *ô*, with the resultant sense, "I will hope *in him*"! Most of the ancient versions, including the Greek Septuagint and the Latin Vulgate, follow the masoretic recommendation, as do various English translations (e.g., KJ, NIV).

Notice that what the masoretic reading would do is substitute the exact opposite sense for the original. In all fairness, however, this should not be represented, as sometimes is done, as a flat-out

---

[85] To be precise, the text itself does not ask this question. It "unleashes" it only insofar as its substitution of terms prompts readers to reflect on the logic of the substitution.

obscuring of the text the Masoretes received.[86] The masoretic practice was not to alter or efface what was given but to add to it by registering a proposed reading in the margin. Called *kĕtîb-qĕrê*, the practice was a way of annotating the text, somewhat analogous to footnoting. And that is what we have here. If there is an effort to obscure, it is at the level of translation, both those earlier ones that centralize the marginal note, and the later ones that scorn its witness.

What I would argue is that this particular *kĕtîb-qĕrê* is a significant canonical witness. It witnesses to the fact that, for the religiously interested reader, the issues of the text do spill over its borders and that how we read does indeed make demands on what we bring to the text and how we live when we leave it. The Masoretes' marginal, bordering on extra-textual, witness represents a reading informed by innumerable liturgical and ethical factors. It reflects an overall construal of scripture as pointing to the love and wisdom and praiseworthiness of God. Informed by that construal, it reflects an editorial grasp of both the beginning and ending of the book, and of the book's place in the larger testimony of the canonical corpus. Notably, in the Jewish canon Job comes immediately after, in the Christian canon immediately before, the Psalter. The Psalter includes a wide assortment of hymns, supplications, bitter laments, even vituperative complaints, that despite their variety are collectively called and canonically conceived as *tehillîm*, i.e., "Praises." Thus, they are to be read and repeated as offerings of the full human self to God.

However intentional or unintentional the placement of the two books may be, there seems to be a shared spirit shaping both Psalter and Job. It is that spirit the community of faith seeks to embrace in its reading. The masoretic note in Job 13:15 is a witness of faith to what can be called the canonical sense of the text of scripture, what for centuries of Jewish and Christian readers was the literal sense: that God will bring hope out of hopelessness, and that therefore we best read hopefully, and in the spirit of praise.

But spirit is elusive. The more one talks about it, the more slippery it gets. On this point Kierkegaard should have the penultimate word. In the introduction to the Discourse (*ED*, 11-13),[87] he praises not only Job, but the reader whose life most accords with Job and who thereby interprets Job's text with her life, in

---

[86] So Tilley, "God and the Silencing of Job," 258f., following Marvin Pope, *Job*, The Anchor Bible 15, 3rd edition (Garden City: Doubleday, 1973), xliv-xlv.

[87] *EUD*, 111-13.

circumstances of her own testing and not another's. Only such a person "interprets the word correctly," he confesses. And he contrasts that existential understanding of the word, in which one's life interprets the word such that she never need even speak of it, with the prolixity of "the one who spent a whole lifetime in explaining this one word."

The latter of course is himself. It is his own "human wisdom," "eloquence," and "fluency" that he denigrates in the closing paragraph of his prelude. The effect is to refuse the reader the luxury of resting with another—even Kierkegaard's own—"explanation" of the word. For the unappropriated verbal understanding proves a deception. At the same time, he salvages a margin of utility for his writing, that process of reflective communication to which he and we are consigned. If the reader take care "not to ensnare himself in the splendid words of human persuasiveness," those words might at least help position him to appropriate Job when the right circumstances arise: "Perhaps the reflection would sometime become significant to him." With that slighting self-justification, Kierkegaard dares to interpret Job.

In the final chapter, we shall see another example of this tendency of Kierkegaard's to ironically cancel himself while justifying himself, in the service of the reader's edification. Meanwhile, to conclude this chapter, we should note that his emphasis on life as the medium for interpreting the word has returned us to the reading-loving-living nexus developed throughout this book.

To read "scripture," Kierkegaard showed us in chapter 1, one has to answer Christ's call to "follow me"; to perceive and understand the love of which scripture speaks, one has to "go and do likewise." In chapter 2 he reminded us that making sense of scripture is a matter of matching deeds to words *à la* James 1:22. Scripture is to be practiced—and it exists *for* practice, for practice in the art of interpreting one's neighbor in love. We learned in chapter 3 that practice with both scripture and neighbor would involve attentive silence, mitigating explanations, and forgiveness, so as to cover the multiplicity of sins (1 Peter 4:8). Then, in chapter 4, the focus was the confidence of a humble receptivity and gratitude toward God, by which all things can be seen as good gifts (James 1:17), including scripture and one's neighbor. And now this chapter has added praise to the list of love's components: a spirit of doxology in confronting the hard sayings of scripture and in embracing the ordeals of life. The hermeneutics of love is a rich mix—almost too much to imagine.

It is to this extravagant task of imagining that we turn now for a final word on Kierkegaard, scripture, and the Rule of faith.

Chapter 6

POSTSCRIPT: THE CANONICAL IMAGINATION

Given Kierkegaard's penchant for paradox, it was inevitable that a study of his use of scripture should have turned out to be a study of the problematics of Christian reading. These problematics were referred to as the "embarrassments" of the Rule of faith in chapter 2, and they reappeared in such forms as the conflict between giving and covering offense in chapter 3, the "conundrum of sorrow" in chapter 4, and the "double binds" of chapter 5. Deeply implicated in each instance was the imagination. As Kierkegaard was well aware, a fierce dialectic of the imagination was working itself out throughout his corpus.[1] I promised in the Introduction to return for some closing comments on that dialectic. Let me attempt to do that now by way of summary. In the process we will review the workings of the imagination at a variety of levels, the scope of the imagination when it is put to work in the context of the canon, and finally the perennial threat the imagination poses to faithful reading, as illustrated in the person of Kierkegaard.

From the outset it was emphasized that to read the Bible as canonical "scripture," in contrast to reading it as a "classic," was to choose one *"imaginative* construal" over another. There is a definite logic to the terminology. By construal we mean *Gestalt*, the large-scale, overall conception one has of the Bible, what one sees it *as*. Insofar as neither construal, scripture or classic, is inevitable, there is an element of freedom in their adoption. If the reader is at all self-aware, he or she makes a choice between them, and choosing among options entails *imagining* them: comparing them in the mind's eye,

---

[1] The definitive study of Kierkegaard's dialectic of the imagination is David Gouwens's book of that title (New York: Peter Lang, 1989), to which I have referred throughout the present work and which reappears in the notes below.

grasping their forms, projecting the processes and probable effects of their application. This is part of what it means to call the construals "imaginative."[2]

Another part of what it means is that any given construal consists of one or more dominant *images*. In the case of scripture, we have argued, the Rule of faith prescribes a constellation of images summarized under the rubric of the love of God, the paradigm of which is provided by the gospel story of Jesus. Images being the stuff of story, the construal of the Bible as scripture is irreducibly, inescapably, inexhaustibly imaginative.[3] That implies a degree of persistent open-endedness in interpretation. No discursive, propositional formulation of the Rule of faith can so circumscribe any one of the gospel's images as to preclude further argument over its meaning, even within the context of the canon and the community of faith.

Why has it been necessary to insist on this point? Partly to answer various critics of the postmodern canon-contextual approach to scriptural exegesis, who claim that this approach remains, like pre-critical orthodoxies, oppressively closed-ended, "dogmatic" in the pejorative sense. But also to answer Brevard Childs, the father of the approach, who gives the critics their window of opportunity when he writes the following about the "new Yale theology":

> ...I am critical of any theological method which speaks of the Bible as a type of literary or symbolic construct (e.g. narrative, realistic novel, classic), but does not feel

---

[2] These examples do not begin to exhaust the scope of the term "imagination" in either Kierkegaard or this book. To quote Gouwens,

...the imagination proves to be not a simple capacity, but a dialectically complex concept that can name an activity, a capacity or faculty, a long-term disposition of a person, a medium (especially the poet's medium), and a passion. (6)

...Kierkegaard looks beyond the surface of imagining to discover the immense differences in the *contexts* of being imaginative. ...The "imagination" is finally not adequately understood if it is seen merely as the name for a discrete internal activity or process, or for a form of consciousness. In contemporary terms, the imagination cannot be understood apart from attending to the different contexts of the imagination's uses; to understand the imagination, we must attend not only to "what" one imagines, but to "how" a person imagines. ...So too, the difference between any form of aestheticized Christianity...and ethico-religious existence is in the "how." (278, my emphasis)

[3] This is part of what it means to do "narrative" theology within the context of the canon. Canon-contextual criticism must take the irreducibly imagistic, and thus imaginative, quality of scripture with utmost seriousness.

constrained to engage in continuous exegesis of the Bible itself as the indispensable ground for all Christian theological reflection. For a variety of theological reasons I find it basically unsatisfactory to assign the Bible a subordinate role with the creative imagination of the church where it functions merely as a source of imagery without a determinate meaning.[4]

There is little in Childs's statement I would disagree with. Certainly, promoting "continuous exegesis" has been a key objective of this book, and practicing it has been, I trust, conspicuous in the method. As for the second sentence, far from subordinating the Bible to the creative imagination of the church, I have argued that giving scripture its due as *formative* of the church's creative imagination involves recognizing that the relationship between the two, scripture and imagination, is nonetheless dialectical.

The area of ambiguity, or dispute, is with Childs's phrase "a determinate meaning." Obviously, imagery without any meaning is *not* what the canon is about. Scripture's concern with historical particularity and extra-textual realities is too pronounced for that to be the case. Moreover, we have spoken of how context helps to establish an expression's literal sense. In the context of the canon—a context broadly conceived as entailing liturgical, devotional and ethical activities, plus a whole host of human dispositions, all of which help constitute an interpretive community—a reasonable consensus can often be reached on the literal sense of a biblical image or text. Or so I have argued. What context cannot do is limit an image/text's meaning to one meaning, and thereby make meaning *fully* "determinate." The practical upshot is that the canon may settle some arguments over what a piece of scripture means, and what it means to be a Christian, but it cannot settle all of them. Differences rooted in image and imagination will remain.[5]

In any case, Kierkegaard was not one to understate the role of the imagination in the Christian reading of scripture. As we saw in the focus text for chapter 2 (the "love sleuth" passage from "Love Covers the Multiplicity of Sins"), *Works of Love* was as much a panegyric to the imagination as it was to love, for the simple reason

---

[4] Childs, *The New Testament as Canon: An Introduction* (Philadelphia: Fortress, 1984), 545f.

[5] See above, pp. 66 n. 29, 71 and 75f. n. 50, for my earlier statements of this argument.

that love is a work of the imagination. Not that the work is simple. As we saw in chapter 3, covering sin with silence or with a mitigating explanation or with forgiveness requires strenuous exertions of will and discernment. It also requires exertions in the thought and feeling that accompany our reading, since scripture may be one of the "neighbors" whose sins need covering. Part of the point of chapters 1 and 2, after all, was to show how inextricably living and reading are related, how the skills of each become the skills of the other, and how the skills require constant practice. To adapt one of Kierkegaard's formulas, the imagination is not so much a *what* as a *how*, not so much a *thing* as a *way*.[6] Kierkegaard's emphasis on the role of imagination in reading scripture by love, therefore, was a call to a certain quality of consciousness, a call to live imaginatively. Imagination, for him, meant a highly disciplined way of being.

On the other hand, Kierkegaard did not want to overstate the role of the imagination either. The focus text in chapter 2, which spoke of the imagination as a capacity with which humans are "endowed," should allay Childs's anxieties. If the imagination is a gift of God, it remains under God's sovereignty. That point was reinforced by what we discovered in our historical review of the Rule of faith, namely, that the development of the Rule included the notion of "inspired interpretation." Kierkegaard was entirely in tune with scripture and the early church in representing the human imagination as a prime locus for the work of the Holy Spirit.[7]

In the same vein, Kierkegaard's image of the Bible as a love letter from God was clearly intended to affirm God's initiative in the divine-human relationship. And his image of scripture as a mirror, which he drew from the Epistle of James and which served as a corollary to that of the love letter, spoke to the same point, since ultimately, by God's grace, the "face" that the mirror reflects is that of Christ, who is God's decisive self-enactment in the world. By

---

[6] One version of the formula was cited on p. 36 above, from *WL*, 30. That in turn was an echo of the following in *CUP*: "*The objective accent falls on WHAT is said, the subjective accent on HOW it is said*" (181, Kierkegaard's emphasis). Yet another version came in the *Attack Upon Christendom* where Kierkegaard speaks, under the figure of "the eternal," of how one conceives of God: "But the eternal is not a thing which can be had regardless of the way in which it is acquired; no, the eternal is not really a thing, but *is the way* in which it is acquired" (100, my emphasis.) See also *JP* I, #678 ("What and—How"), 317f.

Kierkegaard's emphasis on imagining as a how is also reflected in the Gouwens quotations in n. 2 above. Gouwens gives the idea particularly elegant expression in his remark that "...being ethical is a *way* of being imaginative" (211, my emphasis).

[7] See pp. 66f., 70.

combining these two images of scripture, Kierkegaard helps prevent theology from dissolving into anthropology, the transcendence of God from being transmogrified into an aesthetic faculty fully immanent within humans.[8]

But again, the importance of the imagination as an immanent human capacity grows in proportion to the concreteness with which its manifestations are detailed, and Kierkegaard was lavish with the details. It was an essential function of his parabolic discourse, we saw in chapter 3, to concretize for his readers the work of the imagination. Just as Hawthorne's parable "Young Goodman Brown" (or Kierkegaard's own "Diary of the Seducer") fleshed out the "sick imagination," *WL* and the Edifying Discourses on James and Job drew scene after scene representing the healthy imagination. Desire—as obvious an activity of the imagination as can be named, and as universal an ingredient of our humanity—he both figured and named repeatedly. For instance, the "anticipation of joy" (my term), which we identified as one of the affective components of the Rule of faith in chapter 2 (with reference to the parable of the love sleuth in "Love Covers the Multiplicity of Sins"), appeared as "the expectation of comfort" (his term) in chapter 4, where Kierkegaard instructed us in how to read James's words about desiring gifts. Again, much of who we are as particular individuals seems to depend very specifically upon what and how we desire. The particulars are crucial.

To detail desire as a work of imagination is to recognize desire as a key element of human *subjectivity*, and subjectivity, we recall from chapters 2 and 5, is the basis for the human God-relationship, since "God is a subject and therefore exists only for subjectivity in inwardness."[9] In chapter 4 we saw how Kierkegaard personified other desire-related "elements of subjectivity"—humility, confidence, sorrow, and gratitude—as he strove to show what it would be like to imagine God as the Giver of everything and everything as the good gift of God. One effect was to show how potentially crushing the task is. Indeed, the task of imagining all God's "gifts" as good and God as therefore ever praiseworthy—and then imagining how actually to praise God in the midst of loss and suffering—proves something of an ordeal. By placing such extreme demands on the imagination, religious

---

[8] Cf. *CUP*, 514, where Climacus warns against confounding "what comes from God, and what comes from man."

[9] The quotation is from *CUP* and was cited above in chapter 2, p. 34, and nn. 3 and 71; and in chapter 5, n. 9.

ordeals provoke theodicies. That fact supplied the topic for chapter 5.

Chapter 5 showed that different theodicies entail, once again, different imaginative construals of the Bible. What I called the metaphysical and the sociological theodicies illustrated "foundationalist"[10] construals whereby the Bible was primarily imagined either as a product of philosophical theory or as a source, proof, or defense of theological doctrine. By contrast, the Book of Job, particularly as read by Kierkegaard, following the Rule of faith, seemed to suggest an entirely different way of doing theodicy, i.e., by doing it doxologically. There again was the hermeneutic circle: under the imaginative construal of God as ever praiseworthy and of scripture as the primary witness to God's praiseworthiness, the Book of Job was found to perform and generate praise.

Again, the imagination had to flex athletically to achieve this construal. One of the feats of Kierkegaard's doxological reading of Job was that it took seriously the canonical shape of the text, interpreting the prose portions of the book in dialectical relationship with the poetry. We thus observed the strain on the imagination required to take seriously the story's "fairy-tale" ending. "Who would have *imagined* this ending?" exclaimed one of the characters of Kierkegaard's novel *Repetition*. "Repetition" was Kierkegaard's term for the self-building process in the ethical sphere and the self-losing and -restoring process in the religious sphere. As such, repetition was for Kierkegaard the goal of the religious reading of scripture. Imagining the story's ending with God's gratuitous restoration of Job, Kierkegaard maintained, is essential for the reader's repetition of Job's faith, that act of "imaginative self-consciousness by which one receives one's life anew from God."[11].

However great the imaginative strain, the result was a grasp of praise that was compelling in its human complexity. With sympathetic precision Kierkegaard articulated how in Job, when read canonically, praise encompasses protest, and blessing incorporates and overcomes cursing. Of course, he articulated this by the parabolic, fictive rhetoric that characterized all his writings—that is to say, by virtue of his own extraordinary imagination. This indicates a final hermeneutic puzzle, one which, apparently, scandalized Kierkegaard himself.

---

[10] See Introduction, p. ??? and n. 6.
[11] See above, chap. 5, p. ???.

Because he could not be certain that his life, so singly devoted to writing, did not reflect an imagination arrested at the aesthetic stage, Kierkegaard was tempted to take offense at his own imagination. Was his writing an art in the service of existing, or was it art active only in the medium of thought?[12] In the latter, all energy is spent in the imaginative pondering of possibilities, rather than in their enactment, which of course requires imagination, but at another level.[13] That kind of writing, art in which the artist keeps his distance from life, was what he meant by the "eloquence" of the "rhetorician," which Climacus savaged with such rhetorical skill in the *Postscript*,[14] and by the "poesy" that kept coming up for criticism, almost compulsively, in *WL*.

In the first seventy-five pages of *WL*, the figure of "the poet" is virtually omnipresent, serving as the constant reference point for illustrating what neighbor-love is *not*. Kierkegaard's purpose is to draw out the distinction between erotic love and neighbor-love. Since "the poet is the priest" of erotic love (45), the poet merits attention— that is, as a means of illustration. Nevertheless, it is curious how the attention wants to *center* on him, and the illustration, supposedly subordinate to the subject it illustrates, becomes itself the subject.[15] In fact, the poet is the paradigm of erotic love (and friendship), indeed, of the aesthetic sensibility itself. As such, he threatens the very project Kierkegaard is about, fostering Christian love.

Christian love "cannot be sung about," Kierkegaard says, twice for emphasis; "it must be lived"—"it must be fulfilled in reality" (*WL*, 26, 60). Therefore, "no poet, if he understands himself, would think of celebrating it in song" (26). Ironically, in *WL*, Kierkegaard does that very thing, and in the process suggests that "he [Kierkegaard]

---

[12] See for example, *JP* I, #817, p. 373:

There is a striking passage in the beginning of Tertullian's book about patience.... I acknowledge before the Lord God that in a somewhat rash and perhaps even shameless way I have presumed to write about patience—I, who myself am so very deficient.

This reminds me of my own collision: to what extent should a person dare present the ideal of the Christian although he himself is so far from it? A poet-existence which is not at all related in striving to the ideal, but merely presents it, is one thing; it is something else actually to strive oneself, but then poetically to present the ideal which he himself is far from being.

[13] See again the Gouwens statement quoted above in n. 5: "being ethical is a way of being imaginative."

[14] See, for example, *CUP*, 16-20, 46f., and 387-400 (n.b. "the religious orator"). See also p. 69 n. 39.

[15] See especially *WL* 45f., 59-63.

cannot understand himself," that "he himself is a riddle" (45). If *Works of Love* is "poesy," if it is song, if in its doxological, parabolic rhetoric it is irreducibly imaginative, then the one who appends his signature to it is the poet, who, by his own definition, "*qua* poet is not a Christian" (60), one who "cannot vouch for himself," and who quips, rhetorically, "how good is *his* signature?" (73, my emphasis). How good indeed?

This is a suspicious reading of Kierkegaard's text. But Kierkegaard understands that he may not understand himself, and he anticipates a suspicious reading in the penultimate chapter of the text itself, "The Work of Love in Praising Love" (330-43). The chapter asks if the someone who praises love is really loving in his praise. Does he manifest the external sacrificial disinterestedness required by an inward understanding of oneself as nothing before God? And how would he ever manifest such disinterestedness, since every effort to externalize it could just as well be an effort to curry the approval of the reader. Even admitting not to be disinterested in praising love but to be doing so in self-love (341) may only be a ruse to inspire the reader to say, "My, how nobly self-sacrificial this poet is (by pretending to be self-loving)!" Thus, the effort would be not a foolproof sign of one's love of God, but rather a symptom of the self-love it only pretended to feign.

As Louis Mackey observed, *WL* was not the only non-pseudonymous work to call in question the authenticity of its signature in the very act of vouching for it. In *The Point of View for My Work as an Author*—even while insisting under his own name that he was a religious, not an aesthetic, author—Kierkegaard introduces a *poet*, "my poet," to vouch that God is the true author of the entire literature. A poet no less! "He who cannot vouch for himself!" "Soren Kierkegaard was one of his own pseudonyms," concludes Mackey.[16] Kierkegaard could never quite elude the poet in himself, the poet whose religious genuineness (genius?) he knew he could not trust.

Mackey makes a persuasive case for construing Kierkegaard's authorship as a monumental process of sublimation: "As a result of his reflective and dialectical nature, [Kierkegaard's] whole life...is poured into his writings."[17] By analyzing life and writings as a "system

---

[16] Mackey, "Points of View for his Work as an Author: A Report from History," *Points of View: Readings of Kierkegaard* (Tallahassee: Florida State University, 1986), 188.
[17] Mackey, *Points of View*, 179.

of dualities" variously supplemented and relocated (genius/reflection, Father-God/father-Michael, lover-God/Regine-beloved, chastity-constipation/literary prodigiousness), Mackey sees the pseudonyms, including that of Soren Kierkegaard, as all refractions of a self torn by the inescapability of the aesthetic. In *PV* Kierkegaard wanted to say that he *could* escape it. He protested, Mackey says, that "in his writings the poet is 'got rid of' (*PV*, 74n.). This evacuation [*PV*, 84] is essential if he is to actualize his religious potential."[18]

But this purging of the poetic is never complete, so that the evacuation of the writer proves to be "essential" in an ironic as well as the intended sense. Because the poetic emissions are guiltily pleasurable, they *must* be eliminated. This fact Kierkegaard overtly confesses. But because the witness to Christ against Christendom requires the indirection of rhetoric (i.e., the poetic imagination),[19] the emissions continue—can*not* in fact be eliminated. This is the fact his writing proves, despite himself.

But finally, does Kierkegaard's genuineness as a religous writer really matter? Perhaps it does to the literary critic or historian, the "poets" of academe, whose presumed job it is to assess Kierkegaard's place among other poets, philosophers, and theologians. But *qua* poets, Kierkegaard would remind us, the academicians are not religious subjects. Insofar as readers are religious subjects, however, worrying about *ourselves* is the task at hand. Recognizing this, Kierkegaard performs one of his classic vanishing acts at the end of "The Work of Love in Praising Love." "So much for the speaker," he says, after he has established the undecidability of his own authenticity (342). Of course, the move is fully consistent with the purpose of maieutic edification. By dismissing any pretense to the authority his name might have over us, Kierkegaard leaves us to decide for ourselves what to do with his words.

What, then, about the continuing taint of aestheticism in *our* effort to read scripture, since surely we will be no more able to purge the guilty pleasures of self-love from our imaginative readings than Kierkegaard was? Our imagination is required; our imagination is

---

[18] Mackey, *Points of View*, 179.

[19] The poet's presence in *PV* shows that this holds true for the works of so-called "direct communication" as well as the more obviously indirect products. The poet is no less present in the Edifying Discourses, the Christian Reflections, and the *Attack Upon Christendom*. With respect to the *Attack*, for example: where you have satire and hyperbole systematically employed for the rhetorical effect of shaking the audience to their core, there you have the persona of the poet. Polemic is rhetoric.

contaminating; misinterpretations will continue, not to mention plural, conflicting interpretations.

We know what the Rule of faith would urge: that we strive to imagine how others might have lovingly come up with interpretations that differ from ours, and to imagine that ours might possibly be less than fully loving, in which case we have a loving God to correct us. Or, to paraphrase Luther: trust God, and read boldly!

Bibliography

For the works of Kierkegaard, see Abbreviations.

Achtemeier, Paul J. *Mark*, Proclamation Commentaries. Philadelphia: Fortress Press, 1975.

Augustine, St. *On Christian Doctrine*, D. W. Robertson, Jr., trans. New York: Macmillan, 1958.

Balch, David. *Let Wives Be Submissive: The Domestic Code in I Peter*, SBLMS 26. Missoula, MT: Scholars Press, 1981.

Barfield, Owen. "The Meaning of the Word 'Literal,'" *Metaphor and Symbol*, Proceedings of the Twelfth Symposium of the Colston Research Society, L. C. Knights and Basil Cottle, eds. London: Butterworths, 1960: 48-63.

Barr, James. *Holy Scripture: Canon, Authority, Criticism*. Oxford: Oxford University Press, 1983.

Barth, Karl. *Church Dogmatics*, IV/3/i, G. W. Bromiley, trans. Edinburgh: T. & T. Clark, 1961.

Bell, Richard, ed. *The Grammar of the Heart: Thinking with Kierkegaard and Wittgenstein*. San Francisco: Harper, 1988.

Bellah, Robert. *Habits of the Heart: Individualism and Commitment in American Life*. New York: Harper & Row, 1985.

Berger, Peter. *The Sacred Canopy: Elements of a Sociological Theory of Religion*. Garden City, N.Y.: Doubleday, 1969.

Brown, Delwin. "Struggle till Daybreak: On the Nature of Authority in Theology," *Journal of Religion*, 65 (1985): 15-32.

Cady, Linell E. "Relational Love: A Feminist Christian Vision," *Embodied Love: Sensuality and Relationship as Feminist Values*, Paula M. Cooey, et al., eds. San Francisco: Harper & Row, 1987: 136-49.

Cahoy, William. "One Species or Two? Kierkegaard's Anthropology and the Feminist Critique of the Concept of Sin," *Modern Theology*, 11 (1995): 429-54.

Chesterton, G. K. "Man Is Most Comforted by Paradoxes," *Job: A Study and Selected Readings*. Nahum N. Glatzer, ed. New York: Schocken Books, 1969.

Childs, Brevard S. *Introduction to the Old Testament as Scripture*. Philadelphia: Fortress Press, 1979.

_____. *The New Testament as Canon: An Introduction* Philadelphia: Fortress Press, 1984.

_____. "The Sensus Literalis of Scripture: An Ancient and Modern Problem," in *Beitrage zur alttestamentlichen Theologie*, Festschrift für Walther Zimmerli zum 70. Geburtstag, Herbert Donner *et al.*, eds. Göttingen: Vandenhoeck & Ruprecht, 1977, 80-93.

Clines, David J. A. "Deconstructing the Book of Job," *The Bible as Rhetoric: Studies in Biblical Persuasion and Credibility*, Martin Weaver, ed. London: Routledge, 1990, 65-80.

_____. *Job 1-20*, Word Biblical Commentary, vol. 17. Dallas: Word Books, 1989.

Crenshaw, James L. *A Whirlpool of Torment: Israelite Traditions of God as an Oppressive Presence*. Philadelphia: Fortress, 1984 .

_____. "The Shift from Theodicy to Anthropodicy," *Theodicy in the Old Testament*, James L. Crenshaw, ed. Philadelphia: Fortress Press, 1983: 1-16.

Dahl, Nils. "The Particularity of the Pauline Epistles as a Problem in the Ancient Church," *Neotestamentica et Patristica, Festschrift für O. Cullmann*, W. C. van Unnik, ed. Novum Testamentum Supplements 6, 1962: 261-71

Davis, Stephen T., ed. *Encountering Evil: Live Options in Theodicy*. Atlanta: John Knox, 1981.

Derrida, Jacques. *Positions*, Alan Bass, trans. Chicago: University of Chicago Press, 1981.

Des Pres, Terrence. *The Survivor: An Anatomy of Life in the Death Camps*. New York: Oxford, 1976.

Dibelius, Martin. *A Commentary on the Epistle of James*, 11th edn. by Heinrich Greeven; Michael Williams, trans. Philadelphia: Fortress Press, 1975.

Elliott, John. *A Home for the Homeless: A Social-Scientific Criticism of I Peter, its Situation and Strategy*, 2nd edition. Minneapolis: Fortress Press, 1990 (originally, 1981).

Elrod, John. *Kierkegaard and Christendom*. Princeton: Princeton, 1981.

Evans, C. Stephen. *Kierkegaard's* Fragments *and* Postscript: *The Religious Philosophy of Johannes Climacus*. Atlantic Highlands, NJ: Humanities Press International, 1983.

Fish, Stanley. *Is There a Text in This Class? The Authority of Interpretive Communities*. Cambridge: Harvard, 1980.

Fishburn, Janet Forsythe. "Søren Kierkegaard: Exegete," *Interpretation*, 39 (1985): 229-45.

Ford, David, and Daniel Hardy. *Praising God and Knowing God*. Philadelphia: Westminster, 1985.

Frei, Hans. *The Eclipse of Biblical Narrative*. New Haven: Yale University Press, 1974.

Gamble, Harry. *The Textual History of the Letter to the Romans*. Grand Rapids: Eerdmans, 1977.

Ginsberg, H. L. "Job the Patient and Job the Impatient," *Vetus Testamentum Supplements*, 17 (1969): 88-111.

Good, Edwin. "Job and the Literary Task: A Response," *Soundings*, 56 (1973): 470-85.

Gouwens, David J. *Kierkegaard's Dialectic of the Imagination*. New York: Peter Lang, 1989.

_____. "Kierkegaard's Understanding of Doctrine," *Modern Theology*, 5 (1988): 13-22.

Green, Garrett. "'The Bible As...'": Fictional Narrative and Scriptural Truth," *Scriptural Authority and Narrative Interpretation*. Garrett Green, ed. Philadelphia: Fortress Press, 1987: 79-96.

_____. "The Gender of God and the Theology of Metaphor," *Speaking the Christian God: The Holy Trinity and the Challenge of Feminism*, Alvin F. Kimel, Jr. ed. Grand Rapids: Eerdmans, 1992: 44-64.

_____. *Imagining God: Theology and the Religious Imagination*. San Francisco: Harper & Row, 1989.

Greer, Rowan and James Kugel. *Early Biblical Interpretation*. Philadelphia: Westminster Press, 1986.

Gutierrez, Gustavo. *On Job: God-Talk and the Suffering of the Innocent*, Matthew J. O'Connell, trans. Maryknoll: Orbis, 1987

Hauerwas, Stanley. *Against the Nations: War and Survival in a Liberal Society*. Minneapolis: Winston Press, 1985.

_____. *Truthfulness and Tragedy: Further Investigations into Christian Ethics*, with Richard Bondi and David B. Burrell. South Bend: University of Notre Dame Press, 1977.

_____. *Vision and Virtue*. South Bend: University of Notre Dame Press, 1981 (originally, Fides, 1974).

Heschel, Abraham. *The Prophets*, vol. 1. New York: Harper & Row, 1962.

Holmer, Paul L. *The Grammar of Faith* (San Francisco: Harper & Row, 1978.

_____. "Introduction," *Edifying Discourses: A Selection*. New York: Harper & Row, 1958.

Hong, Howard and Edna. "Introduction," *Works of Love*. New York: Harper & Row, 1962: 11-18.

Houlden, J. L. *Ethics of the New Testament*. Harmondsworth: Penguin Books Ltd., 1973.

Johnson, Luke Timothy. "James 3:13-4:10 and the *Topos peri phthonou*," *Novum Testamentum*, 25 (1983): 327-47.

_____. "The Use of Leviticus 19 in the Letter of James," *Journal of Biblical Literature*, 101 (1982): 391-401.

_____. *The Writings of the New Testament: An Interpretation*. Philadelphia: Fortress Press, 1986.

Juel, Donald H. *Mark*, Augsburg Commentary on the New Testament. Minneapolis: Augsburg Press, 1990.

Kelsey, David. "The Bible and Christian Theology," *The Journal of the American Academy of Religion*, 48 (1980): 390-93.

_____. *The Uses of Scripture in Recent Theology*. Philadelphia: Fortress Press, 1975.

Kermode, Frank. *The Genesis of Secrecy: On the Interpretation of Narrative*. Cambridge: Harvard University Press, 1979.

Kingsbury, Jack Dean. *Jesus Christ in Matthew, Mark, and Luke*, Proclamation Commentaries. Philadelphia: Fortress Press, 1981.

Kirmmse, Bruce H. *Kierkegaard in Golden Age Denmark*. Bloomington: Indiana University Press, 1990.

Laws, Sophie. *A Commentary on the Epistle of James*. San Francisco: Harper & Row, 1980.

Lindbeck, George. *The Nature of Doctrine: Religion and Doctrine in a Postliberal Age*. Philadelphia: Westminster Press, 1984.

Lowrie, Walter. *A Short Life of Kierkegaard*. Princeton: Princeton University Press, 1970 (originally, 1942).

Mackey, Louis. *Kierkegaard: A Kind of Poet*. Philadelphia: University of Pennsylvania, 1971.

_____. *Points of View: Readings of Kierkegaard*. Tallahassee: Florida State University, 1986.

MacLeish, Archibald. *J.B.* Boston: Houghton Mifflin, 1986 (originally, 1956).

Marcus, Joel. "Mark 4:10-12 and Marcan Epistemology," *Journal of Biblical Literature*, 103 (1984): 557-574.

McFague, Sallie. *Metaphorical Theology: Models of God in Religious Language*. Philadelphia: Fortress, 1982.

Miller, Patrick. "Enthroned on the Praises of Israel: The Praise of God in the Old Testament," *Interpretation*, 39 (1985): 5-19.

Minear, Paul S. and Paul S. Morimoto, *Kierkegaard and the Bible: An Index*. Princeton: Princeton Theological Seminary, 1953.

Mooney, Edward F. "Understanding Abraham: Care, Faith, and the Absurd," in *Kierkegaard's* Fear and Trembling*: Critical Appraisals*, Robert L. Perkins, ed. University, AL: University of Alabama Press, 1981): 100-114.

Murdoch, Iris. *The Sovereignty of Good*. New York: Schocken, 1970.

Patten, Rebecca. "Kierkegaard"s Hermeneutics." Unpublished paper.

Pelikan, Jaroslav. *The Christian Tradition, 1: The Emergence of the Catholic Tradition*. Chicago: The University of Chicago, 1971.

Peterson, Elaine. "Kierkegaard"s Exegetical Methodology." Unpublished paper read at the Kierkegaard Conference, St. Olaf College, Northfield, MN, June, 1988.

Placher, William. *Unapologetic Theology: A Christian Voice in a Pluralistic Conversation*. Louisville: Westminster/John Knox Press, 1989.

Robertson, David. "The Book of Job: A Literary Study," *Soundings*, 56 (1973): 446-69.

Rosas, L. Joseph. *Scripture in the Thought of Søren Kierkegaard*. Nashville: Broadman and Holman, Publishers, 1994.

Sanders, James A. *Canon and Community*. Philadelphia: Fortress Press, 1984.

_____. *Torah and Canon*. Philadelphia: Fortress Press, 1972.

Sartre, Jean Paul. *Being and Nothingness*, Hazel Barnes, trans. New York: Washington Square, 1966.

Seitz, Christopher. "Job: Full-Structure, Movement, and Interpretation," *Interpretation*, 43 (1989): 5-17.

Sheppard, Gerald T. "Canonical Criticism," *Harper Bible Dictionary*. San Francisco: Harper, 1992, I: 861-66.

_____. "Between Reformation and Modern Commentary: The Perception of the Scope of Biblical Books," *A Commentary on Galatians* by William Perkins, Gerald T. Sheppard, ed. New York: The Pilgrim Press, 1989: xlviii-lxxvii.

Stout, Jeffrey. *Ethics After Babel: The Languages of Morals and Their Discontents*. Boston: Beacon Press, 1988.

Tannehill, R. C. "The Disciples in Mark: The Function of a Narrative Role," *Journal of Religion*, 57 (1977): 386-405.

Taylor, Mark Lloyd. "Ordeal and Repetition in Kierkegaard''s Treatment of Abraham and Job," *Foundations of Kierkegaard''s Vision of Community: Religion, Ethics, and Politics in Kierkegaard*, George B. Connell and C. Stephen Evans, eds. Atlantic Highlands, NJ: Humanities Press International, 1991: 33-53.

Thiemann, Ronald F. *Revelation and Theology: The Gospel as Narrated Promise*. Notre Dame: University of Notre Dame Press, 1985.

Tilley, Terence. "Incommensurability, Intratextuality, and Fideism," *Modern Theology*, 5 (1989): 87-111.

_____. "The Silencing of Job," *Modern Theology*, 5 (1989): 257-70.

Trollope, Anthony. *The Warden*. Harmondsworth: Penguin Books Ltd., 1994.

Tsevat, Matitiahu. "The Meaning of the Book of Job," *Studies in Ancient Israelite Wisdom*, James L Crenshaw, ed. New York: KTAV, 1976: 341-74 (originally, *Hebrew Union College Annual*, 37 [1966]: 73-106)

Wallace, Mark. "Theology Without Revelation?" *Theology Today*, 45 (1988): 208-13.

Walsh, Sylvia I. "Forming the Heart: The Role of Love in Kierkegaard's Thought," *The Grammar of the Heart: Thinking with Kierkegaard and Wittgenstein*. Richard H. Bell, ed. San Francisco: Harper & Row, Publishers, 1988: 234-56.

Westphal, Merold. *Kierkegaard's Critique of Reason and Society*. Macon, GA: Mercer University Press, 1987.

Wiesel, Elie. *Messengers of God*, Marion Wiesel, trans. New York: Random House, 1976.

Williams, Rowan D. "The Literal Sense of Scripture," *Modern Theology*, 7 (1991): 121-34.

_____. "Postmodern Theology and the Judgment of the World," *Postmodern Theology: Christian Faith in a Pluralist World*, Frederic B. Burnham, ed. San Francisco: Harper, 1989: 92-112.

Wittgenstein, Ludwig. *Philosophical Investigations*, G.E.M. Anscombe, trans., 3rd edn. (New York: Macmillan, 1958.

Wood, Charles M. *The Formation of Christian Understanding: An Essay in Theological Hermeneutics*. Philadelphia: Westminster, 1981.

_____. "Hermeneutics and the Authority of Scripture," *Scriptural Authority and Narrative Interpretation*, Garrett Green, ed. Philadelphia: Fortress, 1987: 3-20.

_____. "The Knowledge Born of Obedience," *Anglican Theological Review*, 61 (1979): 331-40.

Name and Subject Index

Index of Scriptural References

- Collection of articles on literal sense   — Naomi?
- add 4 to the Herm. course

-